BUREAU FOR PARANORMAL · RESEARCH AND DEFENSE ·

THE BLACK GODDESS

Created by MIKE MIGNOLA

ABE SAPIEN

An amphibious man discovered in a primitive stasis chamber in a long-forgotten subbasement beneath a Washington, D.C., hospital. Recent events have confirmed a previous life, dating back to the Civil War, as scientist and occult investigator Langdon Everett Caul.

LIZ SHERMAN

A fire-starter since the age of eleven, when she accidentally burned her entire family to death. She has been a ward of the B.P.R.D. since then, learning to control her pyrokinetic abilities and cope with the trauma those abilities have wrought.

DR. KATE CORRIGAN

A former professor at New York University and an authority on folklore and occult history. Dr. Corrigan has been a B.P.R.D. consultant for over ten years and now serves as Special Liaison to the enhanced-talents task force.

PANYA

An ancient Egyptian mummy who returned to life during an unrolling ceremony in the nineteenth century. After her resurrection, Panya was a prisoner first of the Heliopic Brotherhood of Ra, and later of the Oannes Society, until she made contact with and subsequently was freed by the B.P.R.D. She has demonstrated psychic abilities, although their precise nature and range remain unknown.

JOHANN KRAUS

A medium whose physical form was destroyed while his ectoplasmic projection was out-of-body. A psychic empath, Johann can create temporary forms for the dead to speak to the living.

MIKE MIGNOLA'S

B.P.R.D. ™

THE BLACK GODDESS

Story by
MIKE MIGNOLA and JOHN ARCUDI

Art by
GUY DAVIS

Colors by
DAVE STEWART

Letters by
CLEM ROBINS

Collection Cover Art by
MIKE MIGNOLA

Original Series Cover Art by
KEVIN NOWLAN

Editor
SCOTT ALLIE

Assistant Editors
RACHEL EDIDIN and FREDDYE LINS

Collection Designer
AMY ARENDTS

Publisher
MIKE RICHARDSON

DARK HORSE BOOKS®

Neil Hankerson ♦ *executive vice president*
Tom Weddle ♦ *chief financial officer*
Randy Stradley ♦ *vice president of publishing*
Michael Martens ♦ *vice president of business development*
Anita Nelson ♦ *vice president of marketing, sales & licensing*
David Scroggy ♦ *vice president of product development*
Dale LaFountain ♦ *vice president of information technology*
Darlene Vogel ♦ *director of purchasing*
Ken Lizzi ♦ *general counsel*
Davey Estrada ♦ *editorial director*
Scott Allie ♦ *senior managing editor*
Chris Warner ♦ *senior books editor*
Diana Schutz ♦ *executive editor*
Cary Grazzini ♦ *director of design & production*
Lia Ribacchi ♦ *art director*
Cara Niece ♦ *director of scheduling*

Special thanks to Jason Hvam

DarkHorse.com

hellboy.com

Published by Dark Horse Books
A division of Dark Horse Comics, Inc.
10956 SE Main Street
Milwaukie, OR 97222

First Edition: November 2009
ISBN 978-1-59582-411-0

3 5 7 9 10 8 6 4 2

Printed at Midas Printing International, Ltd., Huizhou, China

B.P.R.D.: The Black Goddess

This book collects the *B.P.R.D.: The Black Goddess* comic-book series, issues #1–#5, published by Dark Horse Comics.

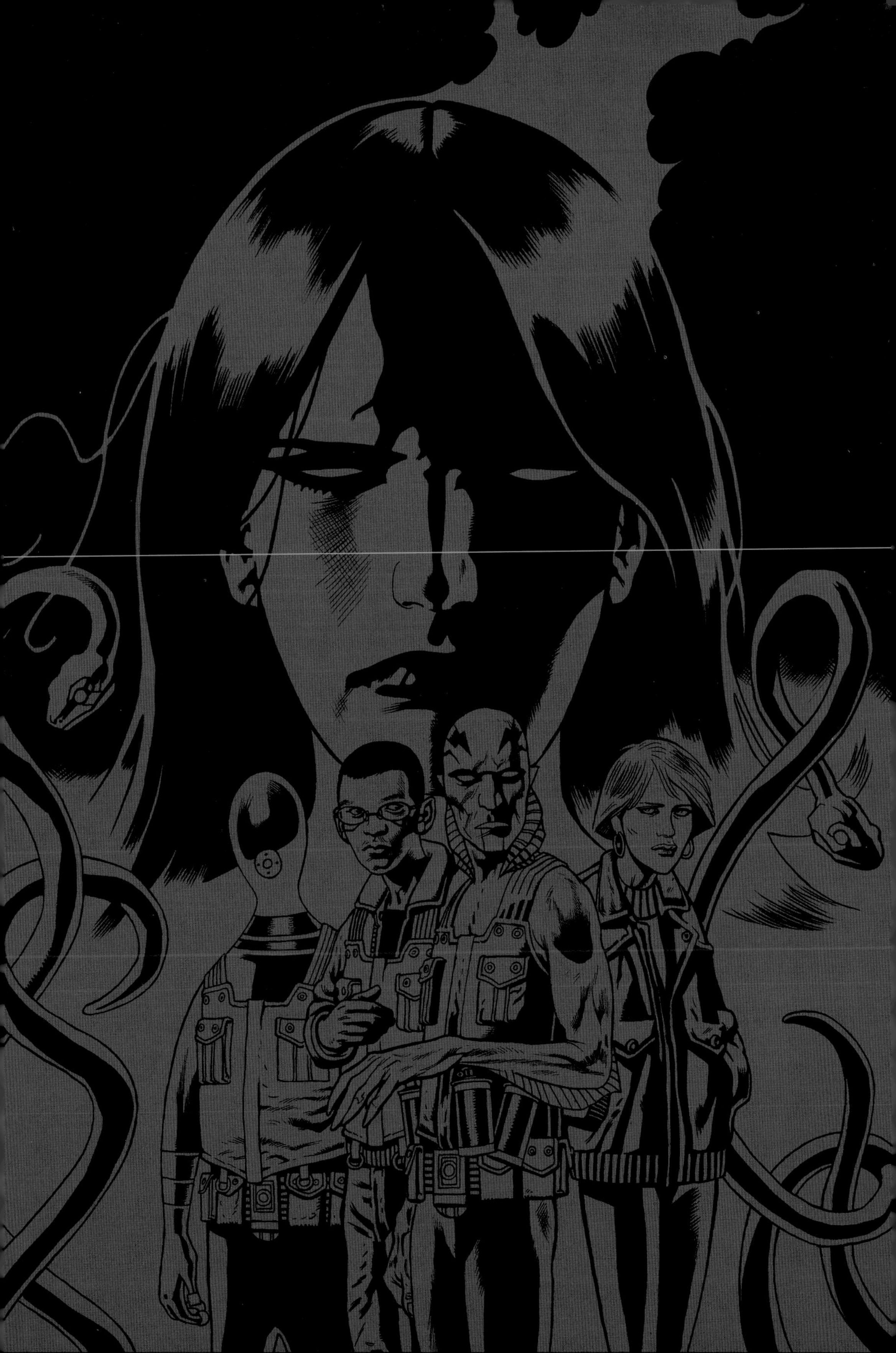

CHAPTER ONE

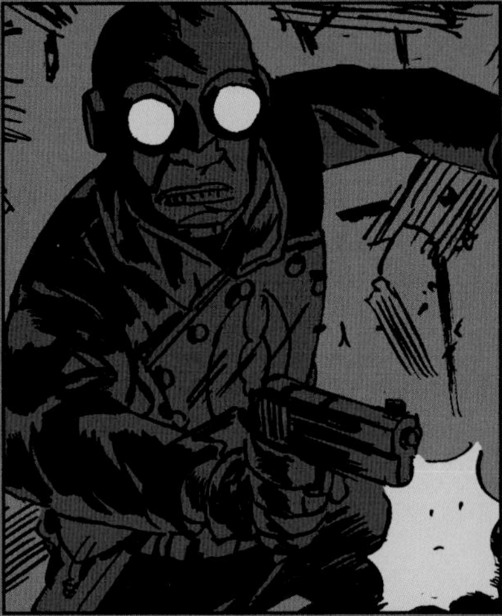

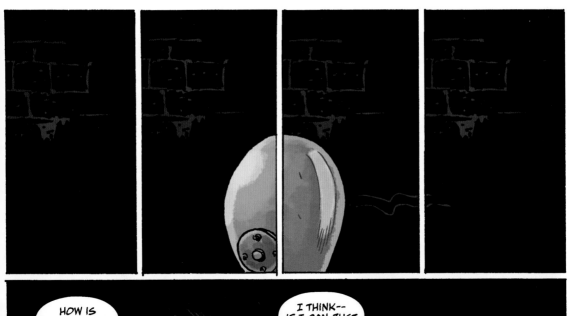

HOW IS THAT COMING ALONG?

I THINK-- IF I CAN JUST GET THIS--

YAA!

HUH.

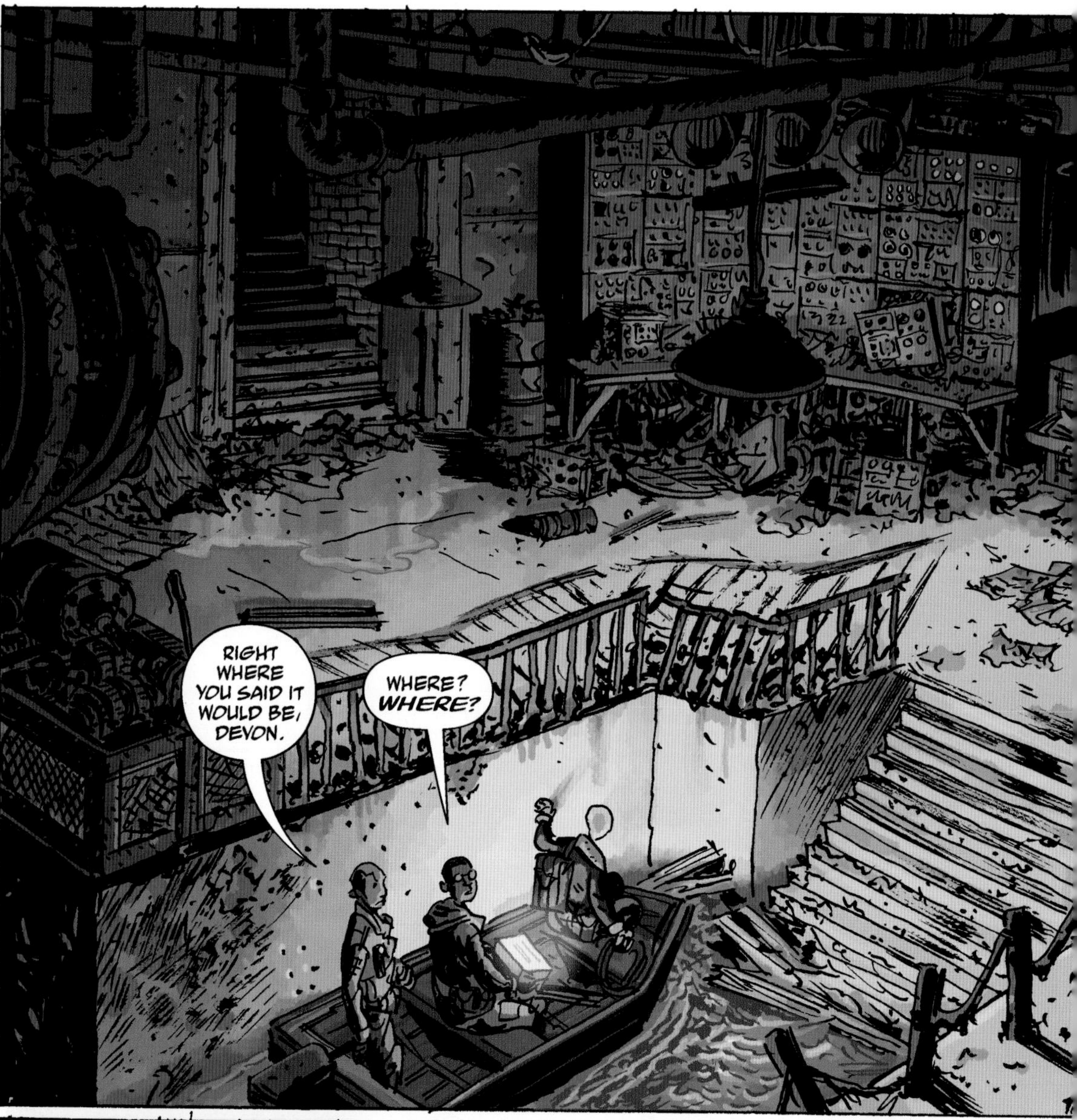
RIGHT WHERE YOU SAID IT WOULD BE, DEVON.
WHERE? WHERE?

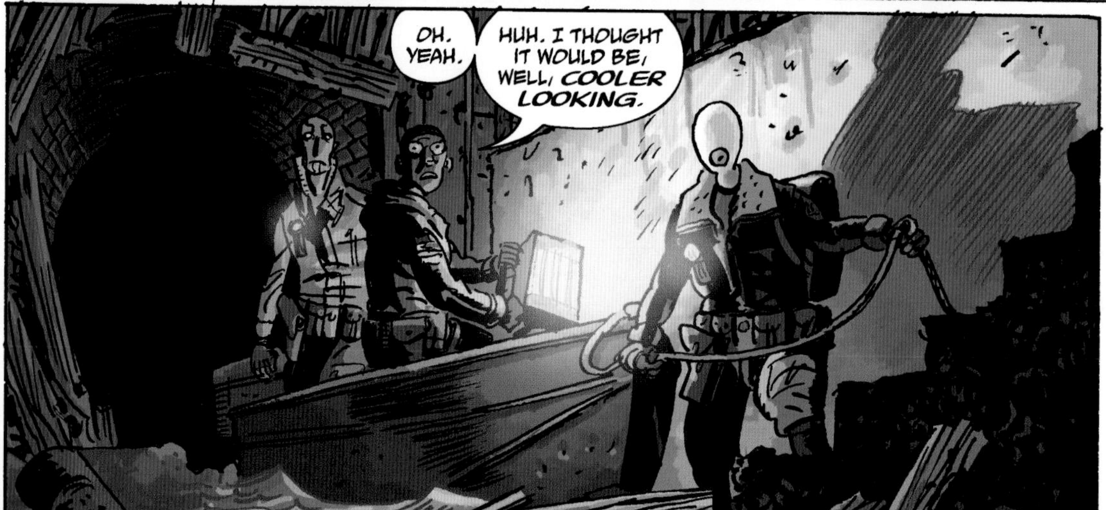
OH. YEAH.
HUH. I THOUGHT IT WOULD BE, WELL, COOLER LOOKING.

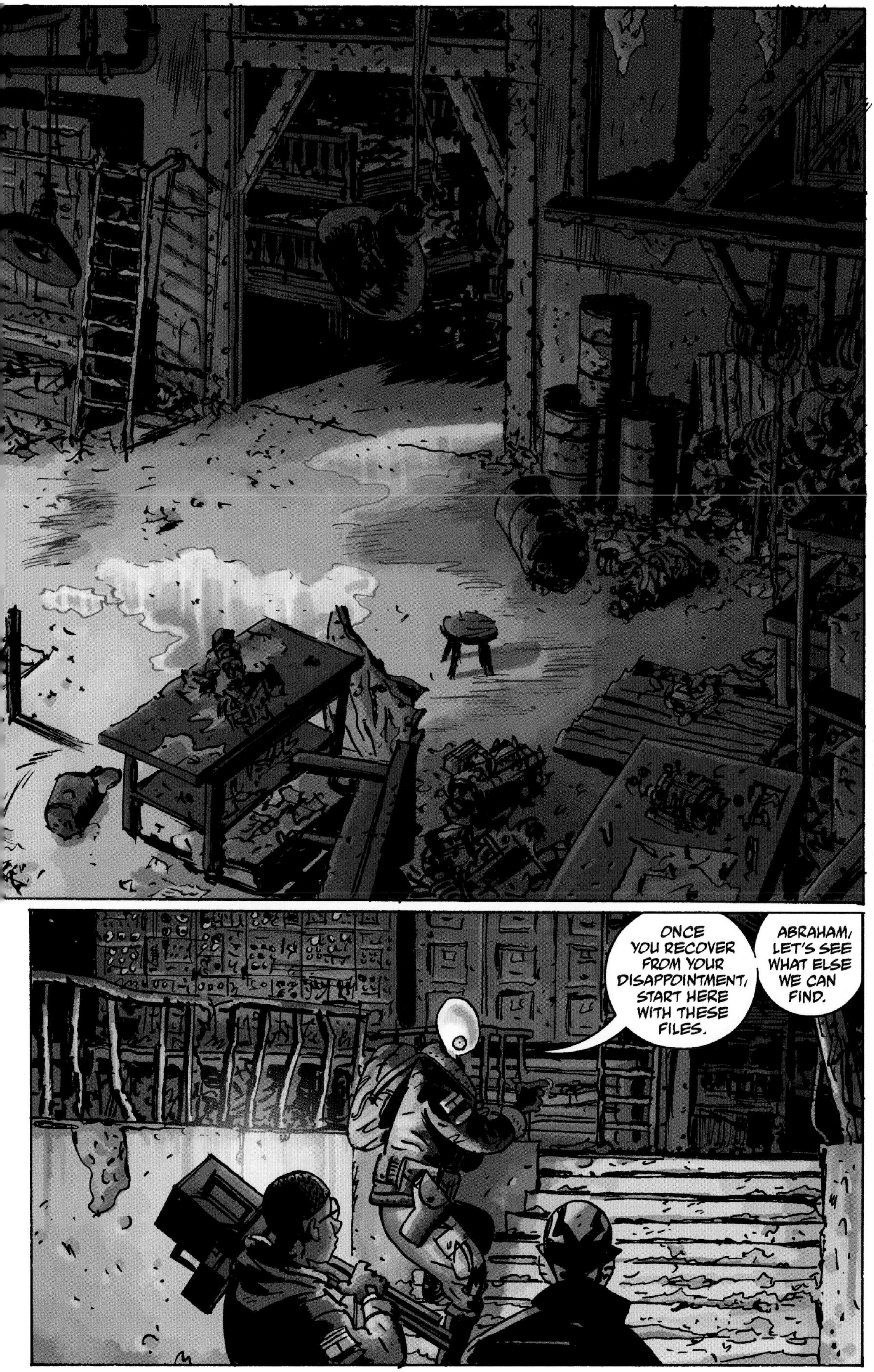
ONCE YOU RECOVER FROM YOUR DISAPPOINTMENT, START HERE WITH THESE FILES.
ABRAHAM, LET'S SEE WHAT ELSE WE CAN FIND.

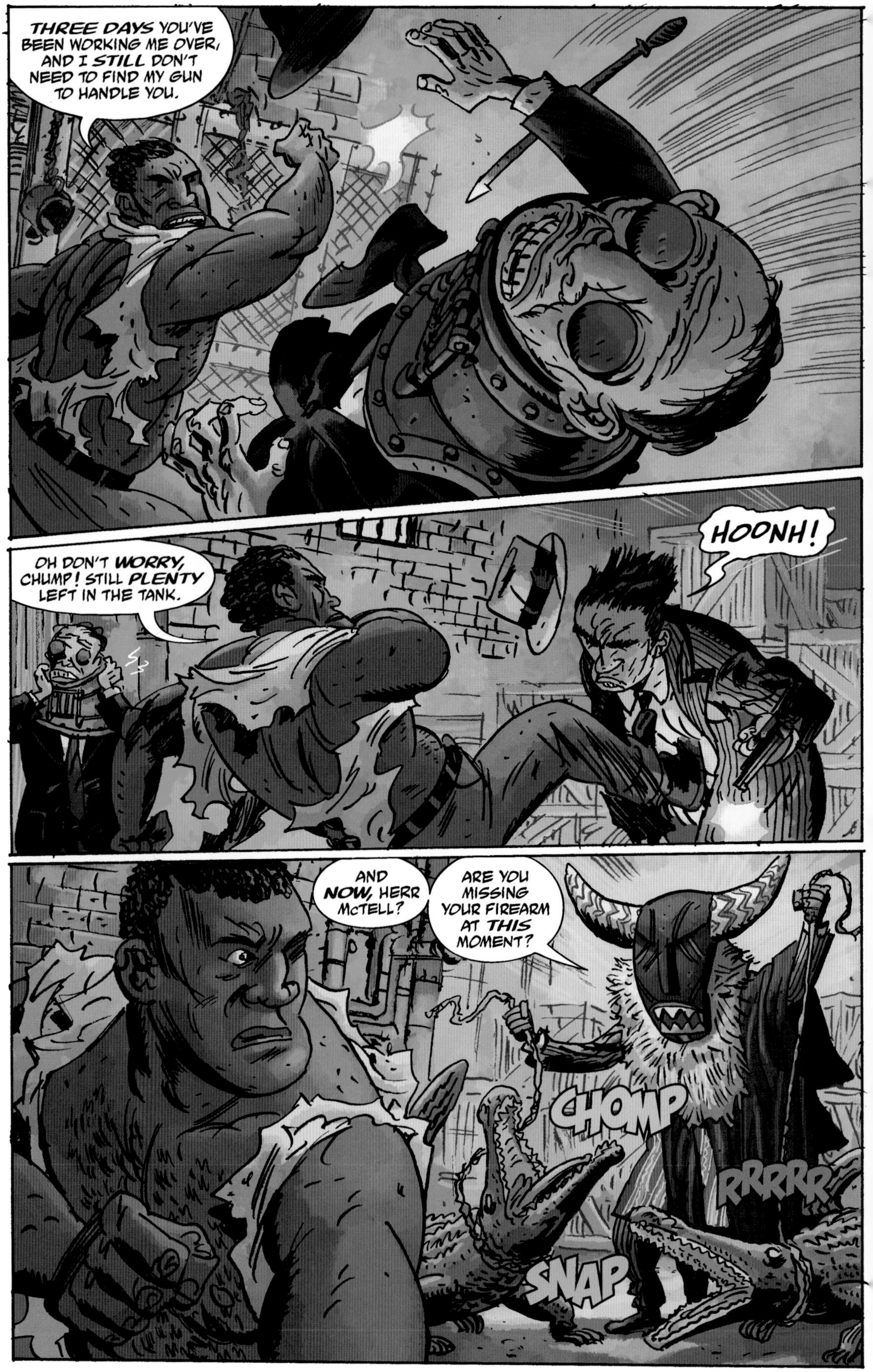

THREE DAYS YOU'VE BEEN WORKING ME OVER, AND I STILL DON'T NEED TO FIND MY GUN TO HANDLE YOU.
OH DON'T WORRY, CHUMP! STILL PLENTY LEFT IN THE TANK.
HOONH!
AND NOW, HERR McTELL?
ARE YOU MISSING YOUR FIREARM AT THIS MOMENT?
CHOMP
RRRRR
SNAP

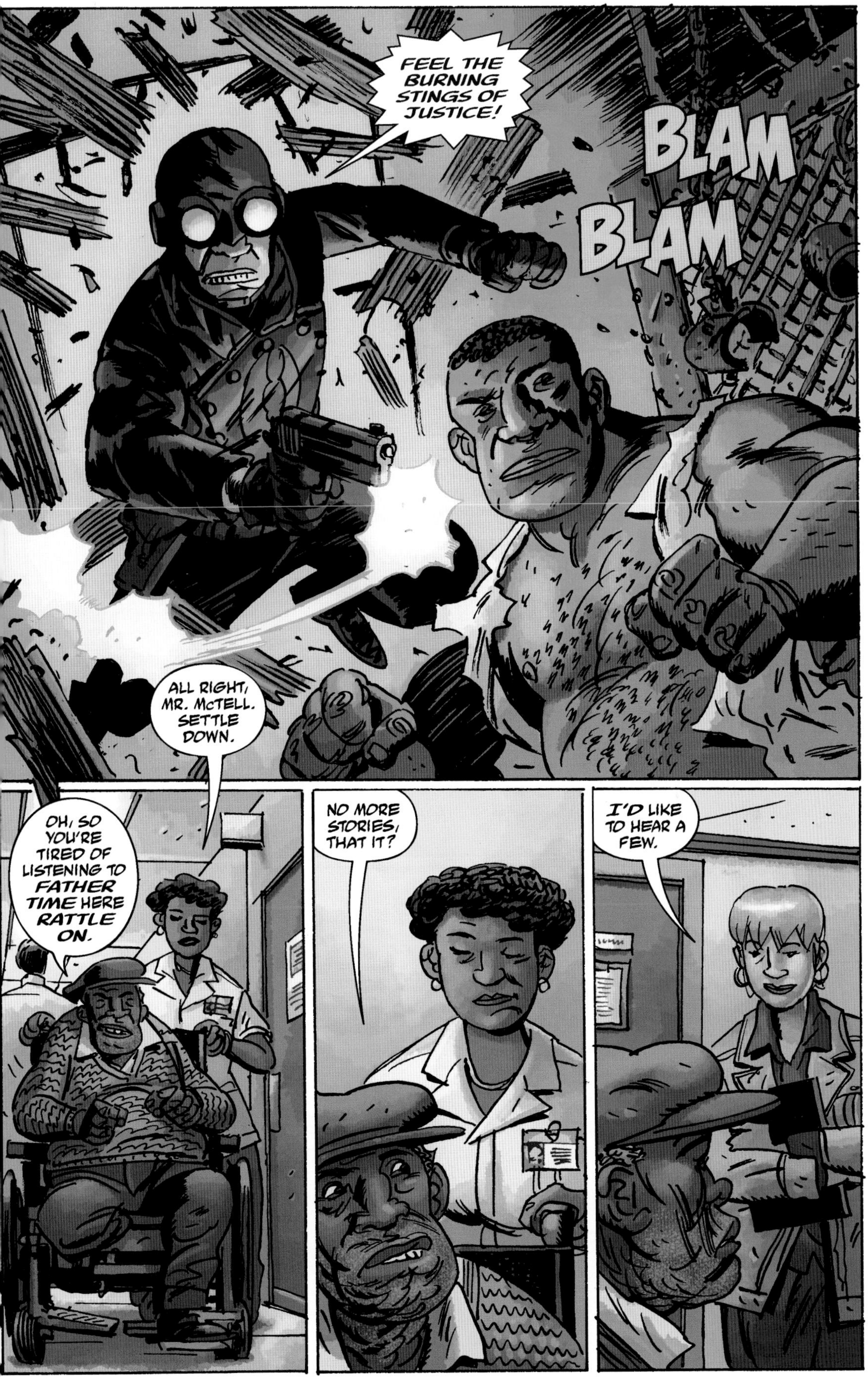
FEEL THE BURNING STINGS OF JUSTICE!
BLAM
BLAM
ALL RIGHT, MR. McTELL. SETTLE DOWN.
OH, SO YOU'RE TIRED OF LISTENING TO *FATHER TIME* HERE *RATTLE ON*.
NO MORE STORIES, THAT IT?
I'D LIKE TO HEAR A FEW.

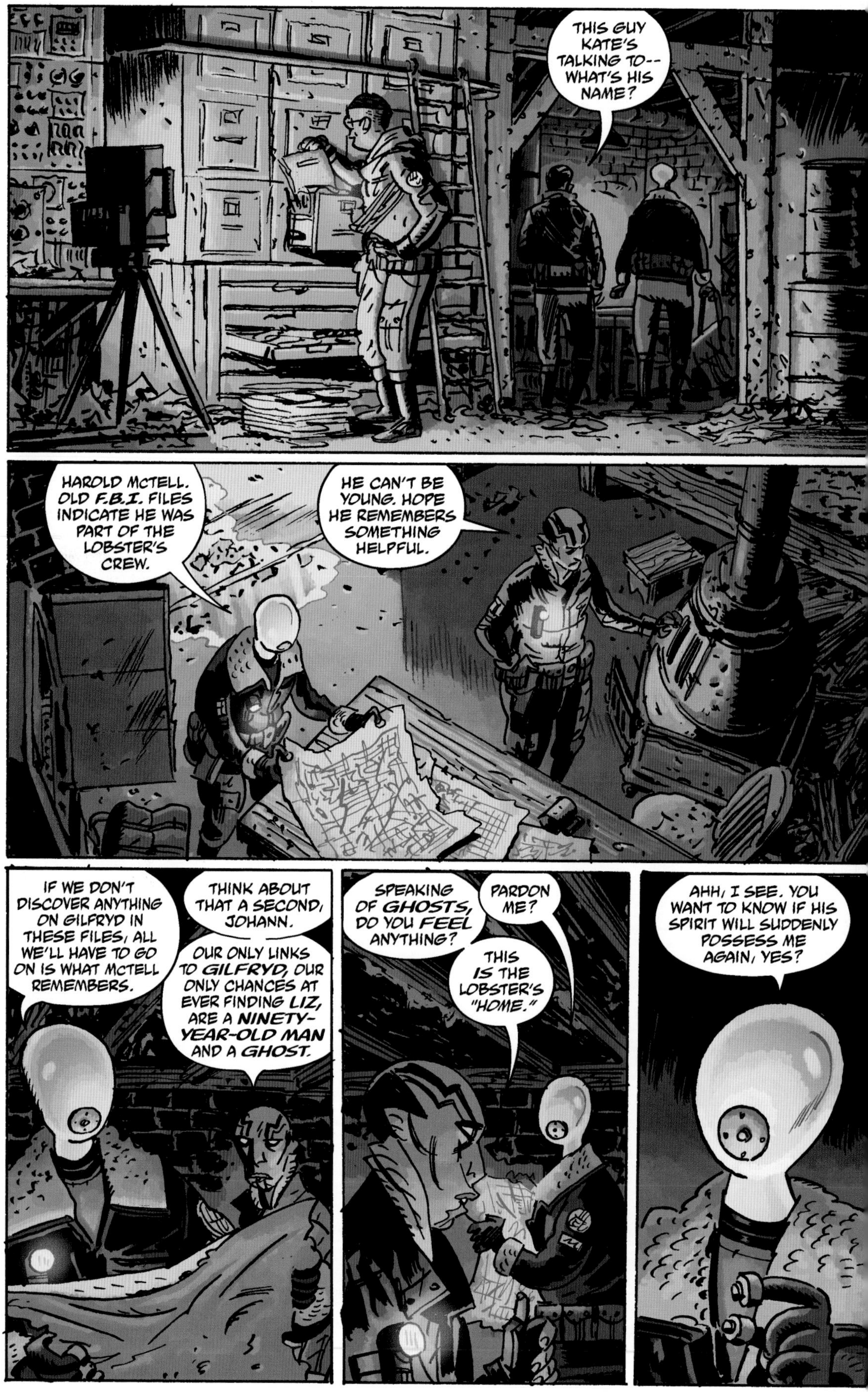
THIS GUY KATE'S TALKING TO-- WHAT'S HIS NAME?
HAROLD MCTELL. OLD F.B.I. FILES INDICATE HE WAS PART OF THE LOBSTER'S CREW.
HE CAN'T BE YOUNG. HOPE HE REMEMBERS SOMETHING HELPFUL.
IF WE DON'T DISCOVER ANYTHING ON GILFRYD IN THESE FILES, ALL WE'LL HAVE TO GO ON IS WHAT MCTELL REMEMBERS.
THINK ABOUT THAT A SECOND, JOHANN.
OUR ONLY LINKS TO GILFRYD, OUR ONLY CHANCES AT EVER FINDING LIZ, ARE A NINETY-YEAR-OLD MAN AND A GHOST.
SPEAKING OF GHOSTS, DO YOU FEEL ANYTHING?
PARDON ME?
THIS IS THE LOBSTER'S "HOME."
AHH, I SEE. YOU WANT TO KNOW IF HIS SPIRIT WILL SUDDENLY POSSESS ME AGAIN, YES?

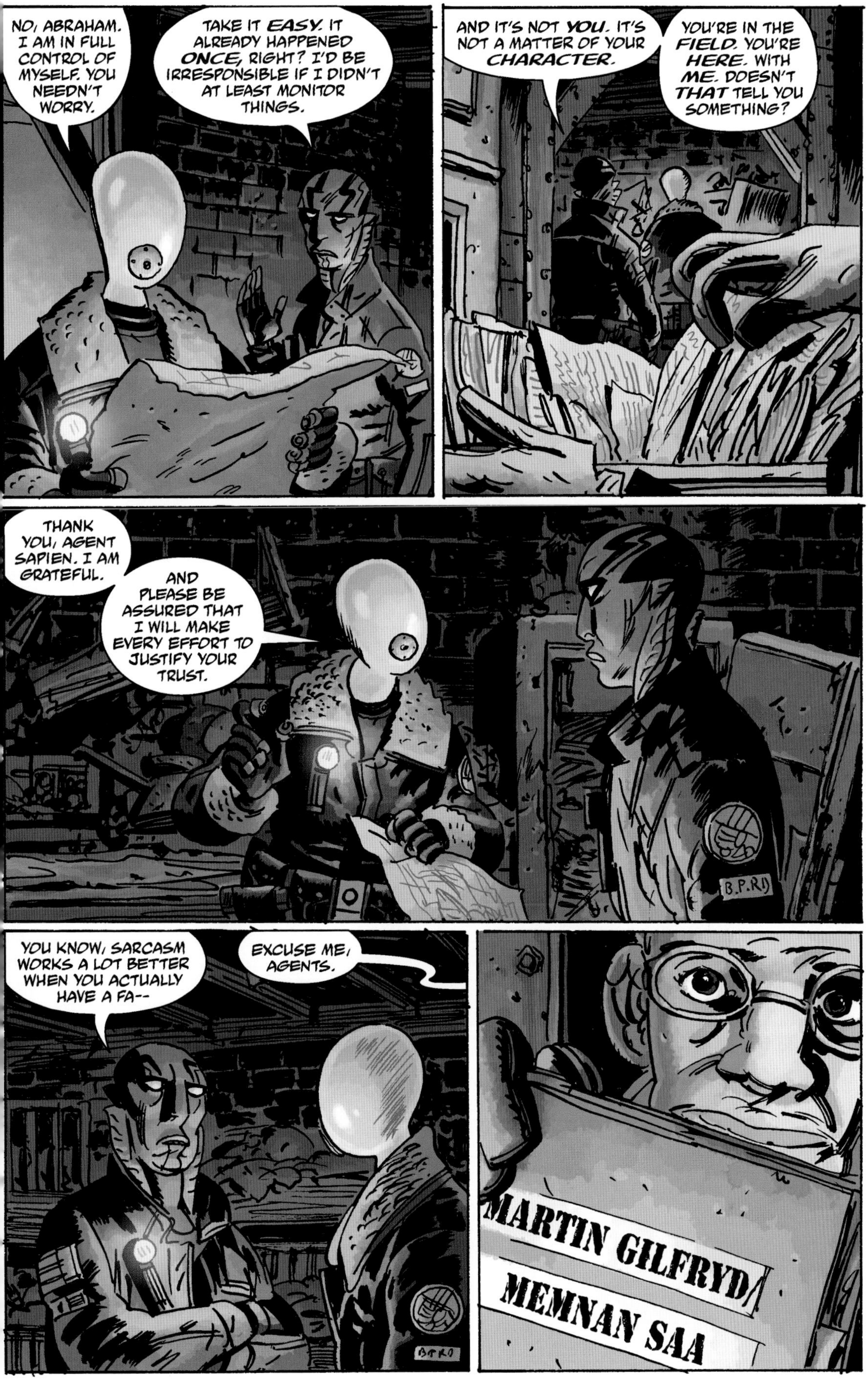
NO, ABRAHAM. I AM IN FULL CONTROL OF MYSELF. YOU NEEDN'T WORRY.
TAKE IT EASY. IT ALREADY HAPPENED ONCE, RIGHT? I'D BE IRRESPONSIBLE IF I DIDN'T AT LEAST MONITOR THINGS.
AND IT'S NOT YOU. IT'S NOT A MATTER OF YOUR CHARACTER.
YOU'RE IN THE FIELD. YOU'RE HERE. WITH ME. DOESN'T THAT TELL YOU SOMETHING?
THANK YOU, AGENT SAPIEN. I AM GRATEFUL.
AND PLEASE BE ASSURED THAT I WILL MAKE EVERY EFFORT TO JUSTIFY YOUR TRUST.
B.P.R.D.
YOU KNOW, SARCASM WORKS A LOT BETTER WHEN YOU ACTUALLY HAVE A FA--
EXCUSE ME, AGENTS.
MARTIN GILFRYD
MEMNAN SAA

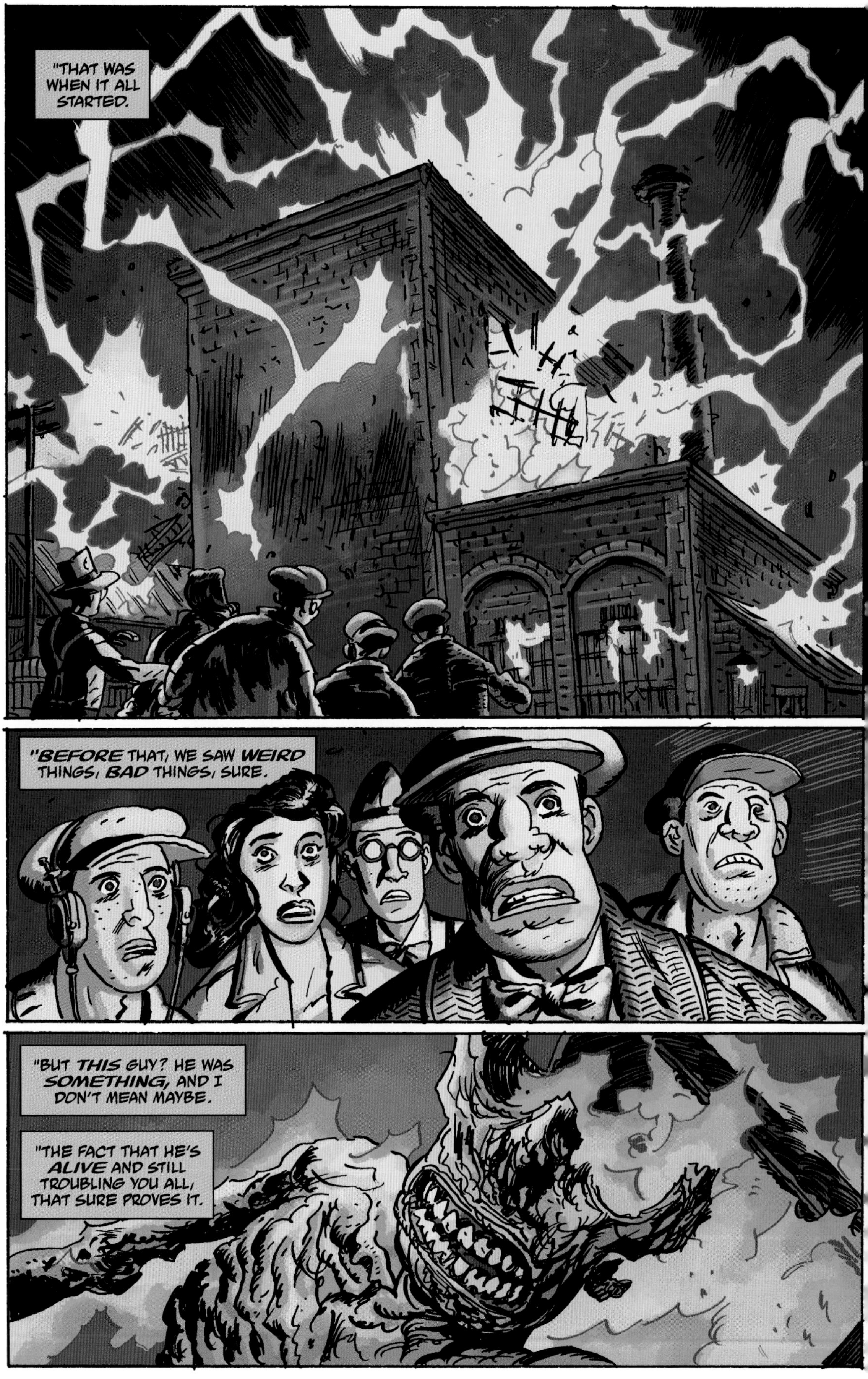
"THAT WAS WHEN IT ALL STARTED.
"BEFORE THAT, WE SAW WEIRD THINGS, BAD THINGS, SURE.
"BUT THIS GUY? HE WAS SOMETHING, AND I DON'T MEAN MAYBE.
"THE FACT THAT HE'S ALIVE AND STILL TROUBLING YOU ALL, THAT SURE PROVES IT.

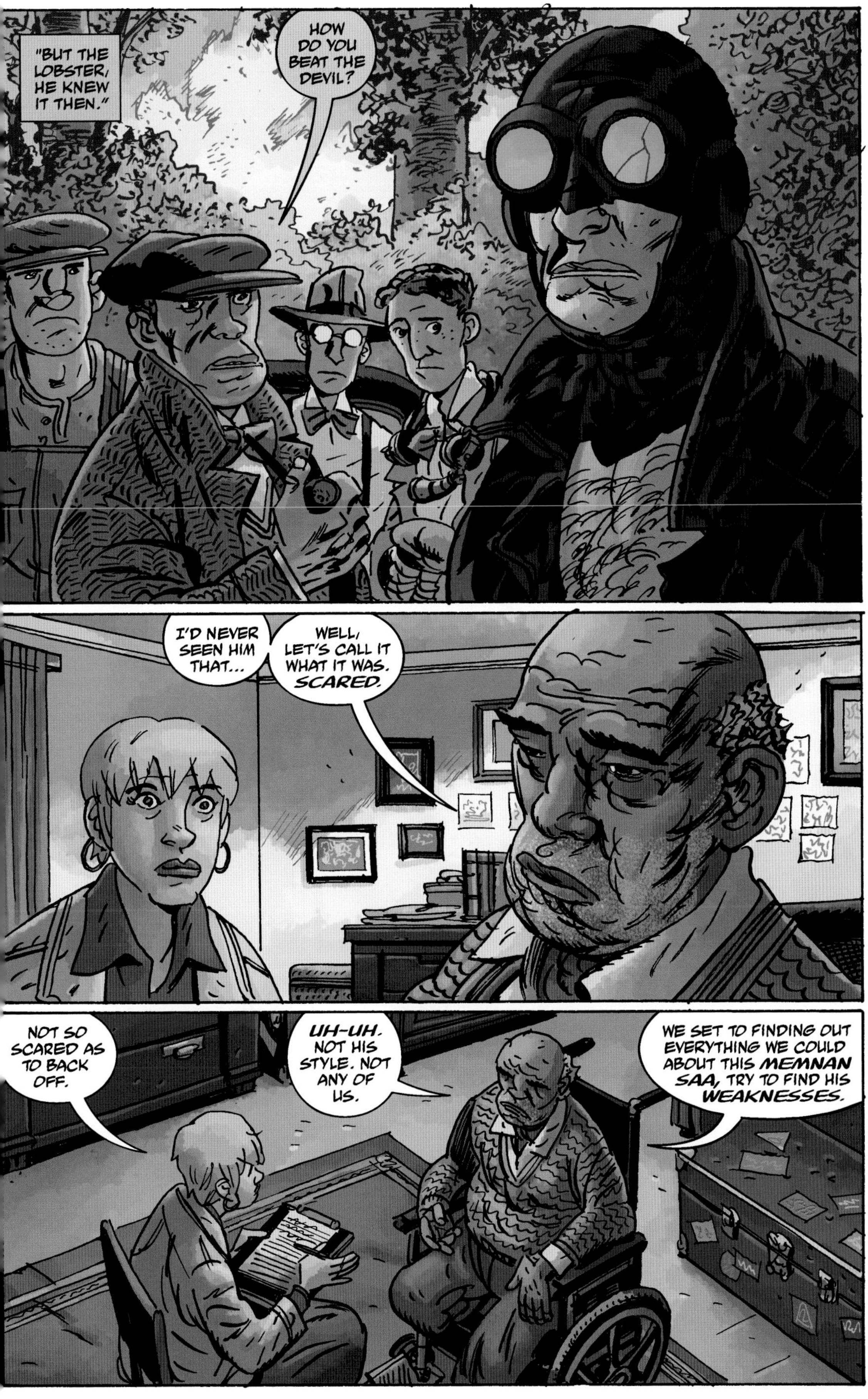
"BUT THE LOBSTER, HE KNEW IT THEN."
HOW DO YOU BEAT THE DEVIL?
I'D NEVER SEEN HIM THAT...
WELL, LET'S CALL IT WHAT IT WAS. SCARED.
NOT SO SCARED AS TO BACK OFF.
UH-UH. NOT HIS STYLE. NOT ANY OF US.
WE SET TO FINDING OUT EVERYTHING WE COULD ABOUT THIS MEMNAN SAA, TRY TO FIND HIS WEAKNESSES.

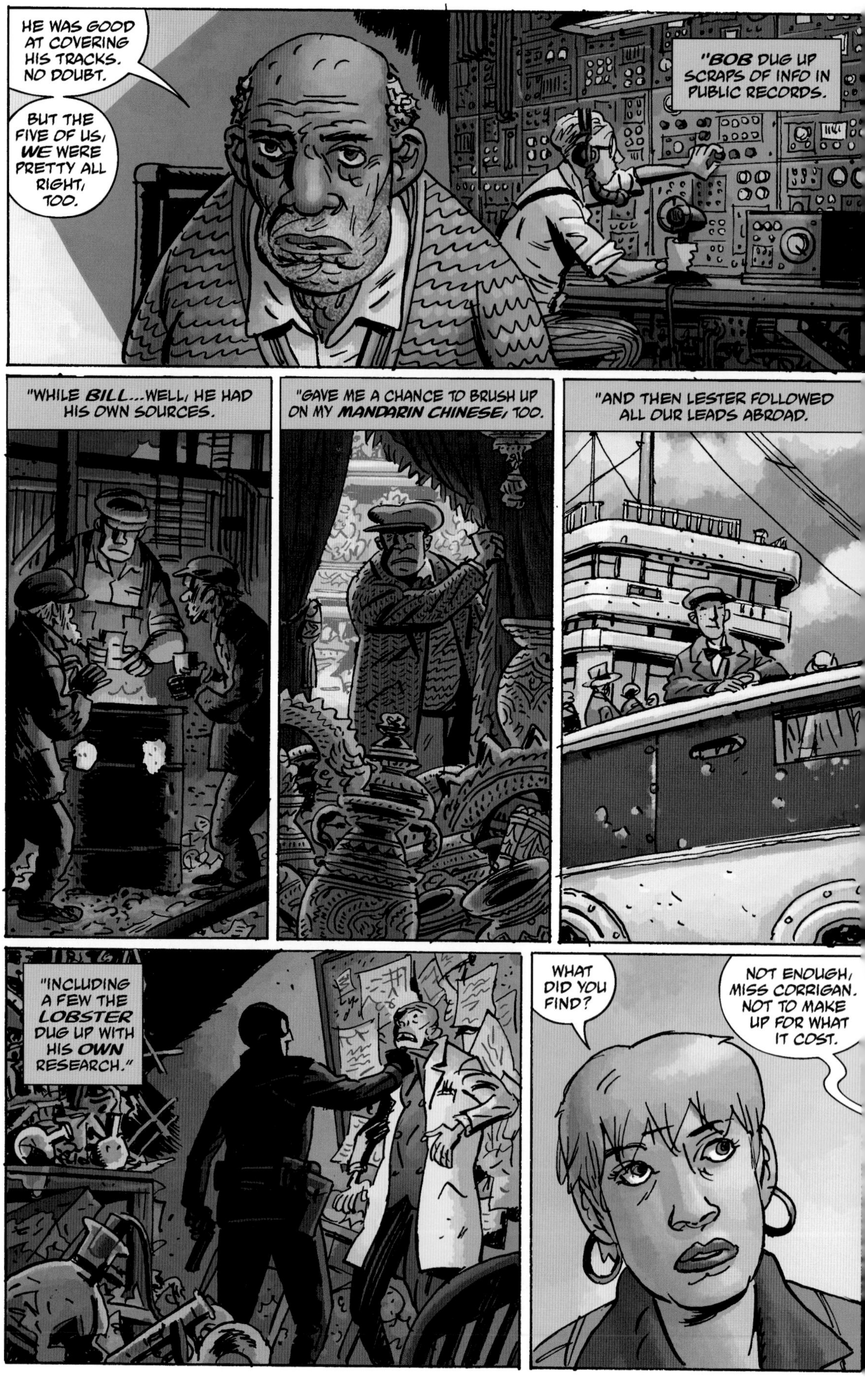
HE WAS GOOD AT COVERING HIS TRACKS. NO DOUBT.
BUT THE FIVE OF US, WE WERE PRETTY ALL RIGHT, TOO.
"BOB DUG UP SCRAPS OF INFO IN PUBLIC RECORDS.
"WHILE BILL...WELL, HE HAD HIS OWN SOURCES.
"GAVE ME A CHANCE TO BRUSH UP ON MY MANDARIN CHINESE, TOO.
"AND THEN LESTER FOLLOWED ALL OUR LEADS ABROAD.
"INCLUDING A FEW THE LOBSTER DUG UP WITH HIS OWN RESEARCH."
WHAT DID YOU FIND?
NOT ENOUGH, MISS CORRIGAN. NOT TO MAKE UP FOR WHAT IT COST.

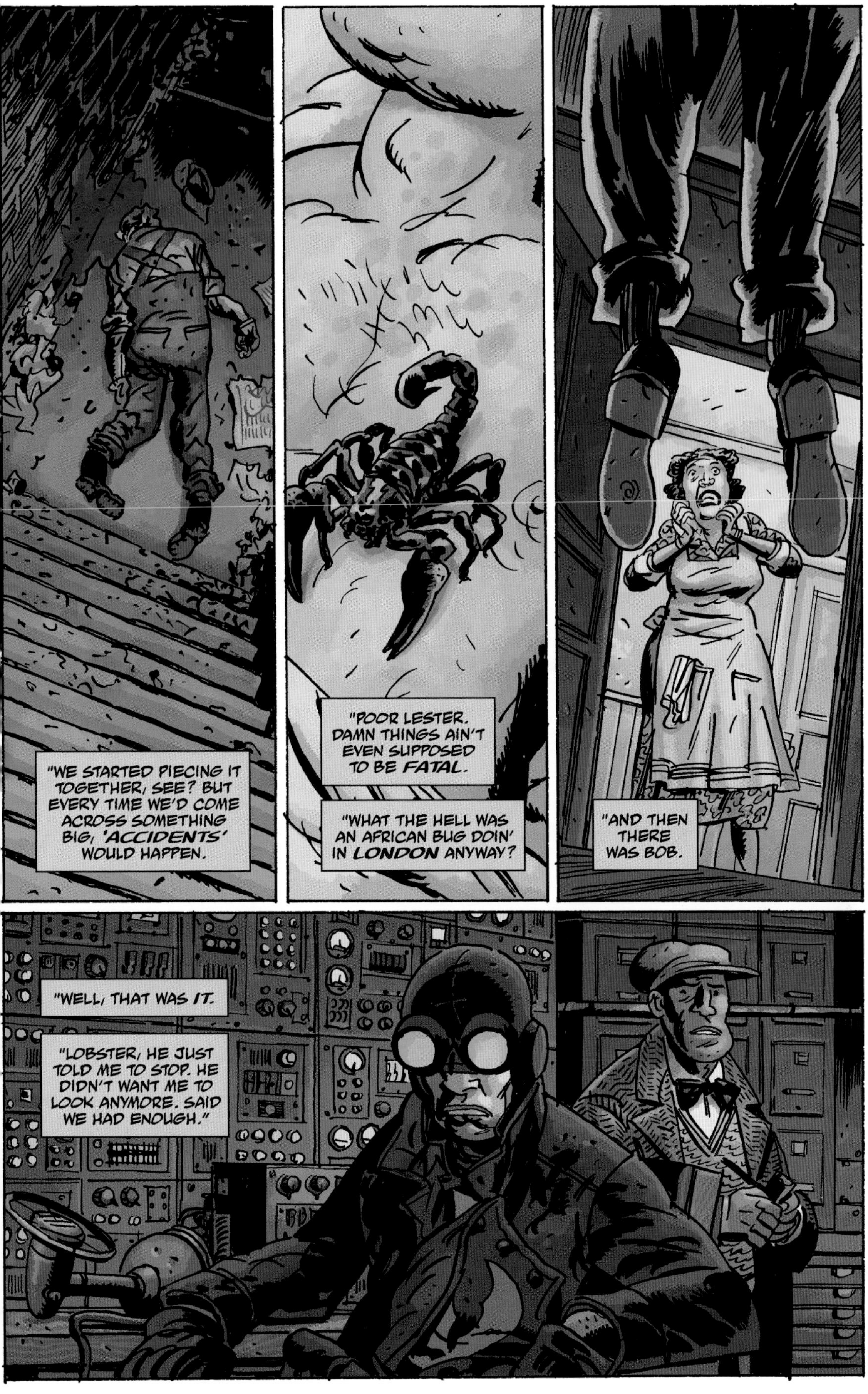
"WE STARTED PIECING IT TOGETHER, SEE? BUT EVERY TIME WE'D COME ACROSS SOMETHING BIG, 'ACCIDENTS' WOULD HAPPEN.
"POOR LESTER. DAMN THINGS AIN'T EVEN SUPPOSED TO BE FATAL.
"WHAT THE HELL WAS AN AFRICAN BUG DOIN' IN LONDON ANYWAY?
"AND THEN THERE WAS BOB.
"WELL, THAT WAS IT.
"LOBSTER, HE JUST TOLD ME TO STOP. HE DIDN'T WANT ME TO LOOK ANYMORE. SAID WE HAD ENOUGH."

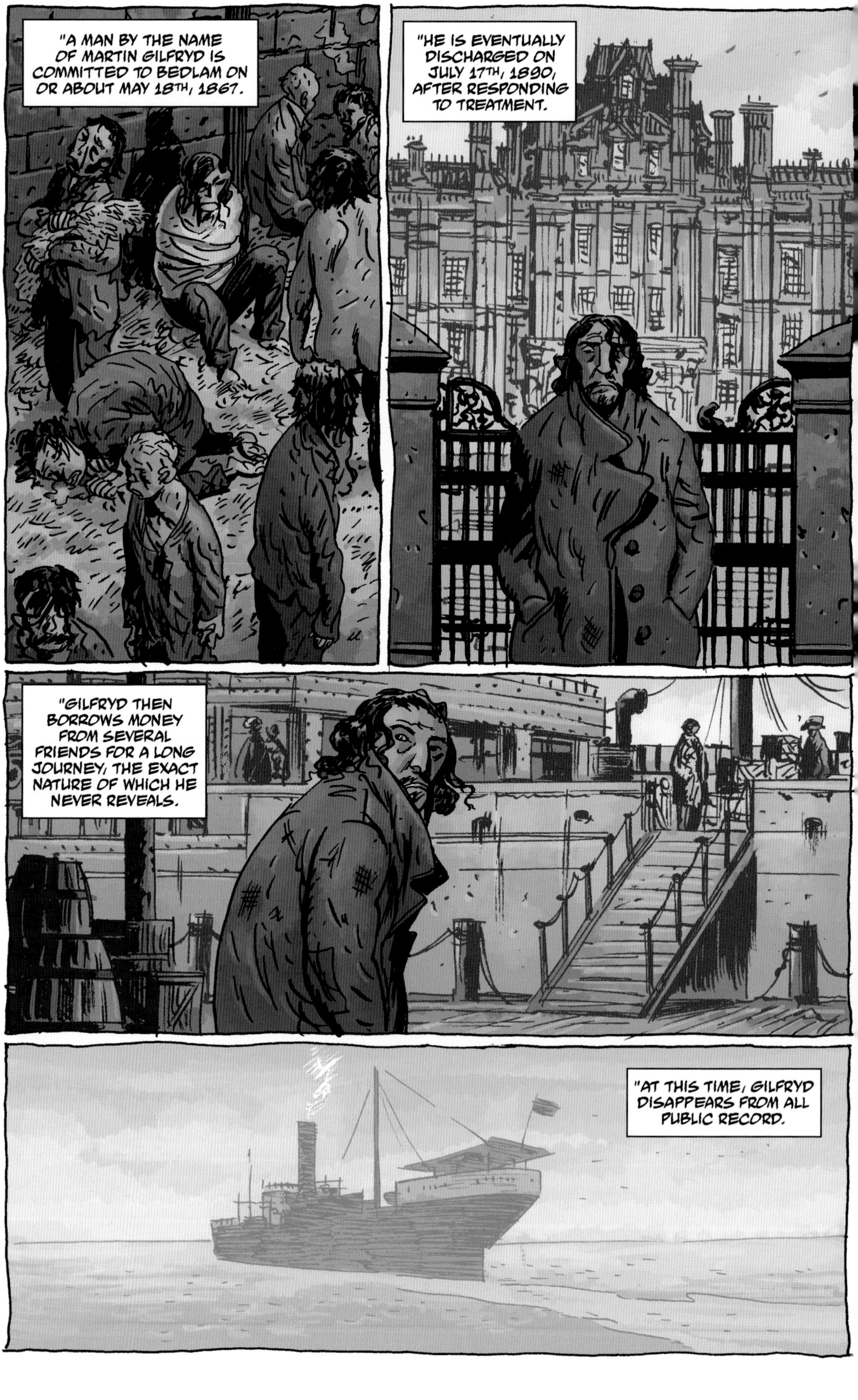
"A MAN BY THE NAME OF MARTIN GILFRYD IS COMMITTED TO BEDLAM ON OR ABOUT MAY 18TH, 1867.
"HE IS EVENTUALLY DISCHARGED ON JULY 17TH, 1890, AFTER RESPONDING TO TREATMENT.
"GILFRYD THEN BORROWS MONEY FROM SEVERAL FRIENDS FOR A LONG JOURNEY, THE EXACT NATURE OF WHICH HE NEVER REVEALS.
"AT THIS TIME, GILFRYD DISAPPEARS FROM ALL PUBLIC RECORD.

"1913. A MAN ASSISTS A MONGOL WARLORD IN A SUCCESSFUL BATTLE THAT ROUTS A RUSSIAN BATTALION.

"THE TRANSLATION FROM THE REPORTS IS AMBIGUOUS, BUT ONE POSSIBLE INTERPRETATION OF HIS NAME COULD BE MEMNAN SAA.

"JUNE 1937. MEMNAN SAA MAKES HIS FIRST CONFIRMED APPEARANCE--THIS TIME IN NEW YORK CITY.

"MARTIN GILFRYD WOULD BE ONE HUNDRED AND ONE YEARS OF AGE AT THIS TIME."

AND?

THAT'S IT. RATHER AN ABRUPT ENDING.

YEAH, WELL, THIS GILFRYD GUY SPECIALIZES IN THOSE, DOESN'T HE?

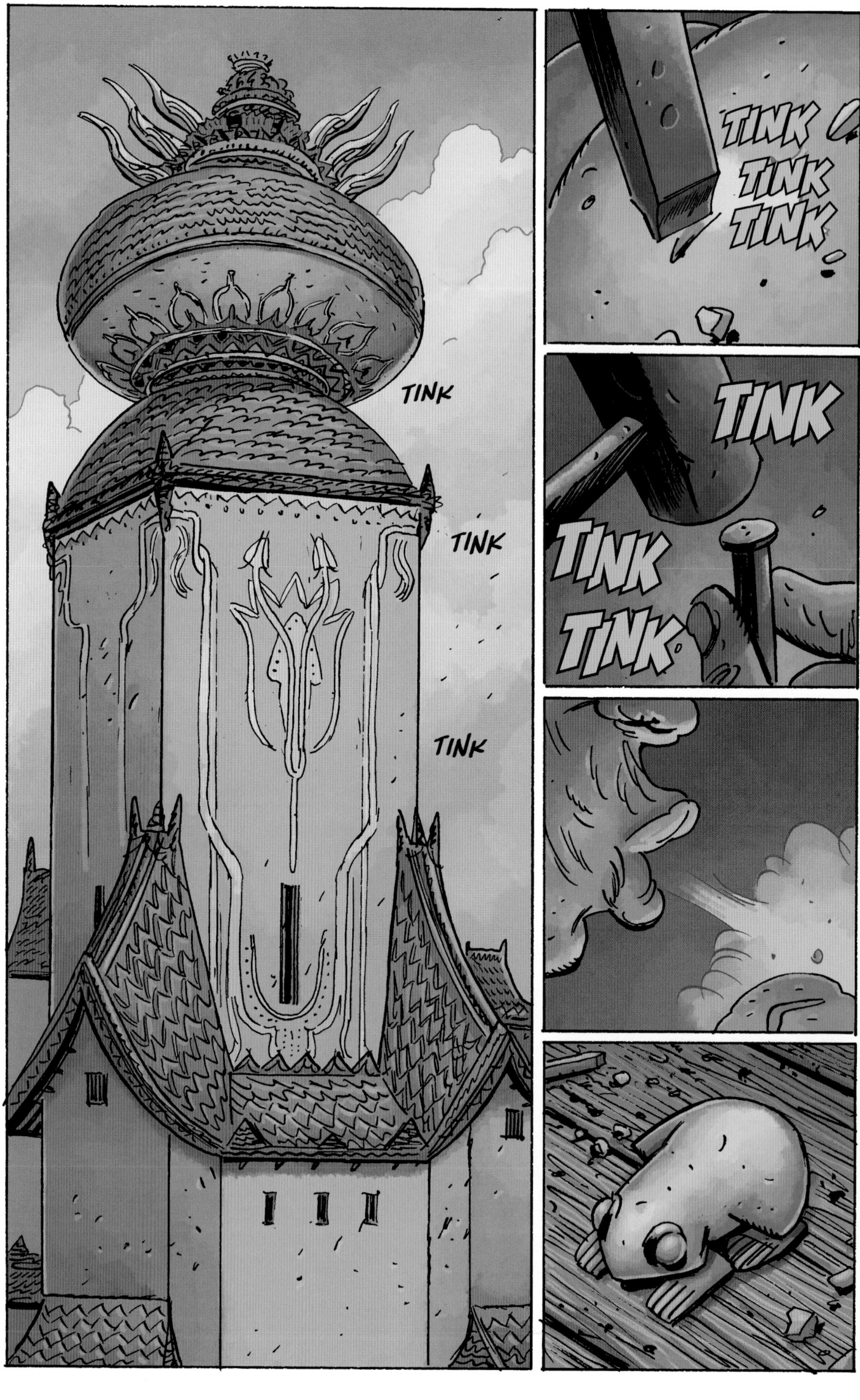
TINK
TINK
TINK
TINK
TINK
TINK
TINK
TINK
TINK

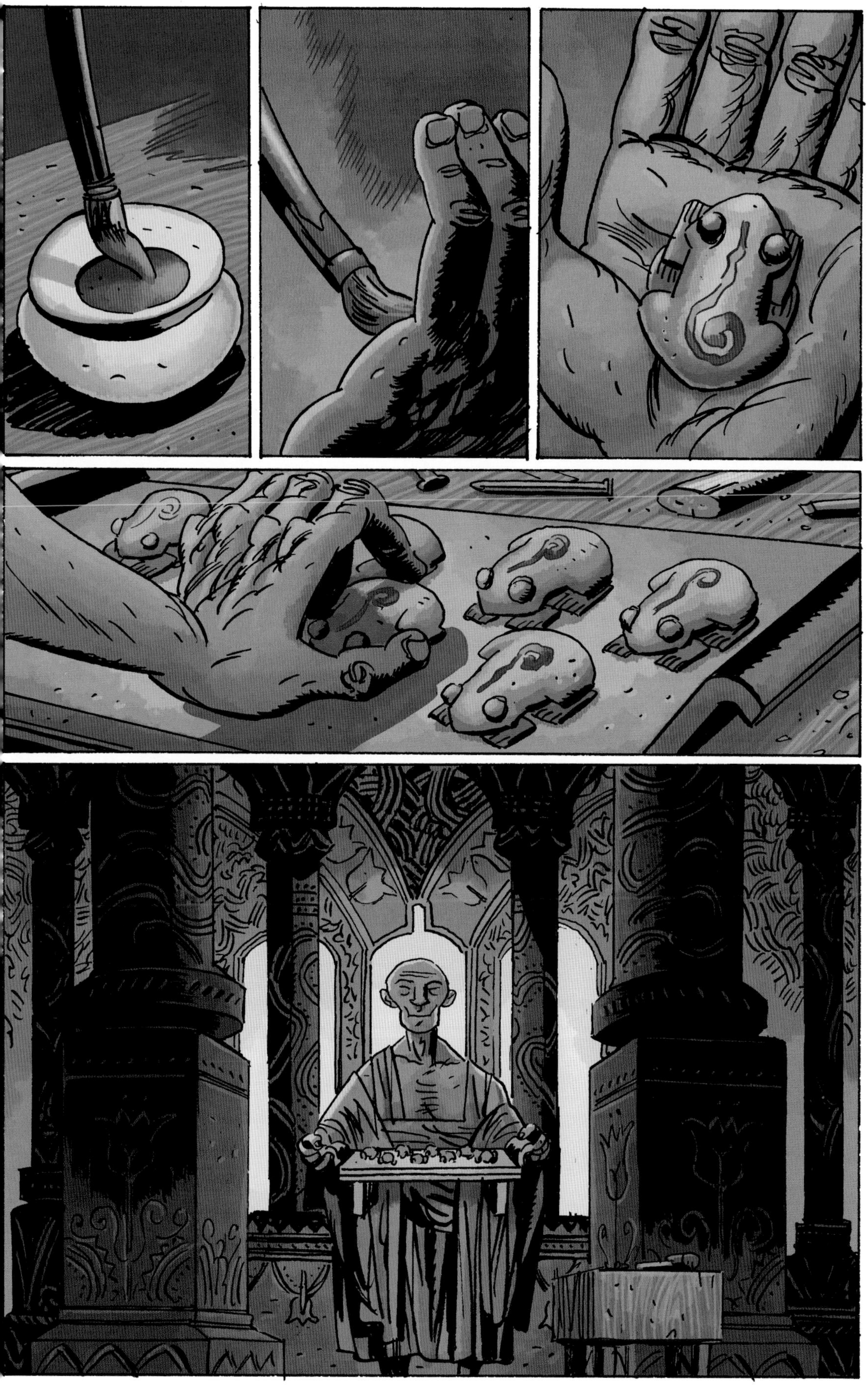

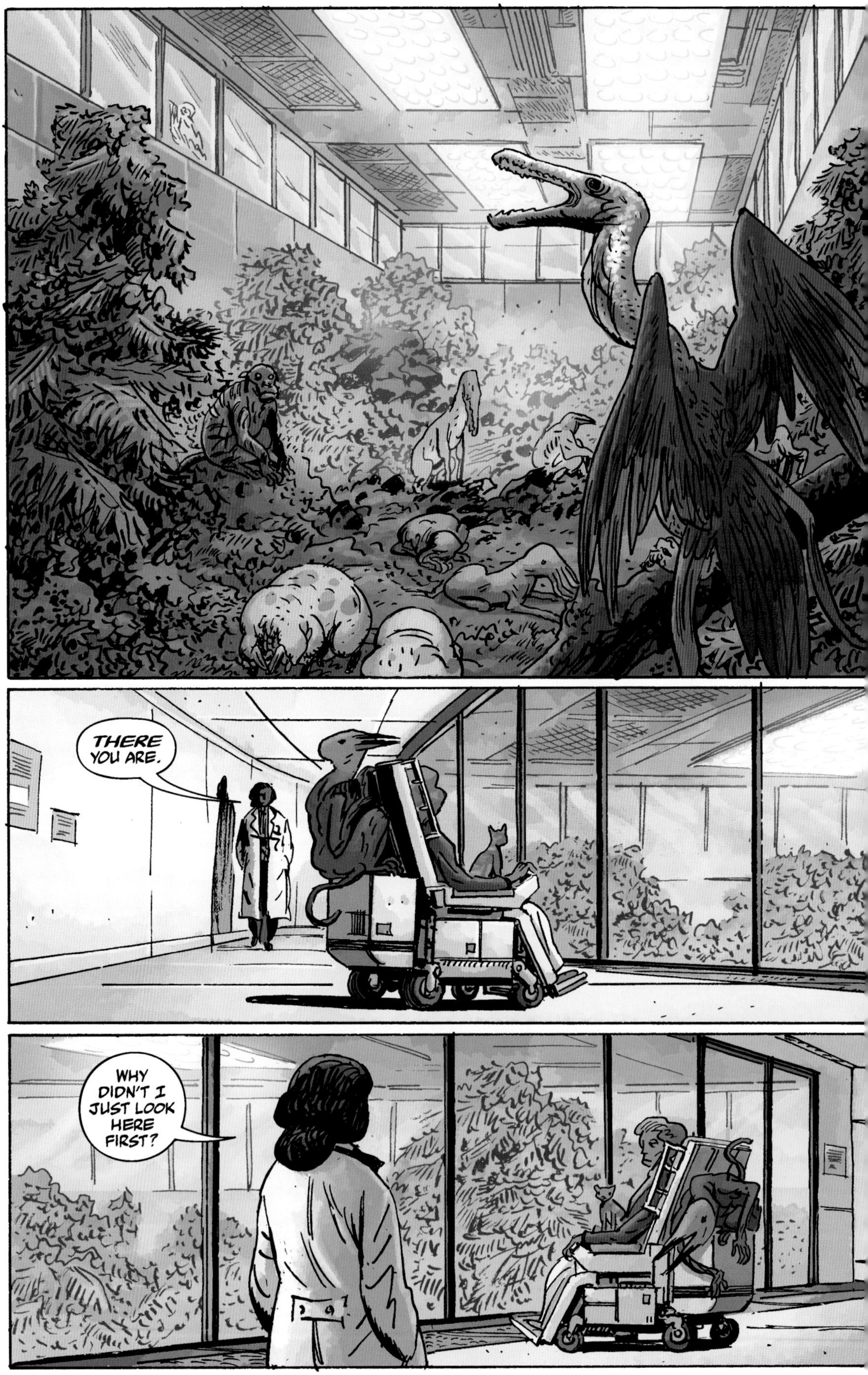
THERE YOU ARE.
WHY DIDN'T I JUST LOOK HERE FIRST?

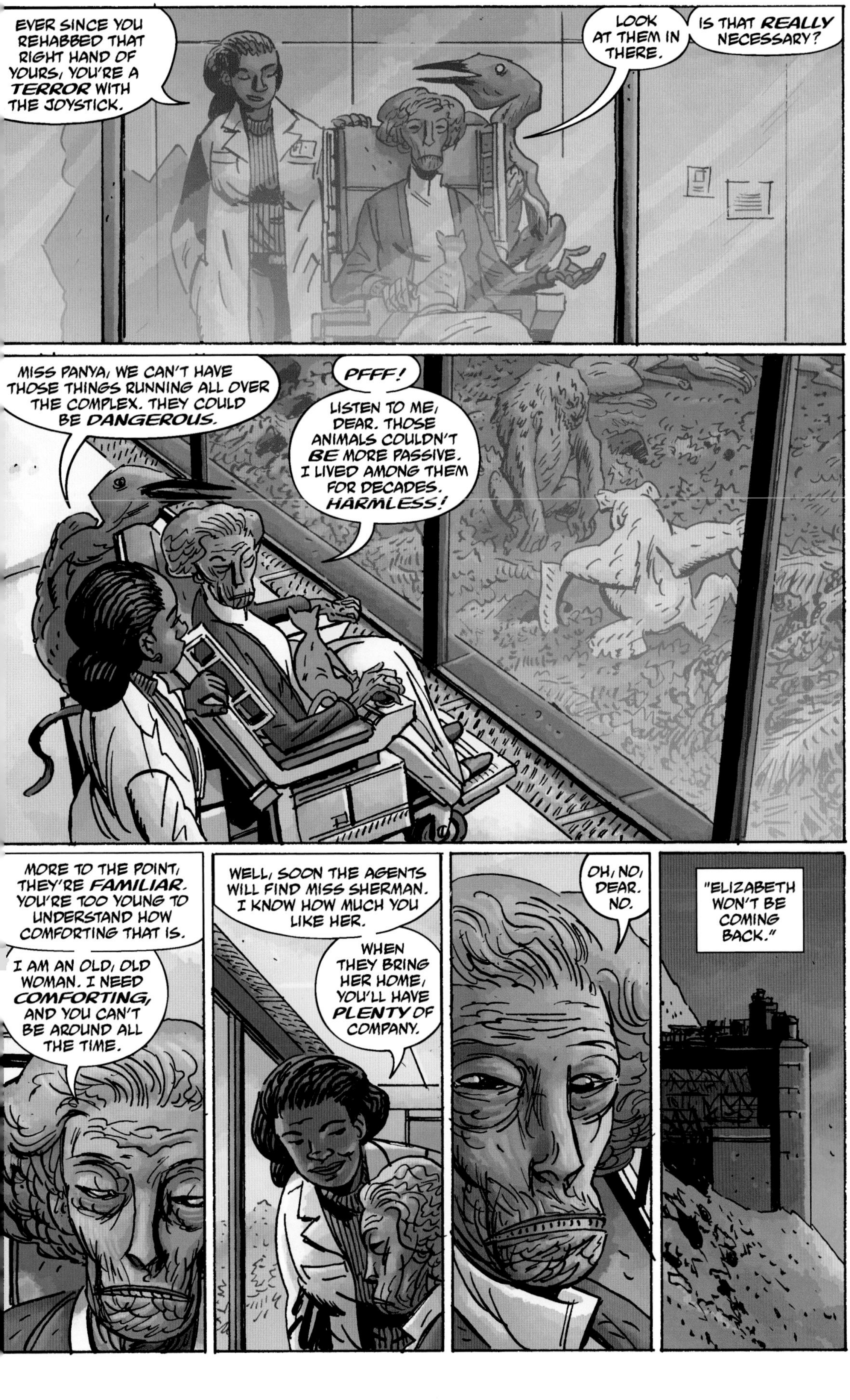
EVER SINCE YOU REHABBED THAT RIGHT HAND OF YOURS, YOU'RE A TERROR WITH THE JOYSTICK.
LOOK AT THEM IN THERE.
IS THAT REALLY NECESSARY?
MISS PANYA, WE CAN'T HAVE THOSE THINGS RUNNING ALL OVER THE COMPLEX. THEY COULD BE DANGEROUS.
PFFF!
LISTEN TO ME, DEAR. THOSE ANIMALS COULDN'T BE MORE PASSIVE. I LIVED AMONG THEM FOR DECADES. HARMLESS!
MORE TO THE POINT, THEY'RE FAMILIAR. YOU'RE TOO YOUNG TO UNDERSTAND HOW COMFORTING THAT IS.
I AM AN OLD, OLD WOMAN. I NEED COMFORTING, AND YOU CAN'T BE AROUND ALL THE TIME.
WELL, SOON THE AGENTS WILL FIND MISS SHERMAN. I KNOW HOW MUCH YOU LIKE HER.
WHEN THEY BRING HER HOME, YOU'LL HAVE PLENTY OF COMPANY.
OH, NO, DEAR. NO.
"ELIZABETH WON'T BE COMING BACK."

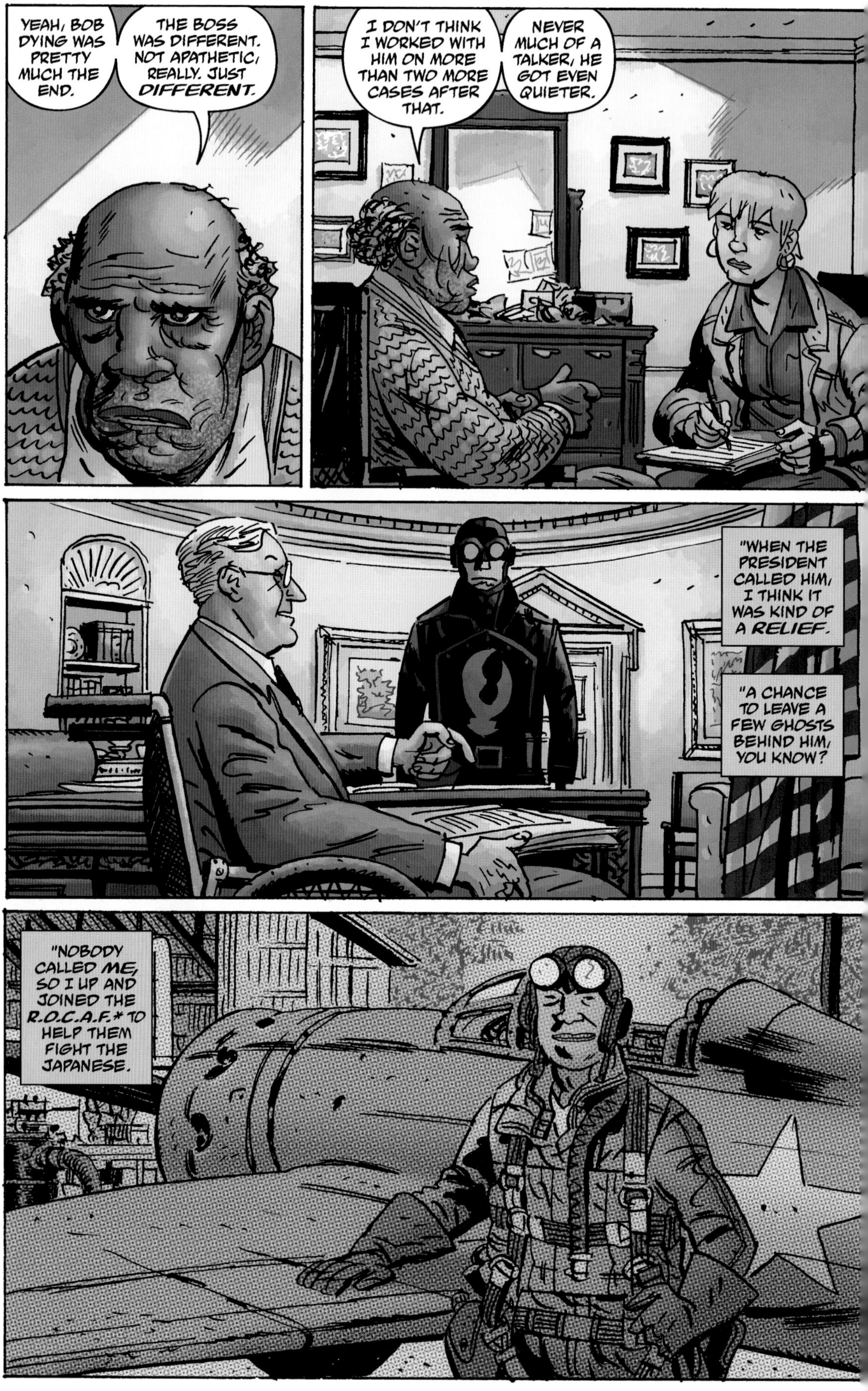

YEAH, BOB DYING WAS PRETTY MUCH THE END.
THE BOSS WAS DIFFERENT. NOT APATHETIC, REALLY. JUST *DIFFERENT*.
I DON'T THINK I WORKED WITH HIM ON MORE THAN TWO MORE CASES AFTER THAT.
NEVER MUCH OF A TALKER, HE GOT EVEN QUIETER.
"WHEN THE PRESIDENT CALLED HIM, I THINK IT WAS KIND OF A *RELIEF*.
"A CHANCE TO LEAVE A FEW GHOSTS BEHIND HIM, YOU KNOW?
"NOBODY CALLED *ME*, SO I UP AND JOINED THE *R.O.C.A.F.** TO HELP THEM FIGHT THE JAPANESE.

*REPUBLIC OF CHINA AIR FORCE

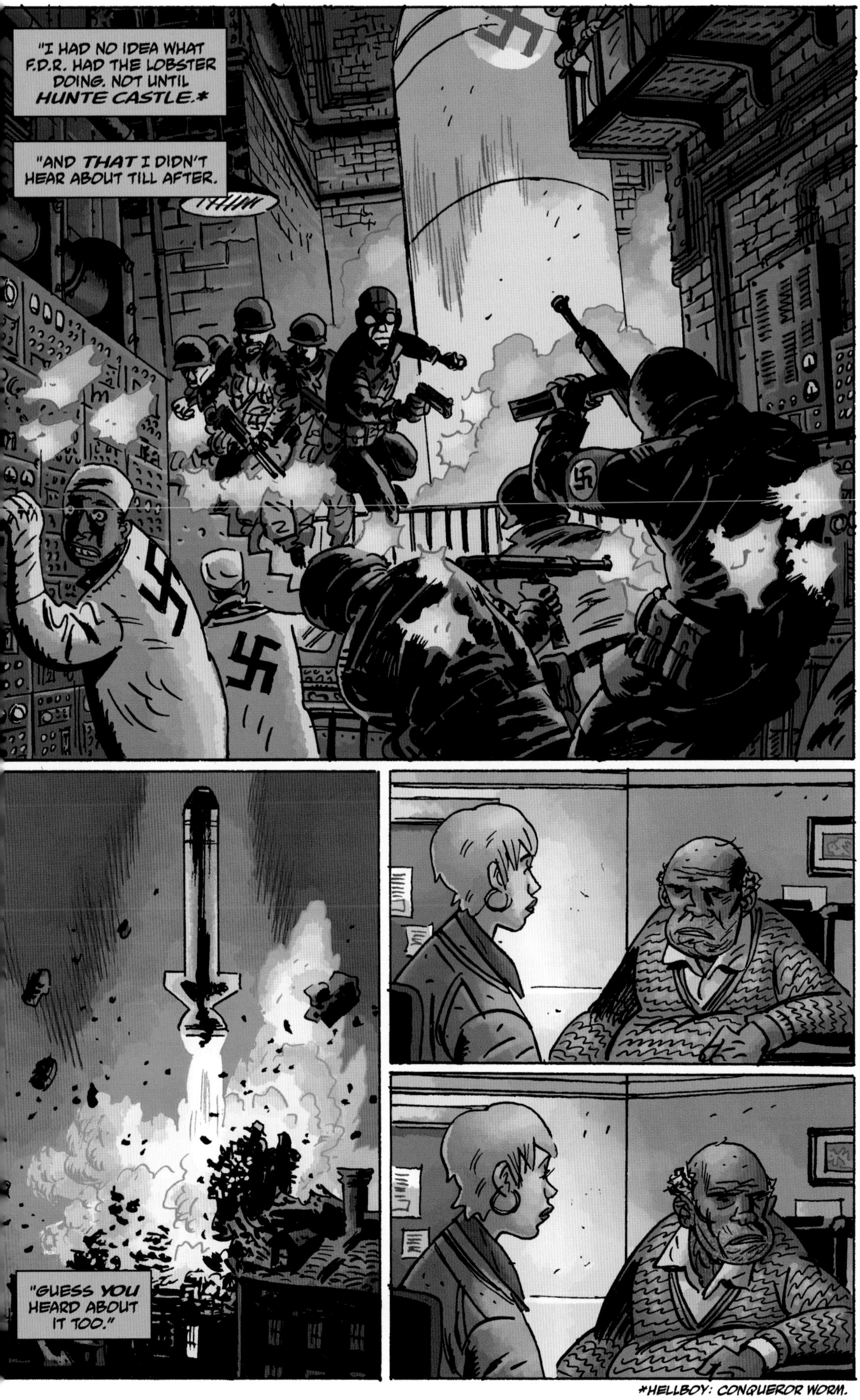
"I HAD NO IDEA WHAT F.D.R. HAD THE LOBSTER DOING. NOT UNTIL HUNTE CASTLE.*
"AND THAT I DIDN'T HEAR ABOUT TILL AFTER.
"GUESS YOU HEARD ABOUT IT TOO."

*HELLBOY: CONQUEROR WORM.

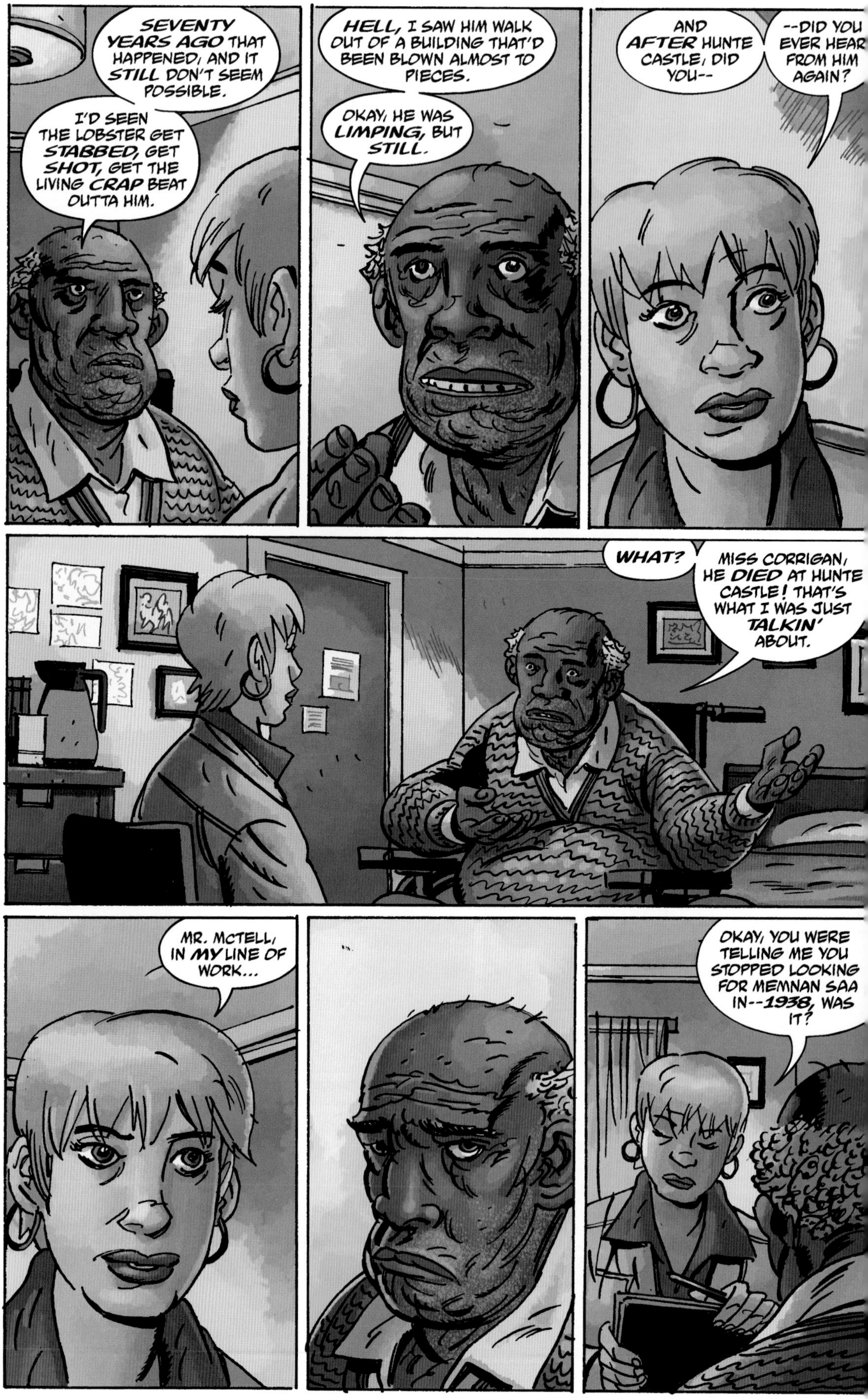
SEVENTY YEARS AGO THAT HAPPENED, AND IT STILL DON'T SEEM POSSIBLE.
I'D SEEN THE LOBSTER GET STABBED, GET SHOT, GET THE LIVING CRAP BEAT OUTTA HIM.
HELL, I SAW HIM WALK OUT OF A BUILDING THAT'D BEEN BLOWN ALMOST TO PIECES.
OKAY, HE WAS LIMPING, BUT STILL.
AND AFTER HUNTE CASTLE, DID YOU--
--DID YOU EVER HEAR FROM HIM AGAIN?
WHAT?
MISS CORRIGAN, HE DIED AT HUNTE CASTLE! THAT'S WHAT I WAS JUST TALKIN' ABOUT.
MR. MCTELL, IN MY LINE OF WORK...
OKAY, YOU WERE TELLING ME YOU STOPPED LOOKING FOR MEMNAN SAA IN--1938, WAS IT?

OH, YEAH. THAT'S WHERE THIS ALL STARTED.

KINDA GOT *OFF TRACK*, DIDN'T I? I DO THAT FROM TIME TO TIME.

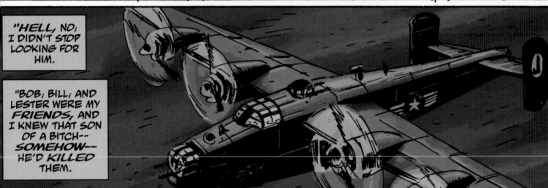

"HELL, NO, I DIDN'T STOP LOOKING FOR HIM.

"BOB, BILL, AND LESTER WERE MY *FRIENDS*, AND I KNEW THAT SON OF A BITCH-- *SOMEHOW*-- HE'D *KILLED* THEM.

"AFTER THE WAR STARTED, I JOINED THE AIR FORCE-- *ARMY AIR FORCE*, IT WAS THEN.

"BECAME A NAVIGATOR SO I COULD GET MY HANDS ON ALL THOSE MAPS."

THIS *SAA* CHARACTER ENDED UP IN EUROPE, BUT HE KEPT STAYING A FEW STEPS AHEAD OF ME.

DID YOU TELL THE ARMY?

AWW, *THEY* DIDN'T CARE ABOUT SOME YELLOW-MENACE WANNABE. AND THEY SURE DIDN'T CARE ABOUT MY *REVENGE*. THERE WAS HITLER, *AND* TOJO.

I JUST WANTED TO KEEP TRACK OF HIM, THEN HUNT HIM DOWN MYSELF LATER.

BUT, YOU KNOW, *STUFF* HAPPENED.

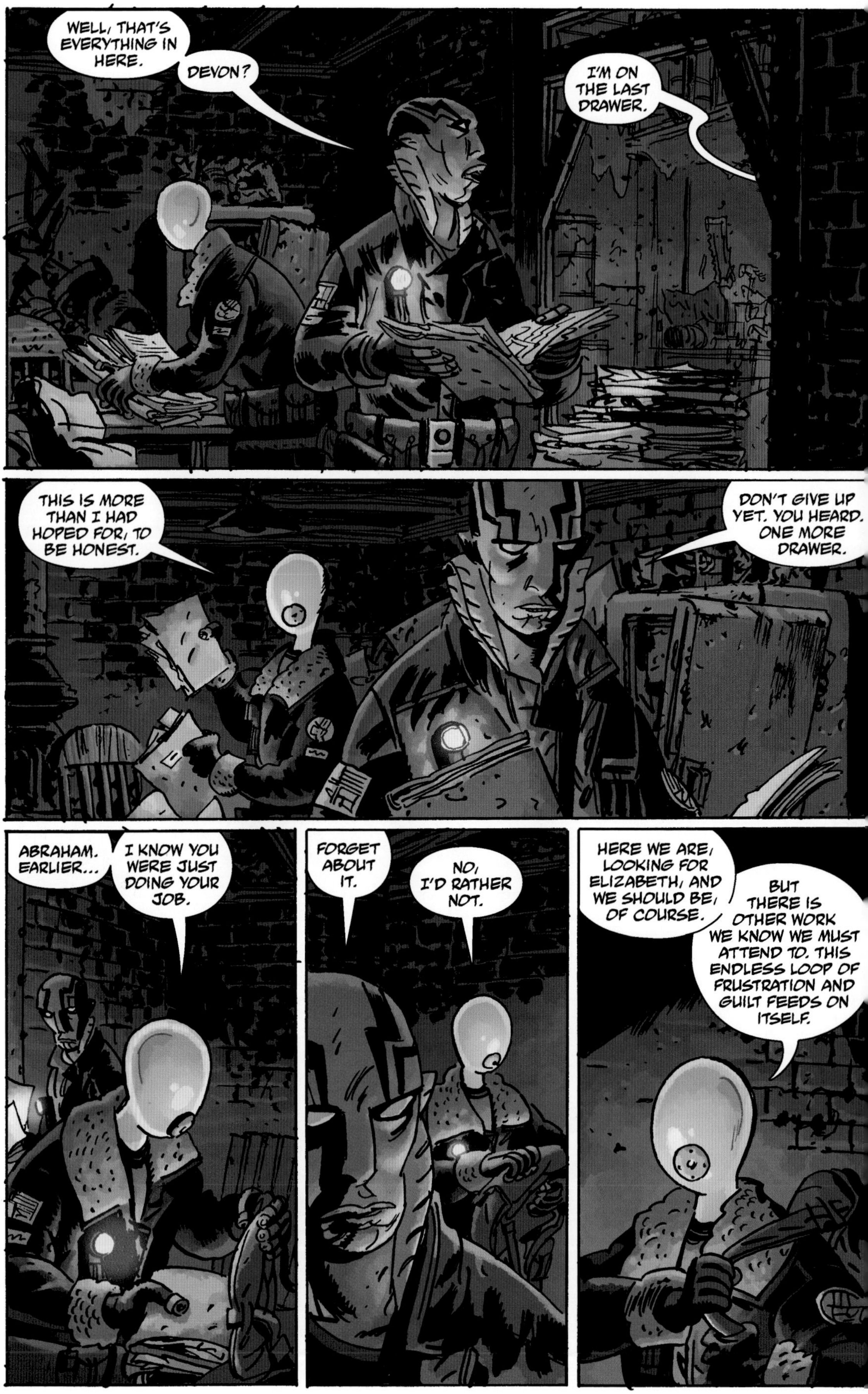

WELL, THAT'S EVERYTHING IN HERE.
DEVON?
I'M ON THE LAST DRAWER.
THIS IS MORE THAN I HAD HOPED FOR, TO BE HONEST.
DON'T GIVE UP YET. YOU HEARD. ONE MORE DRAWER.
ABRAHAM. EARLIER...
I KNOW YOU WERE JUST DOING YOUR JOB.
FORGET ABOUT IT.
NO, I'D RATHER NOT.
HERE WE ARE, LOOKING FOR ELIZABETH, AND WE SHOULD BE, OF COURSE.
BUT THERE IS OTHER WORK WE KNOW WE MUST ATTEND TO. THIS ENDLESS LOOP OF FRUSTRATION AND GUILT FEEDS ON ITSELF.

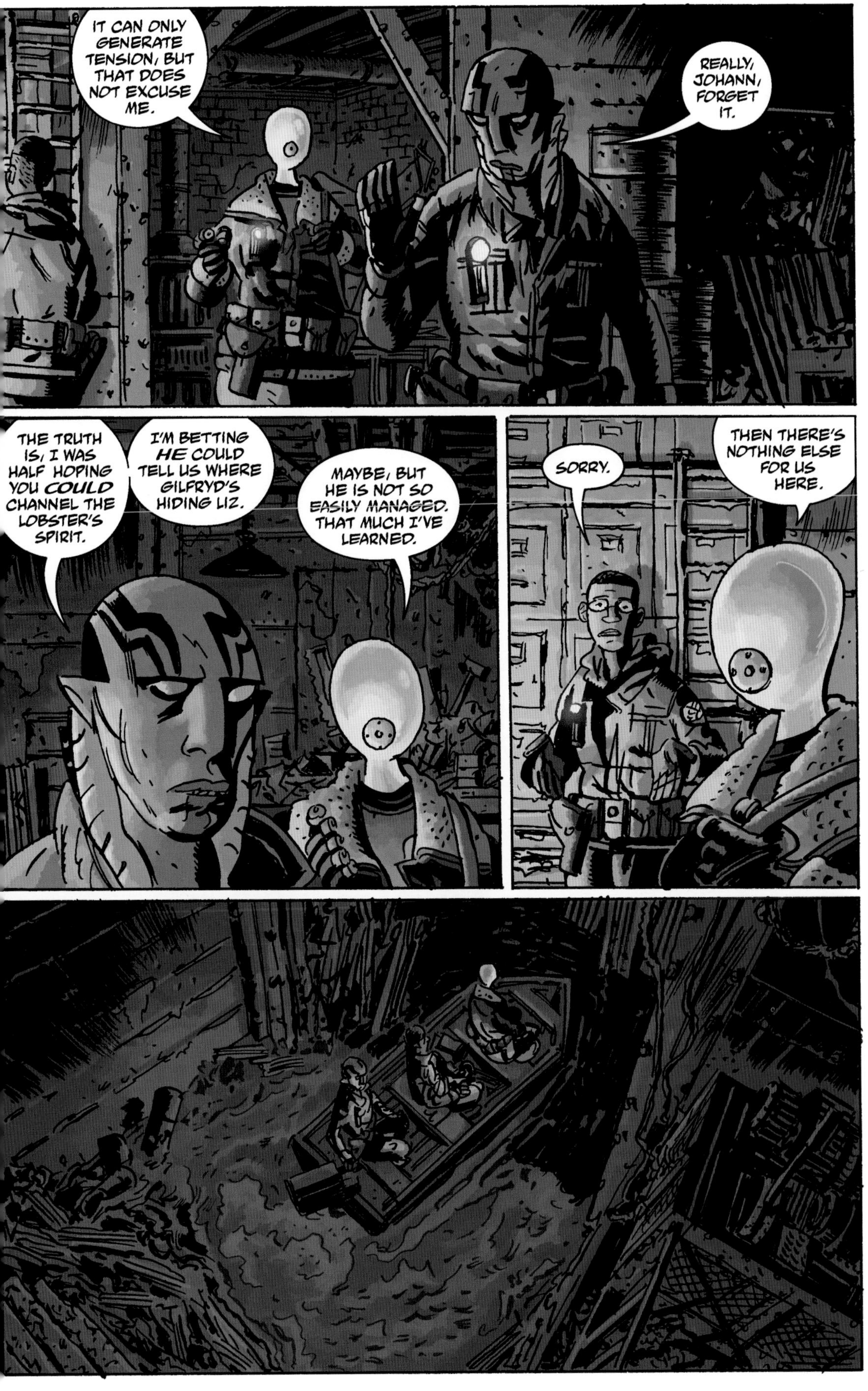
IT CAN ONLY GENERATE TENSION, BUT THAT DOES NOT EXCUSE ME.
REALLY, JOHANN, FORGET IT.
THE TRUTH IS, I WAS HALF HOPING YOU *COULD* CHANNEL THE LOBSTER'S SPIRIT.
I'M BETTING *HE* COULD TELL US WHERE GILFRYD'S HIDING LIZ.
MAYBE, BUT HE IS NOT SO EASILY MANAGED. THAT MUCH I'VE LEARNED.
SORRY.
THEN THERE'S NOTHING ELSE FOR US HERE.

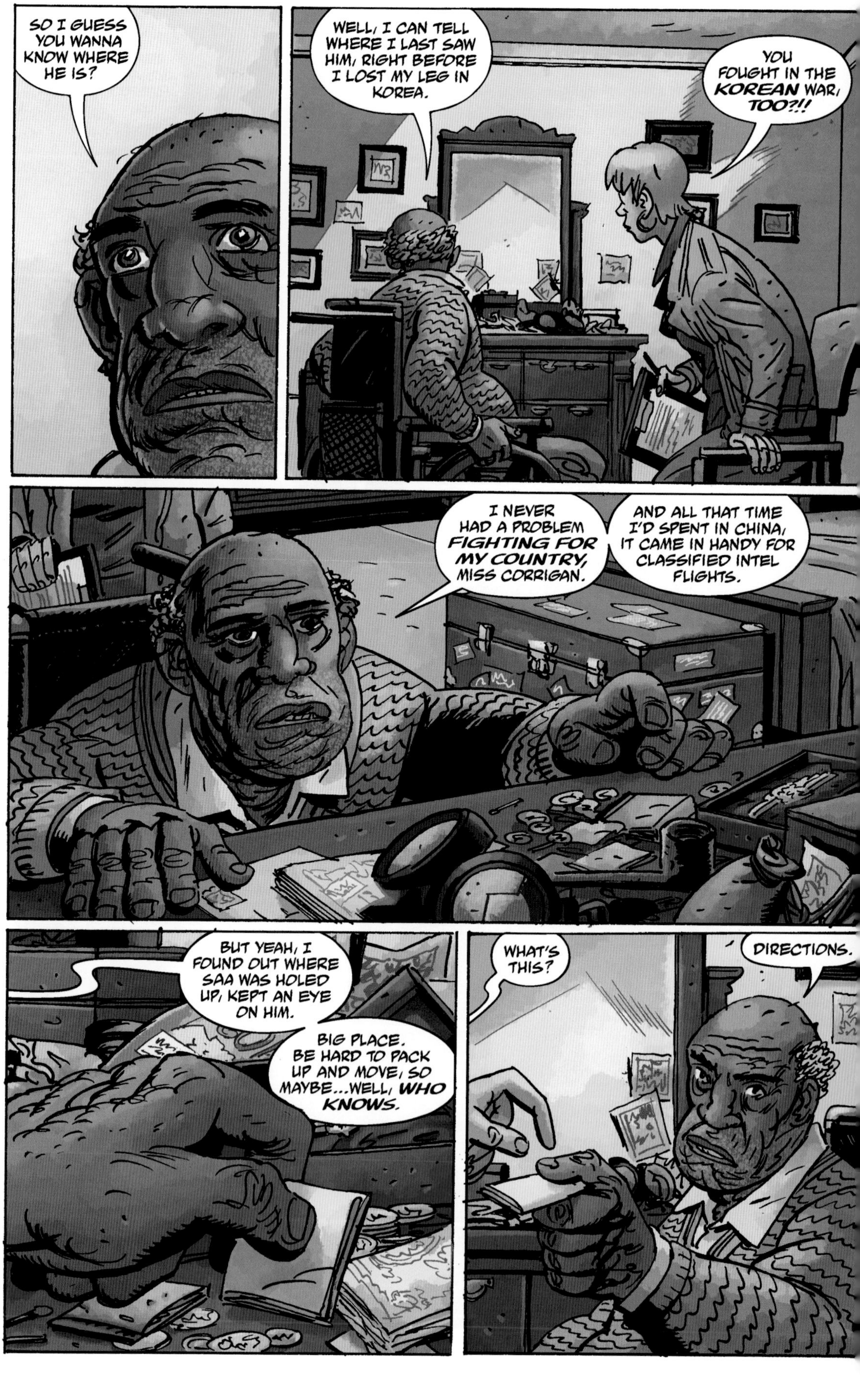
SO I GUESS YOU WANNA KNOW WHERE HE IS?
WELL, I CAN TELL WHERE I LAST SAW HIM, RIGHT BEFORE I LOST MY LEG IN KOREA.
YOU FOUGHT IN THE KOREAN WAR, TOO?!!
I NEVER HAD A PROBLEM FIGHTING FOR MY COUNTRY, MISS CORRIGAN.
AND ALL THAT TIME I'D SPENT IN CHINA, IT CAME IN HANDY FOR CLASSIFIED INTEL FLIGHTS.
BUT YEAH, I FOUND OUT WHERE SAA WAS HOLED UP, KEPT AN EYE ON HIM.
BIG PLACE. BE HARD TO PACK UP AND MOVE, SO MAYBE...WELL, WHO KNOWS.
WHAT'S THIS?
DIRECTIONS.

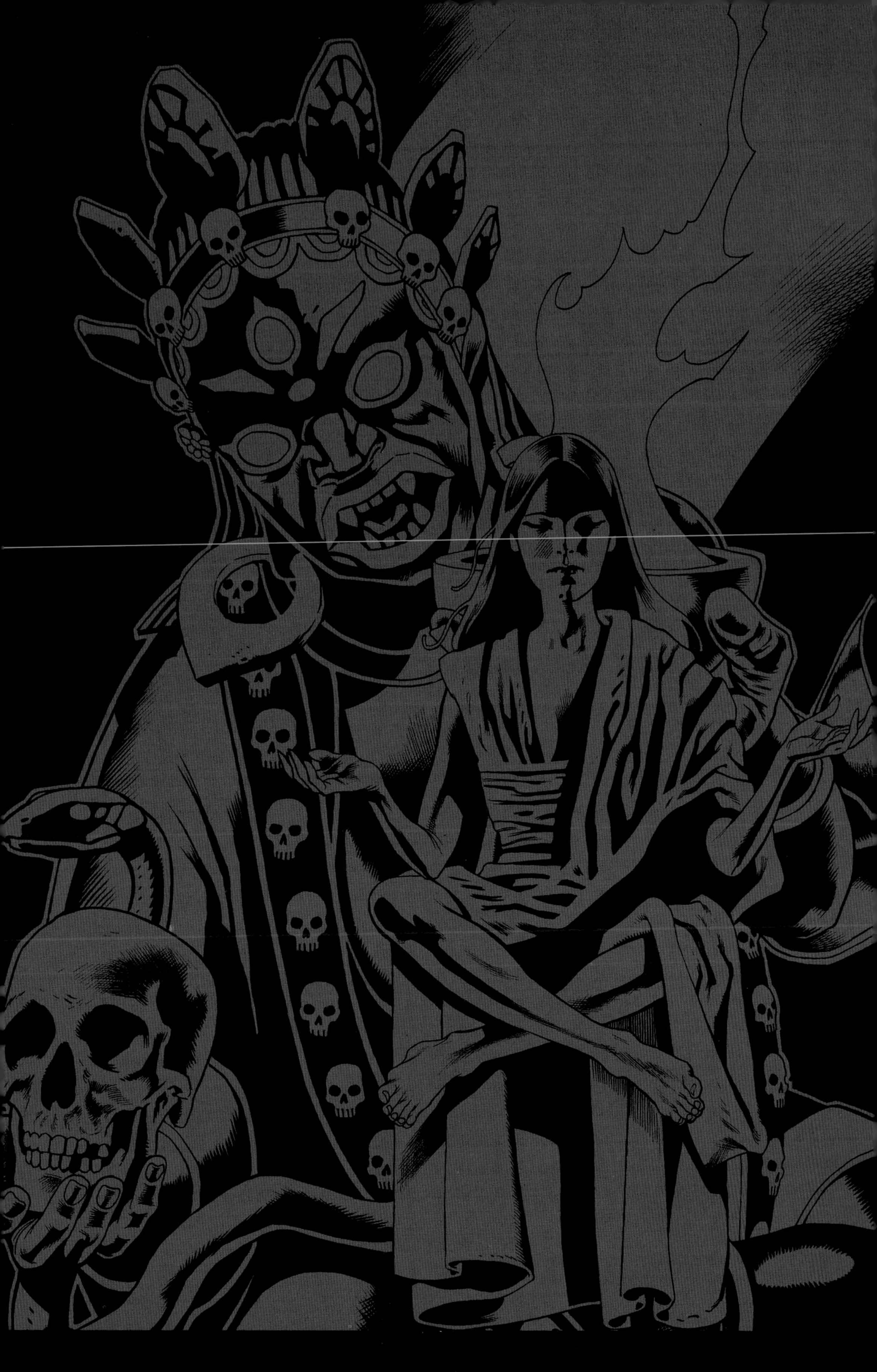

CHAPTER TWO

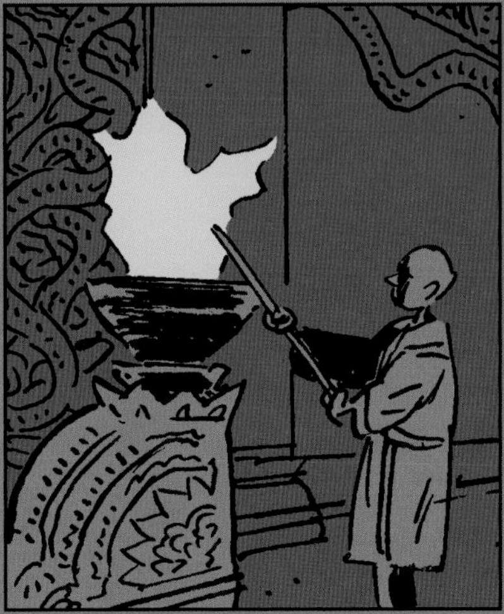

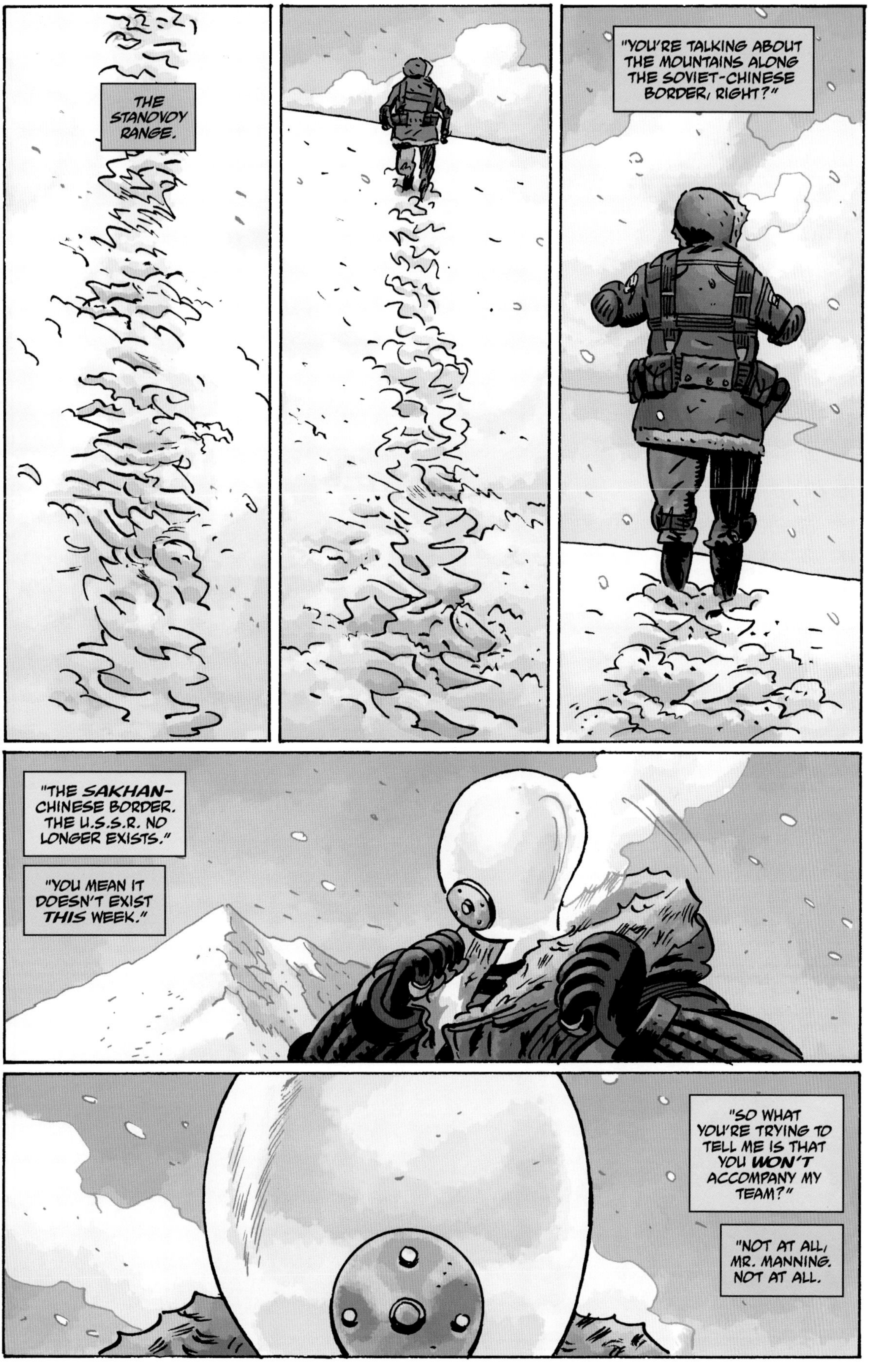
THE STANOVOY RANGE.
"YOU'RE TALKING ABOUT THE MOUNTAINS ALONG THE SOVIET-CHINESE BORDER, RIGHT?"
"THE SAKHAN-CHINESE BORDER. THE U.S.S.R. NO LONGER EXISTS."
"YOU MEAN IT DOESN'T EXIST THIS WEEK."
"SO WHAT YOU'RE TRYING TO TELL ME IS THAT YOU WON'T ACCOMPANY MY TEAM?"
"NOT AT ALL, MR. MANNING. NOT AT ALL.

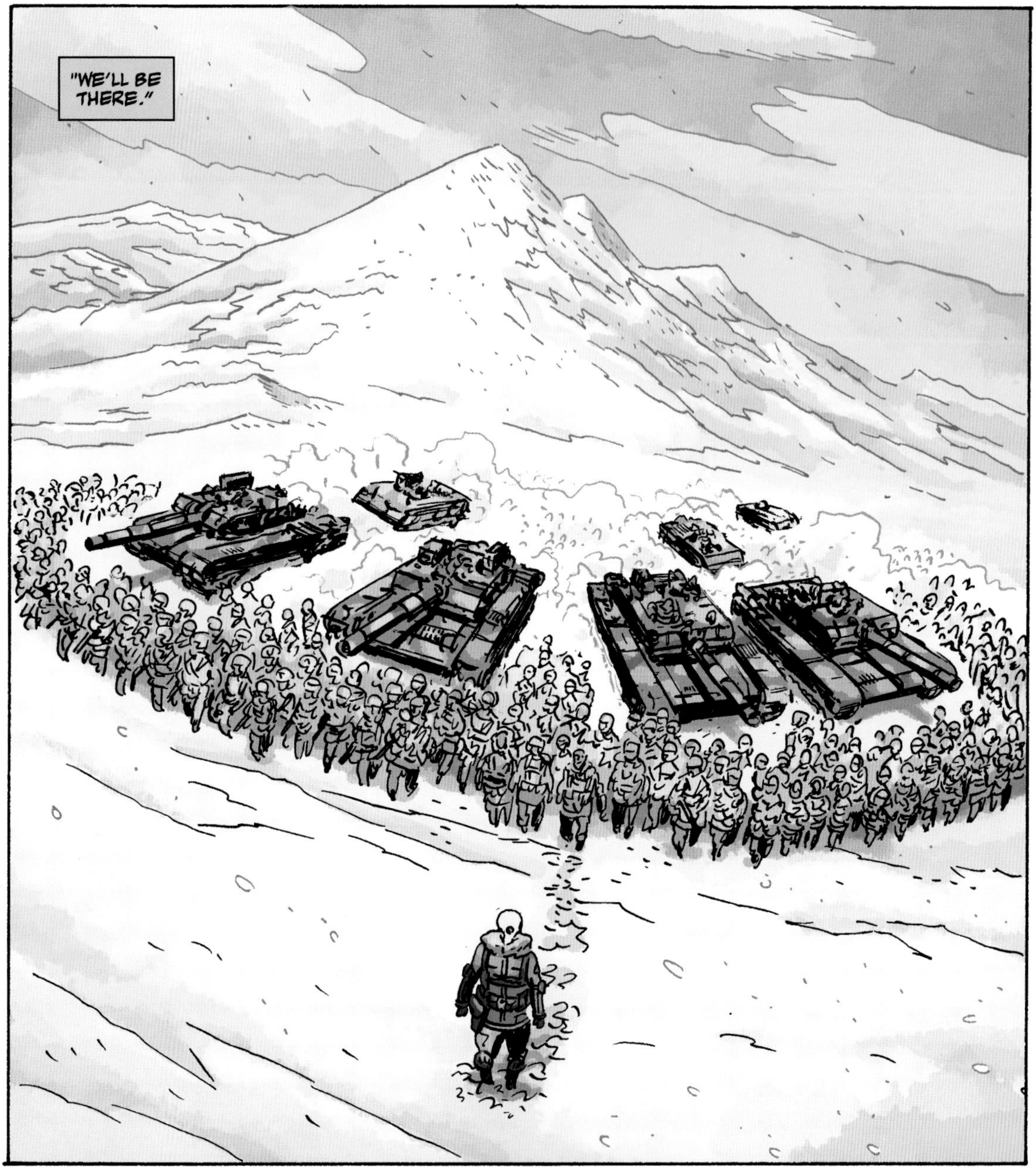
"WE'LL BE THERE."

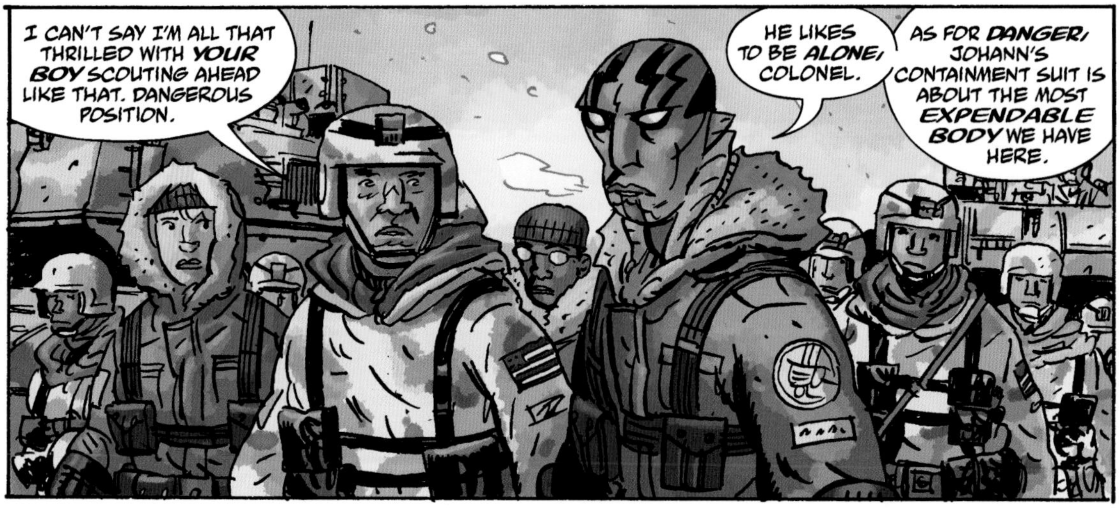
I CAN'T SAY I'M ALL THAT THRILLED WITH YOUR BOY SCOUTING AHEAD LIKE THAT. DANGEROUS POSITION.
HE LIKES TO BE ALONE, COLONEL.
AS FOR DANGER, JOHANN'S CONTAINMENT SUIT IS ABOUT THE MOST EXPENDABLE BODY WE HAVE HERE.

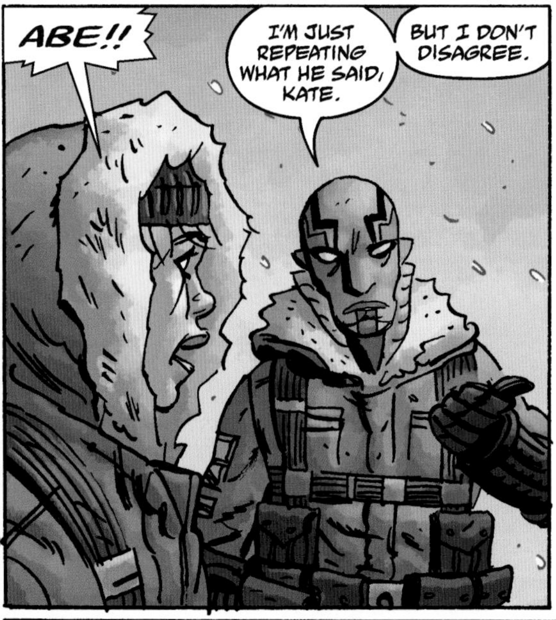
ABE!!
I'M JUST REPEATING WHAT HE SAID, KATE.
BUT I DON'T DISAGREE.

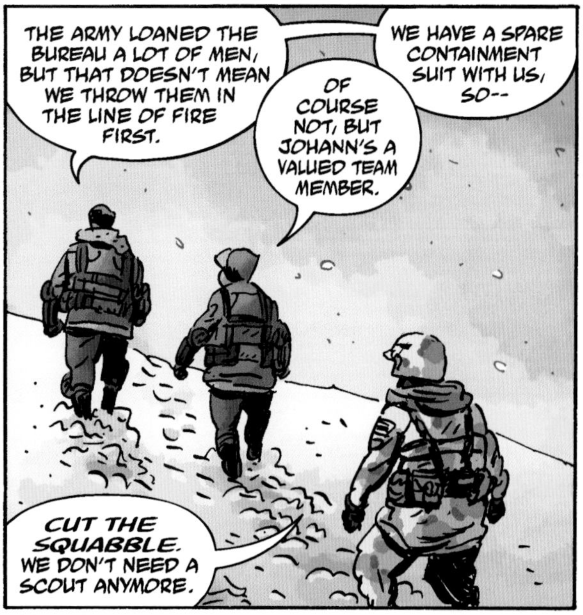
THE ARMY LOANED THE BUREAU A LOT OF MEN, BUT THAT DOESN'T MEAN WE THROW THEM IN THE LINE OF FIRE FIRST.
OF COURSE NOT, BUT JOHANN'S A VALUED TEAM MEMBER.
WE HAVE A SPARE CONTAINMENT SUIT WITH US, SO--
CUT THE SQUABBLE. WE DON'T NEED A SCOUT ANYMORE.

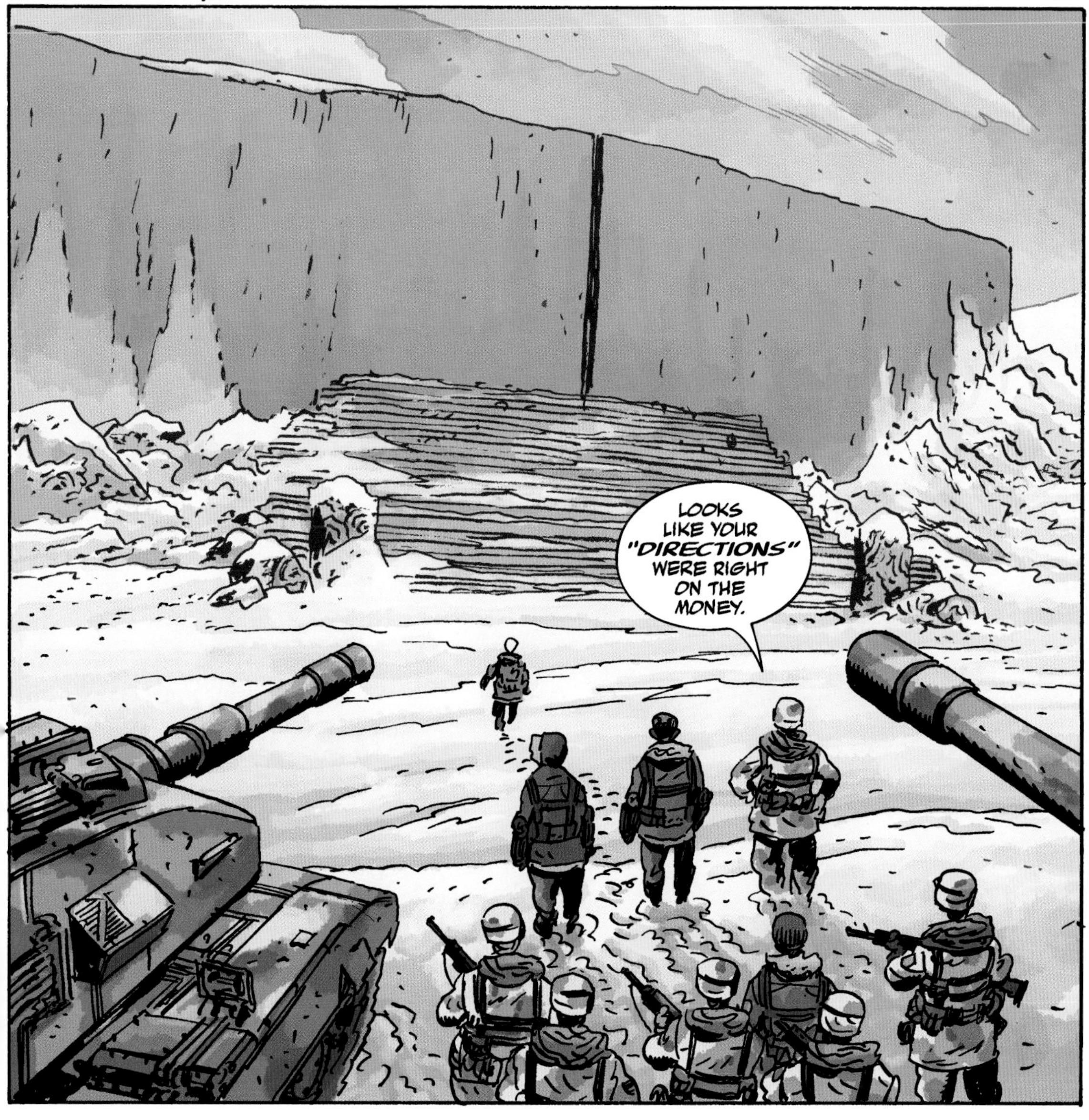
LOOKS LIKE YOUR "DIRECTIONS" WERE RIGHT ON THE MONEY.

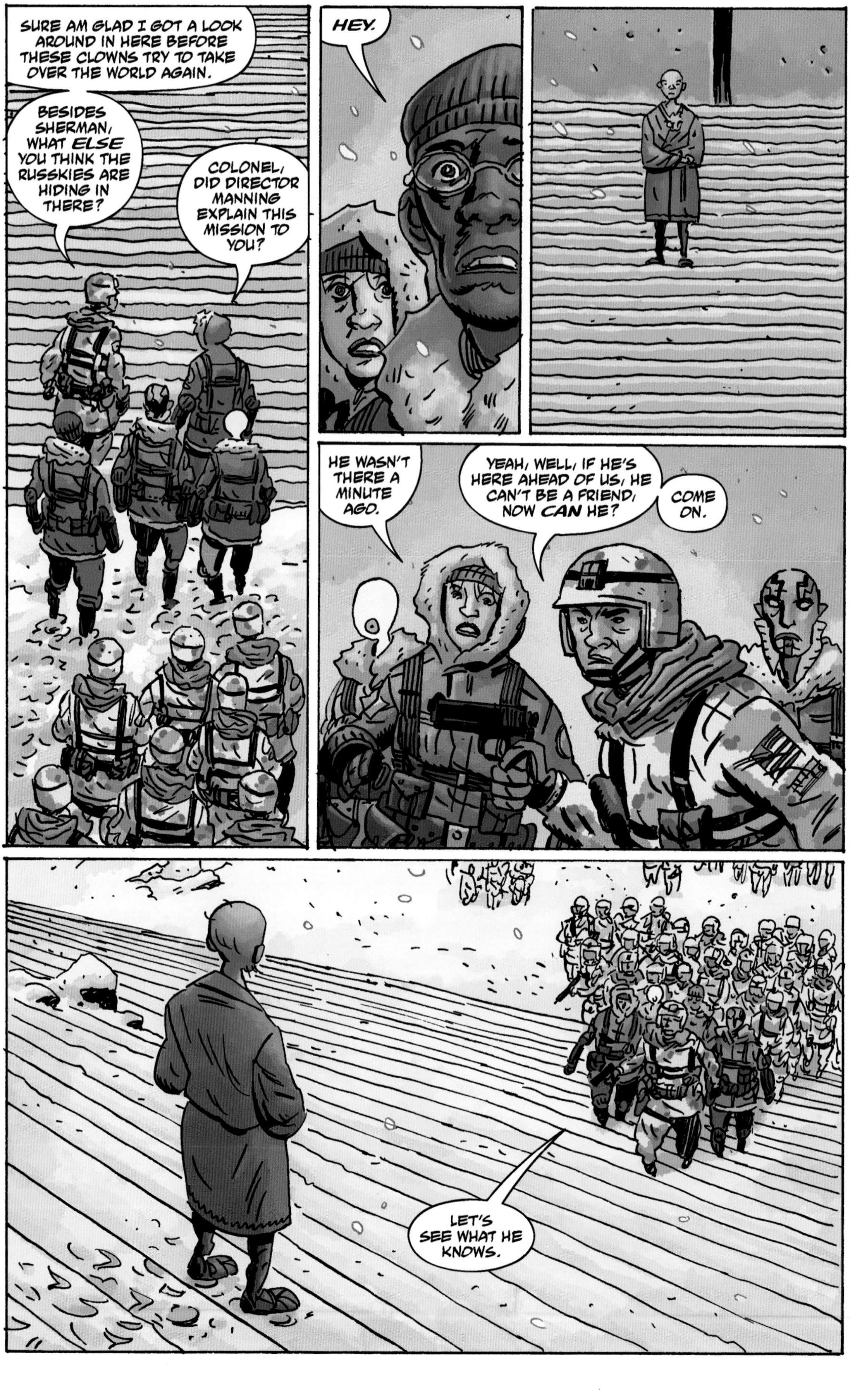
SURE AM GLAD I GOT A LOOK AROUND IN HERE BEFORE THESE CLOWNS TRY TO TAKE OVER THE WORLD AGAIN.
BESIDES SHERMAN, WHAT ELSE YOU THINK THE RUSSKIES ARE HIDING IN THERE?
COLONEL, DID DIRECTOR MANNING EXPLAIN THIS MISSION TO YOU?
HEY.
HE WASN'T THERE A MINUTE AGO.
YEAH, WELL, IF HE'S HERE AHEAD OF US, HE CAN'T BE A FRIEND, NOW CAN HE?
COME ON.
LET'S SEE WHAT HE KNOWS.

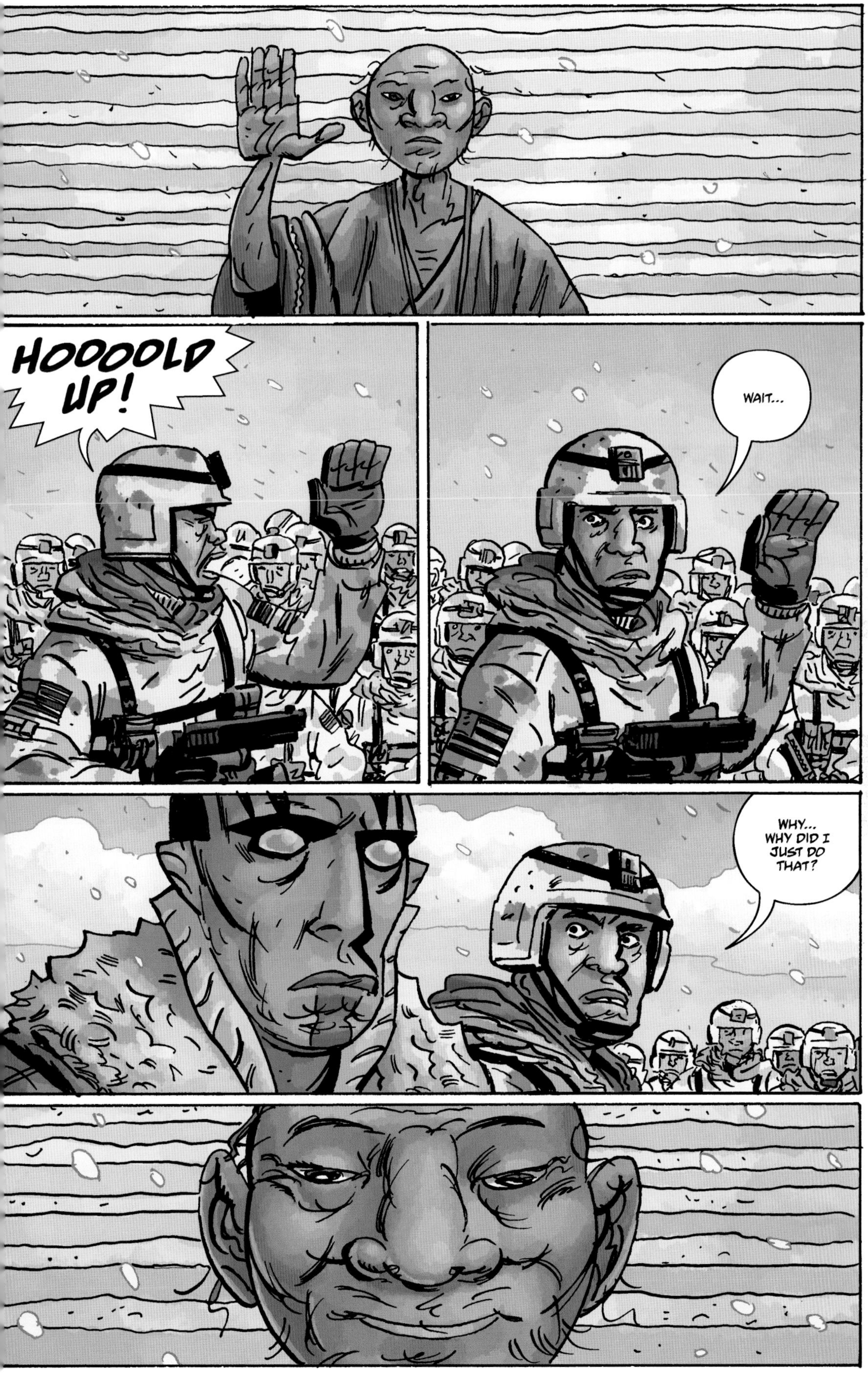
HOOOOLD UP!
WAIT...
WHY... WHY DID I JUST DO THAT?

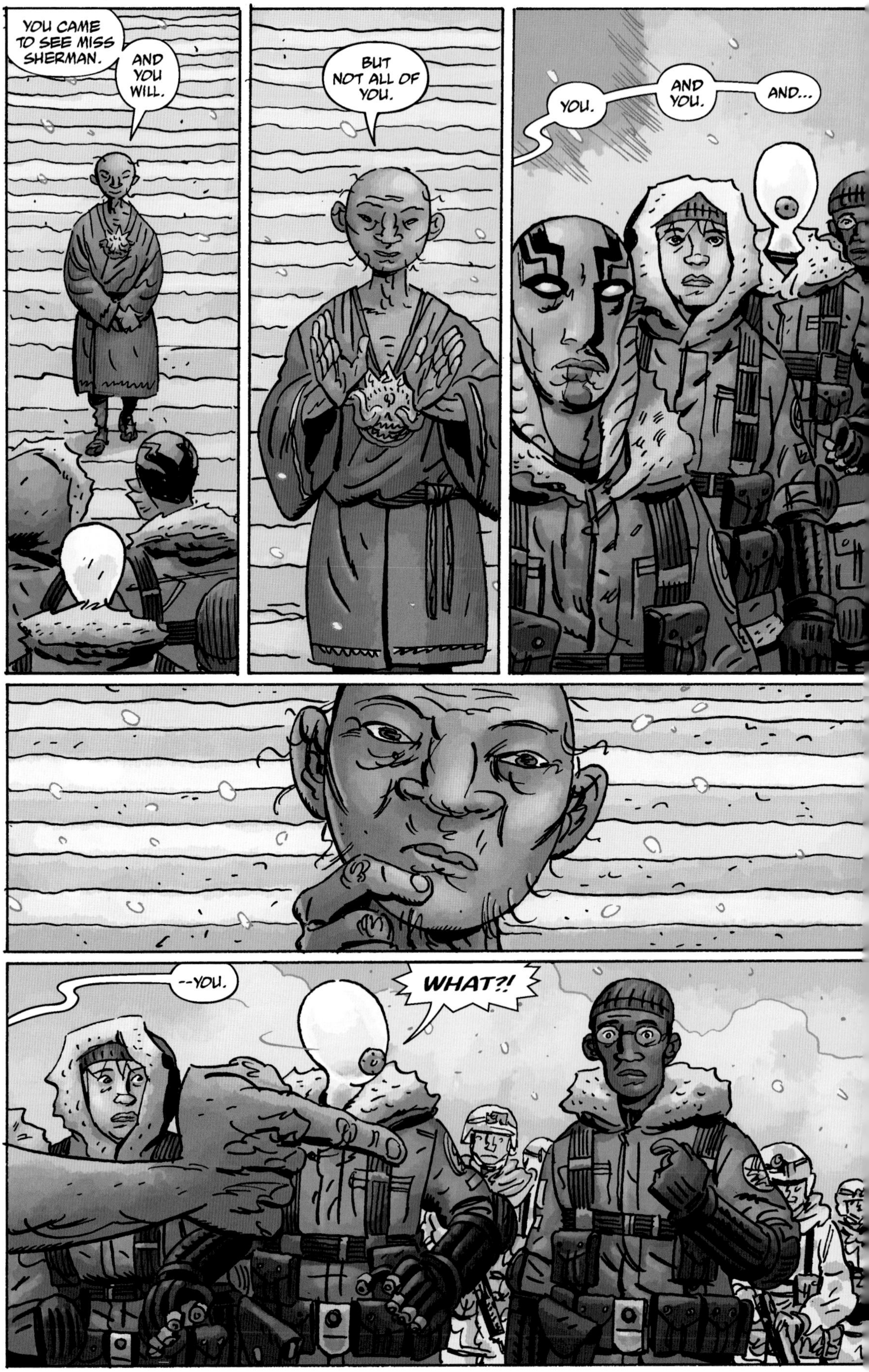
YOU CAME TO SEE MISS SHERMAN.
AND YOU WILL.
BUT NOT ALL OF YOU.
YOU.
AND YOU.
AND...
--YOU.
WHAT?!

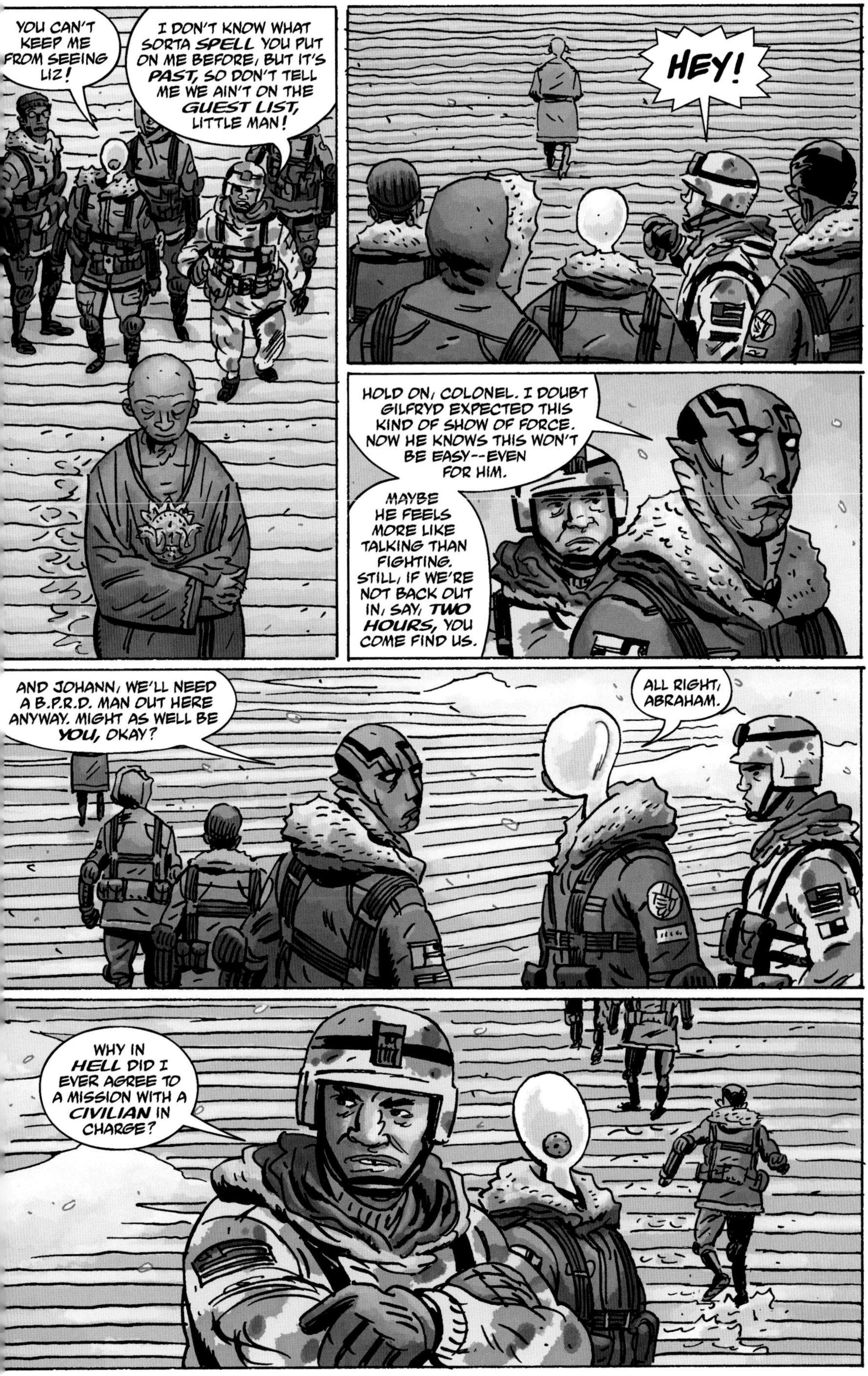
YOU CAN'T KEEP ME FROM SEEING LIZ!
I DON'T KNOW WHAT SORTA SPELL YOU PUT ON ME BEFORE, BUT IT'S PAST, SO DON'T TELL ME WE AIN'T ON THE GUEST LIST, LITTLE MAN!
HEY!
HOLD ON, COLONEL. I DOUBT GILFRYD EXPECTED THIS KIND OF SHOW OF FORCE. NOW HE KNOWS THIS WON'T BE EASY--EVEN FOR HIM.
MAYBE HE FEELS MORE LIKE TALKING THAN FIGHTING. STILL, IF WE'RE NOT BACK OUT IN, SAY, TWO HOURS, YOU COME FIND US.
AND JOHANN, WE'LL NEED A B.P.R.D. MAN OUT HERE ANYWAY. MIGHT AS WELL BE YOU, OKAY?
ALL RIGHT, ABRAHAM.
WHY IN HELL DID I EVER AGREE TO A MISSION WITH A CIVILIAN IN CHARGE?

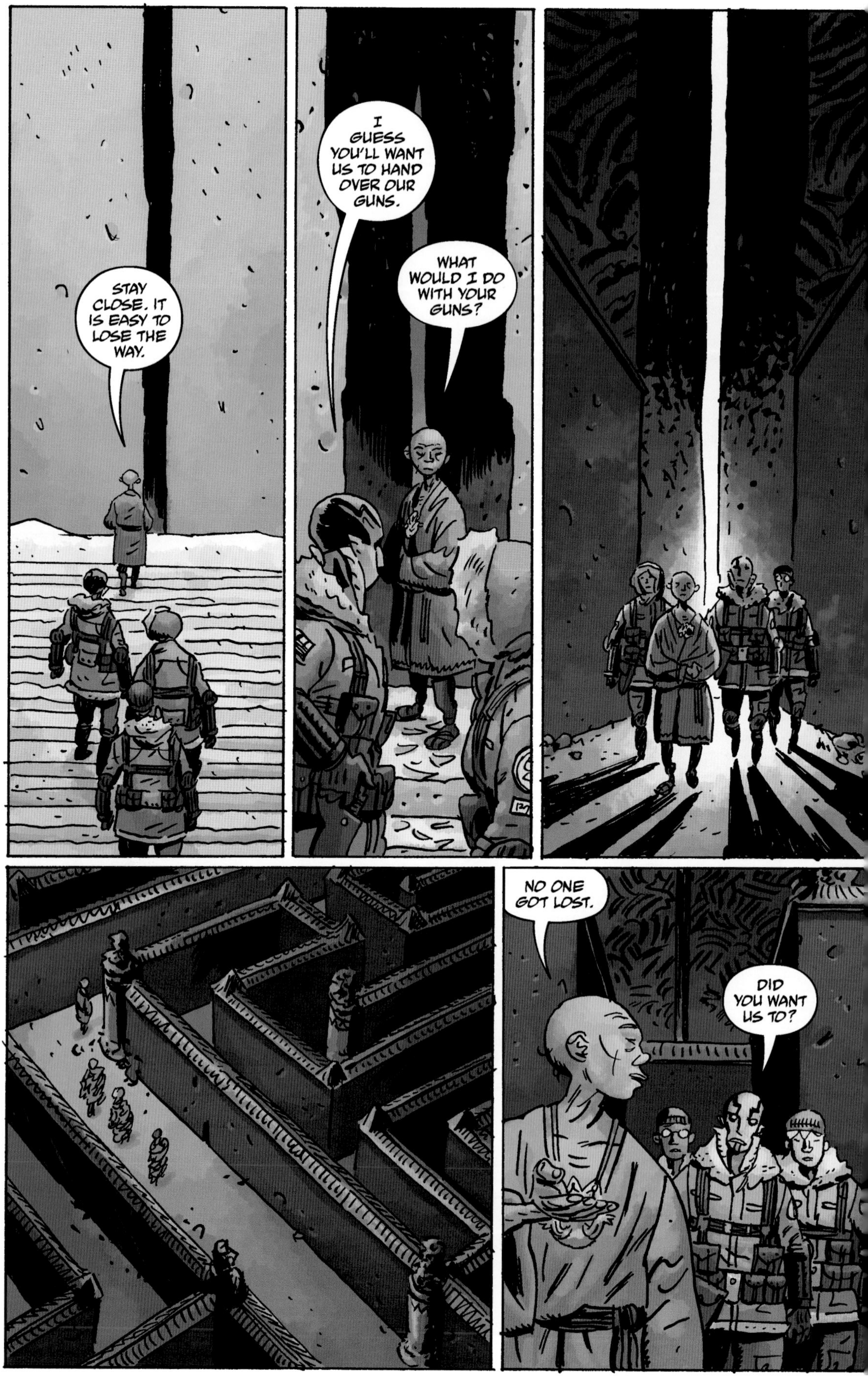
STAY CLOSE. IT IS EASY TO LOSE THE WAY.
I GUESS YOU'LL WANT US TO HAND OVER OUR GUNS.
WHAT WOULD I DO WITH YOUR GUNS?
NO ONE GOT LOST.
DID YOU WANT US TO?

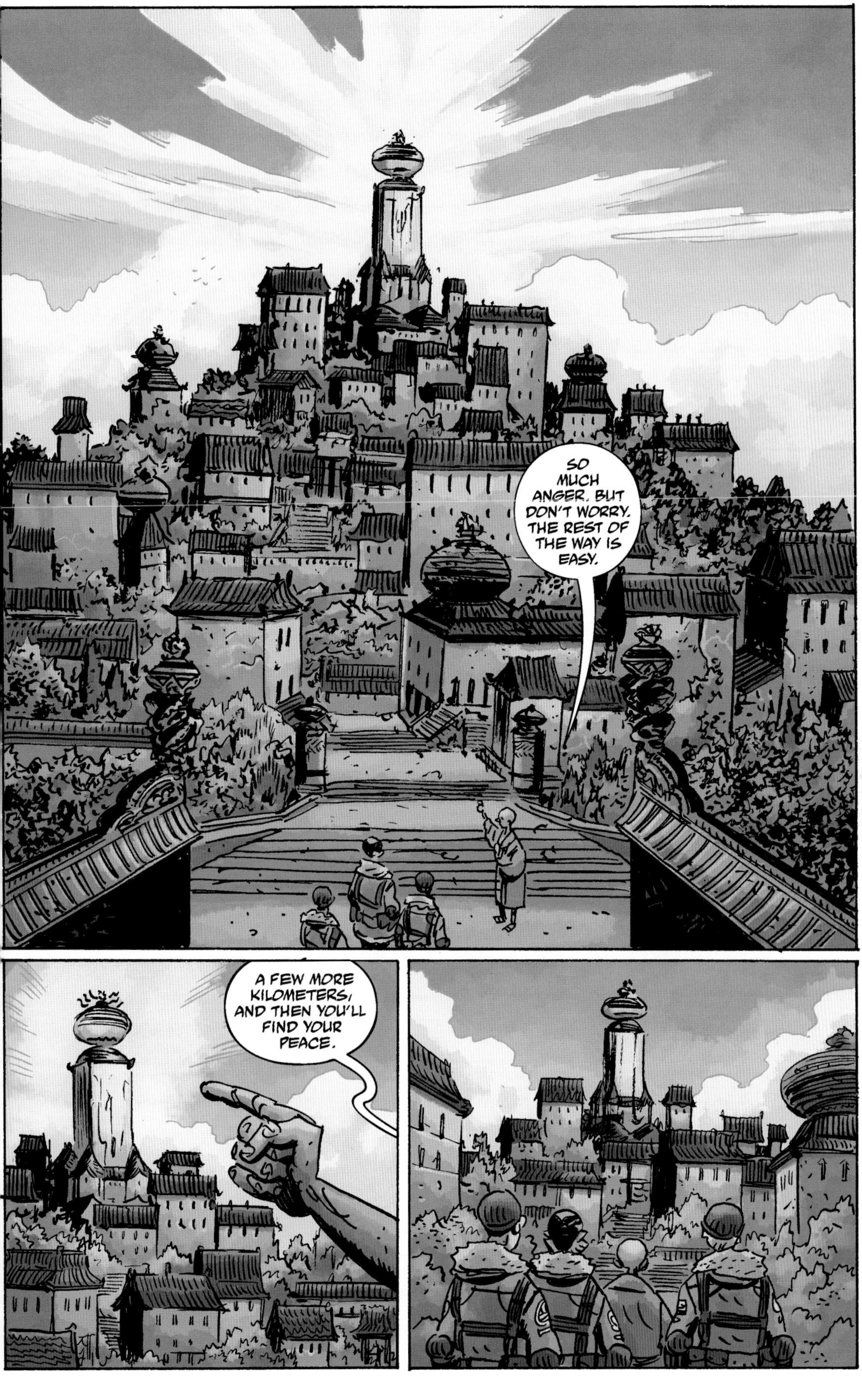
SO MUCH ANGER. BUT DON'T WORRY. THE REST OF THE WAY IS EASY.
A FEW MORE KILOMETERS, AND THEN YOU'LL FIND YOUR PEACE.

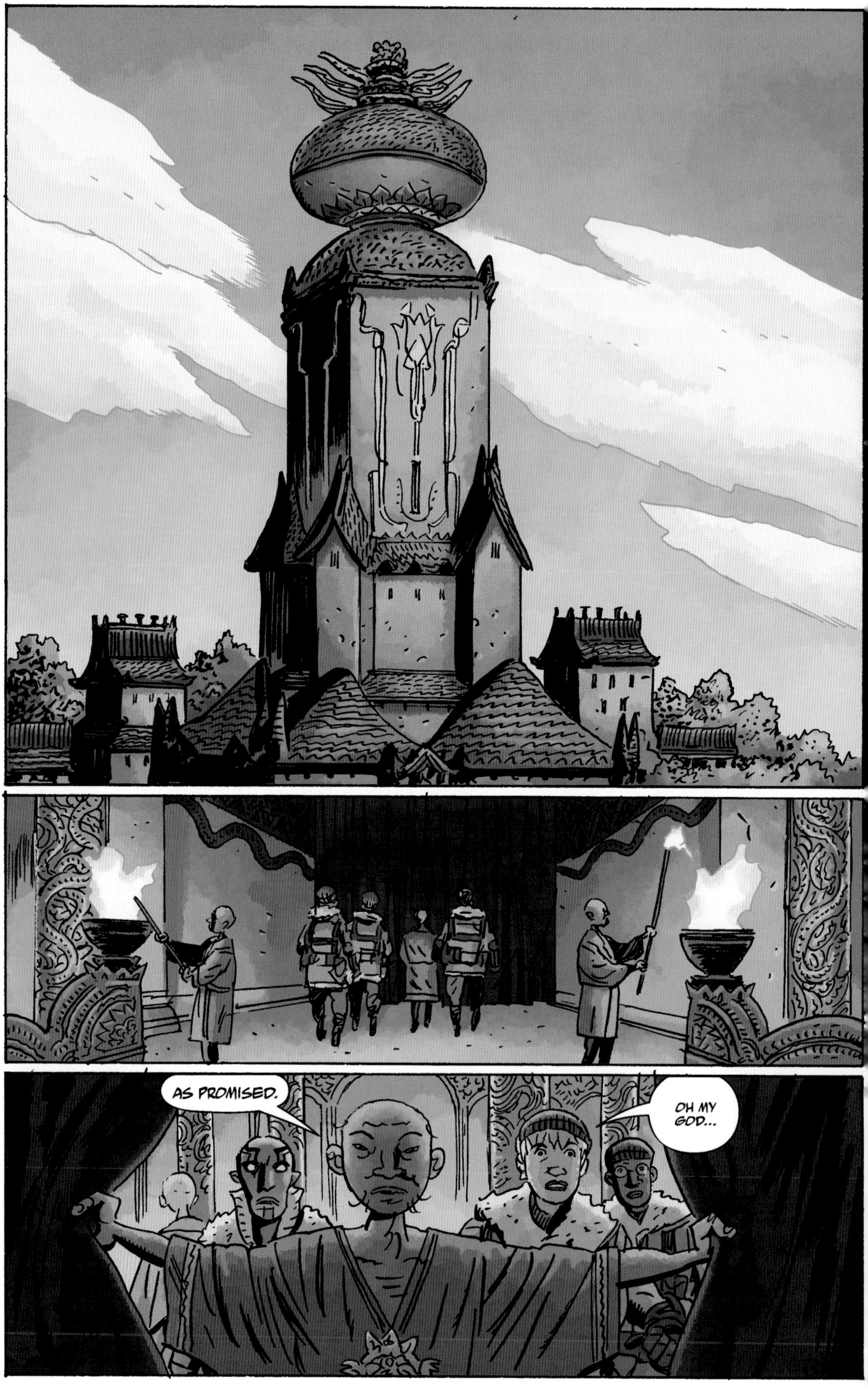
AS PROMISED.
OH MY GOD...

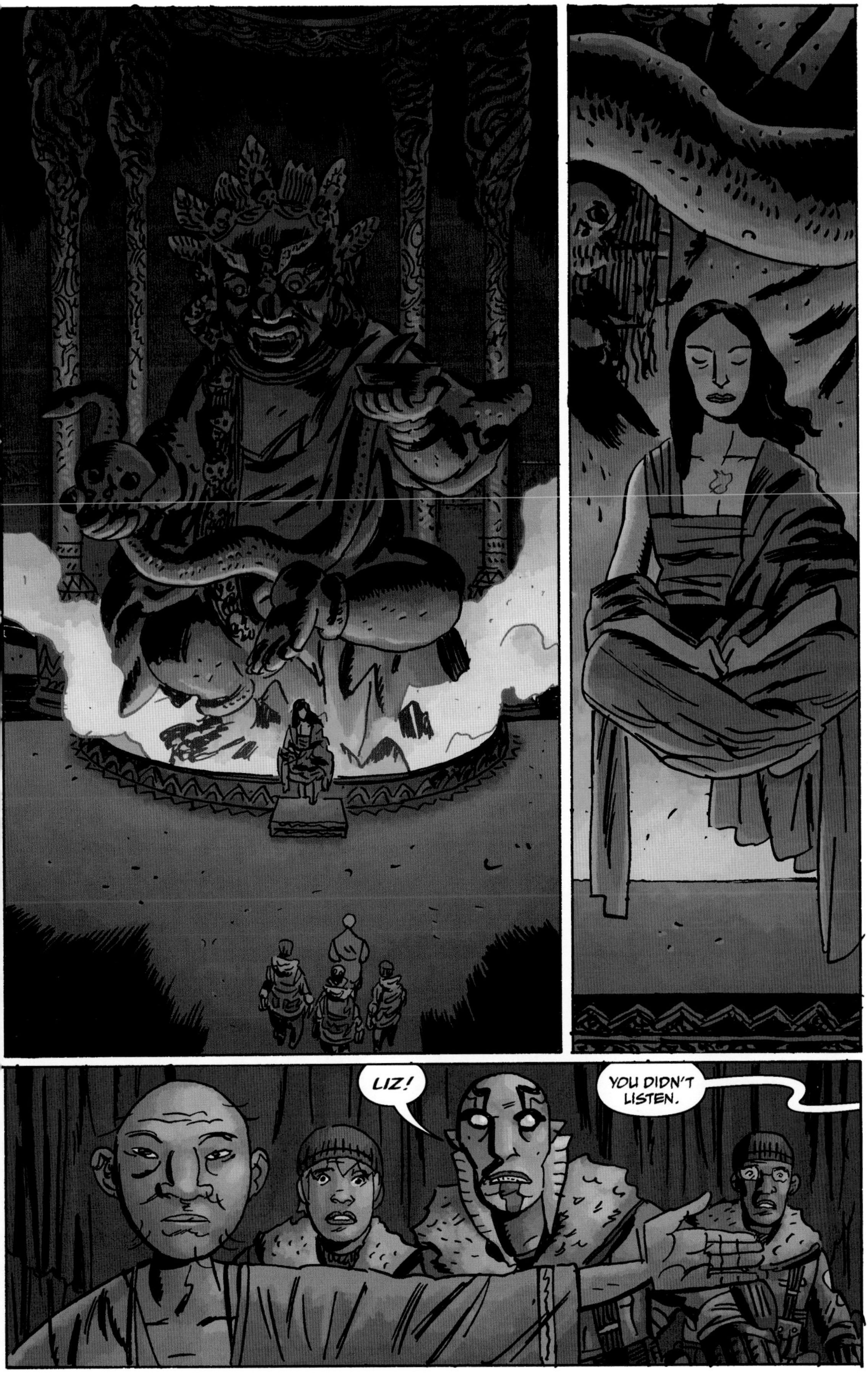
LIZ!
YOU DIDN'T LISTEN.

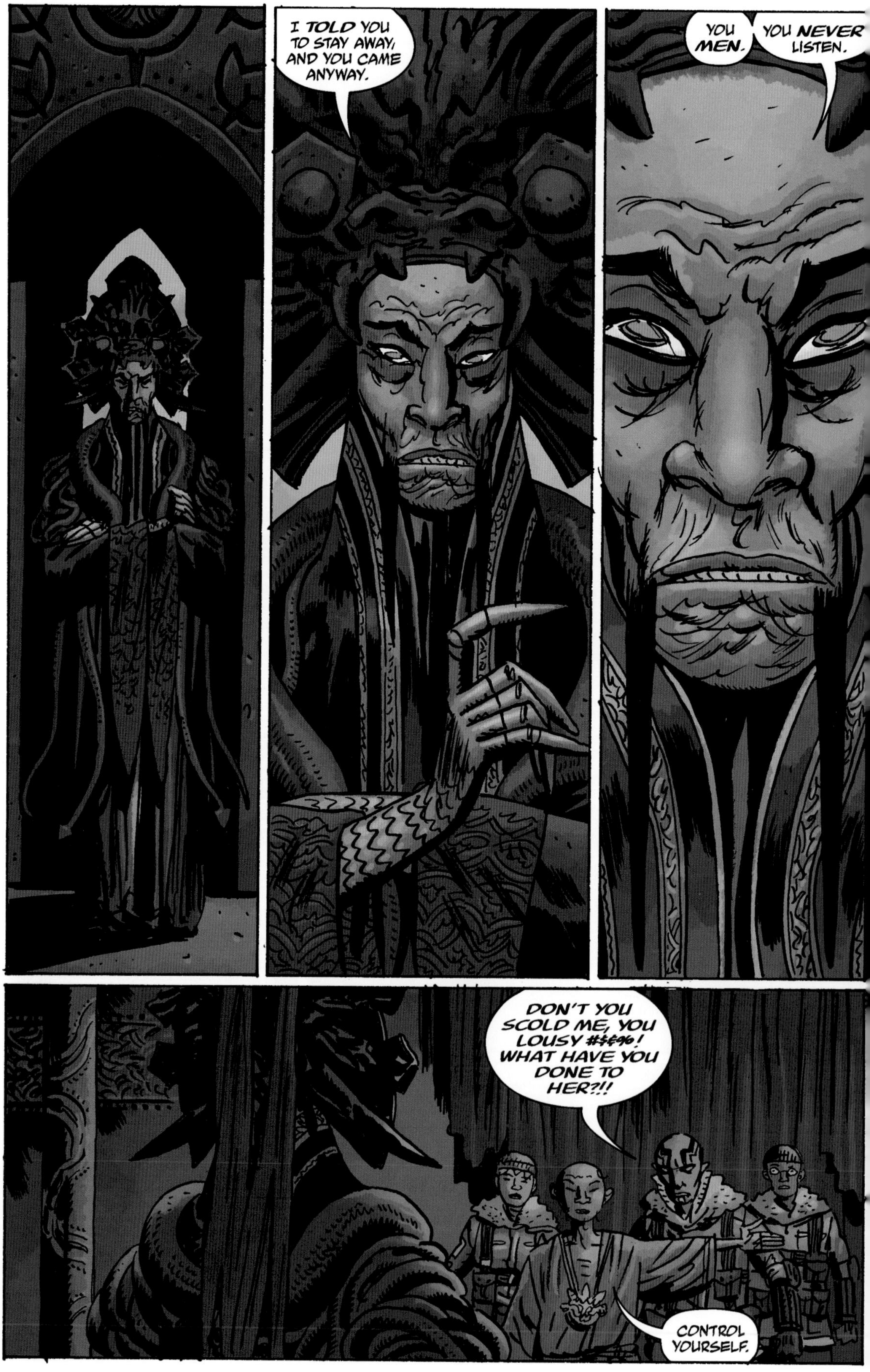
I TOLD YOU TO STAY AWAY, AND YOU CAME ANYWAY.
YOU MEN.
YOU NEVER LISTEN.
DON'T YOU SCOLD ME, YOU LOUSY #$€%! WHAT HAVE YOU DONE TO HER?!!
CONTROL YOURSELF.

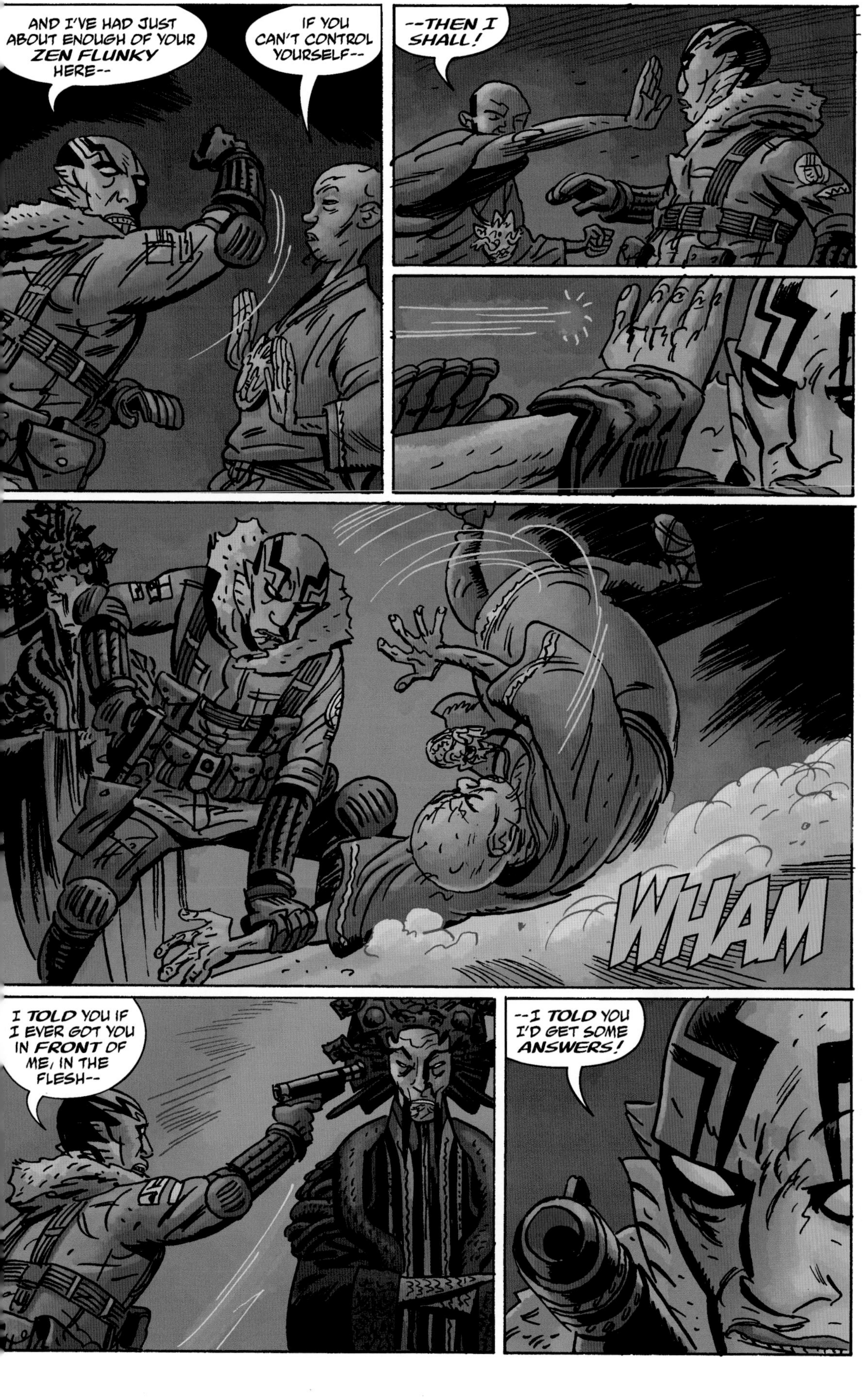
AND I'VE HAD JUST ABOUT ENOUGH OF YOUR ZEN FLUNKY HERE--
IF YOU CAN'T CONTROL YOURSELF--
--THEN I SHALL!
WHAM
I TOLD YOU IF I EVER GOT YOU IN FRONT OF ME, IN THE FLESH--
--I TOLD YOU I'D GET SOME ANSWERS!

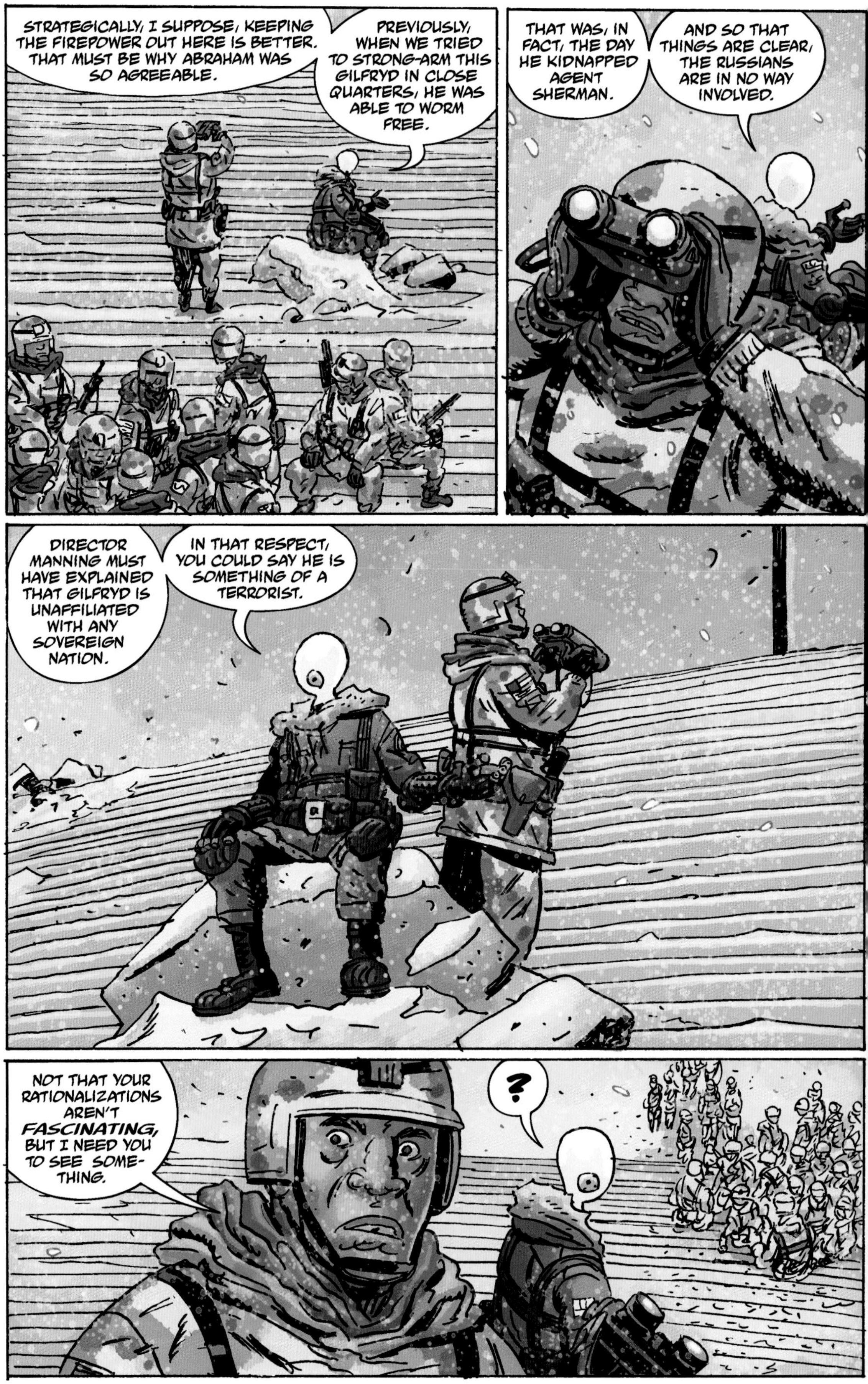
STRATEGICALLY, I SUPPOSE, KEEPING THE FIREPOWER OUT HERE IS BETTER. THAT MUST BE WHY ABRAHAM WAS SO AGREEABLE.
PREVIOUSLY, WHEN WE TRIED TO STRONG-ARM THIS GILFRYD IN CLOSE QUARTERS, HE WAS ABLE TO WORM FREE.
THAT WAS, IN FACT, THE DAY HE KIDNAPPED AGENT SHERMAN.
AND SO THAT THINGS ARE CLEAR, THE RUSSIANS ARE IN NO WAY INVOLVED.
DIRECTOR MANNING MUST HAVE EXPLAINED THAT GILFRYD IS UNAFFILIATED WITH ANY SOVEREIGN NATION.
IN THAT RESPECT, YOU COULD SAY HE IS SOMETHING OF A TERRORIST.
NOT THAT YOUR RATIONALIZATIONS AREN'T *FASCINATING*, BUT I NEED YOU TO SEE SOME-THING.
?

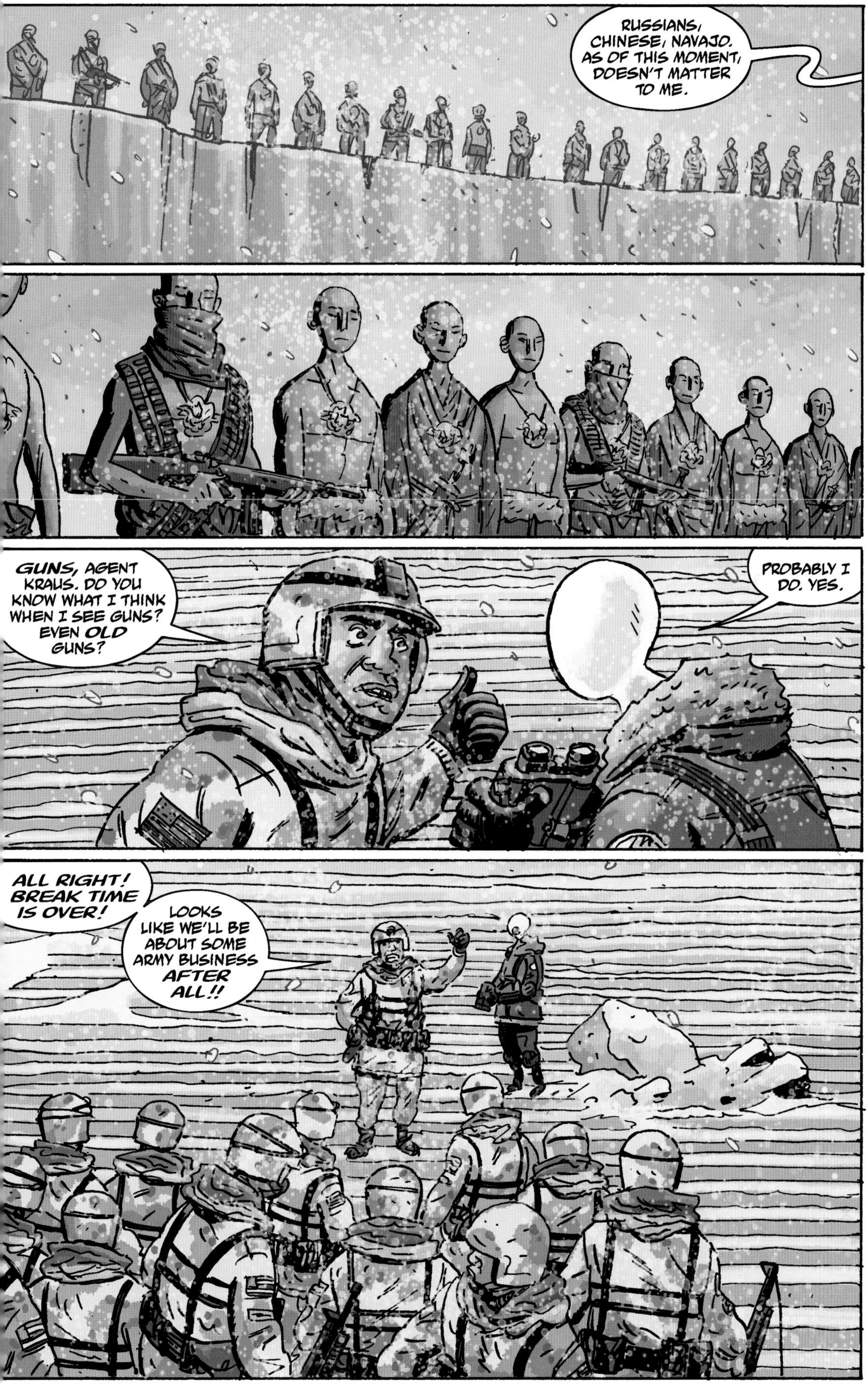
RUSSIANS, CHINESE, NAVAJO. AS OF THIS MOMENT, DOESN'T MATTER TO ME.
GUNS, AGENT KRAUS. DO YOU KNOW WHAT I THINK WHEN I SEE GUNS? EVEN OLD GUNS?
PROBABLY I DO. YES.
ALL RIGHT! BREAK TIME IS OVER!
LOOKS LIKE WE'LL BE ABOUT SOME ARMY BUSINESS AFTER ALL!!

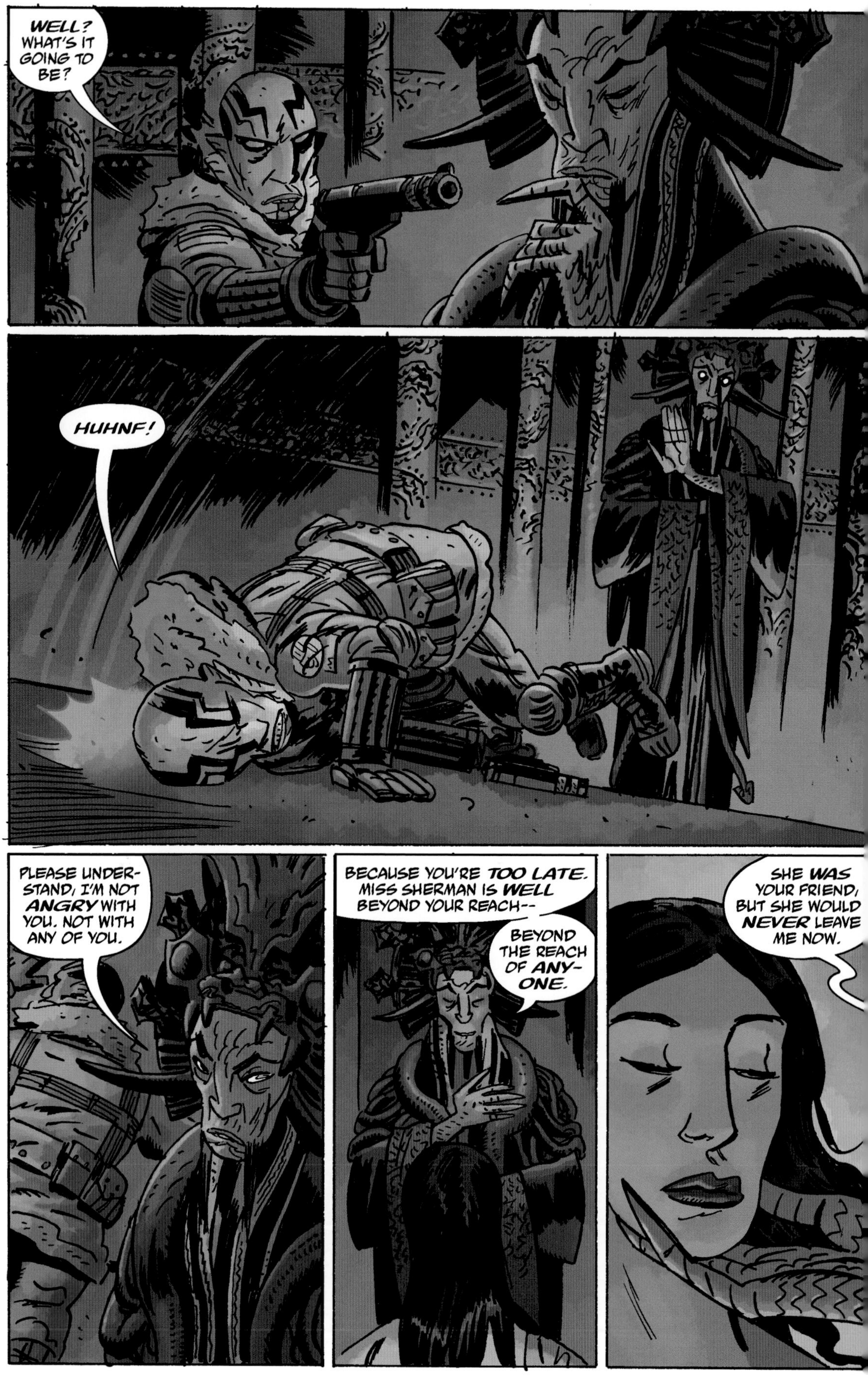
WELL? WHAT'S IT GOING TO BE?
HUHNF!
PLEASE UNDERSTAND, I'M NOT ANGRY WITH YOU. NOT WITH ANY OF YOU.
BECAUSE YOU'RE TOO LATE. MISS SHERMAN IS WELL BEYOND YOUR REACH--
BEYOND THE REACH OF ANYONE.
SHE WAS YOUR FRIEND, BUT SHE WOULD NEVER LEAVE ME NOW.

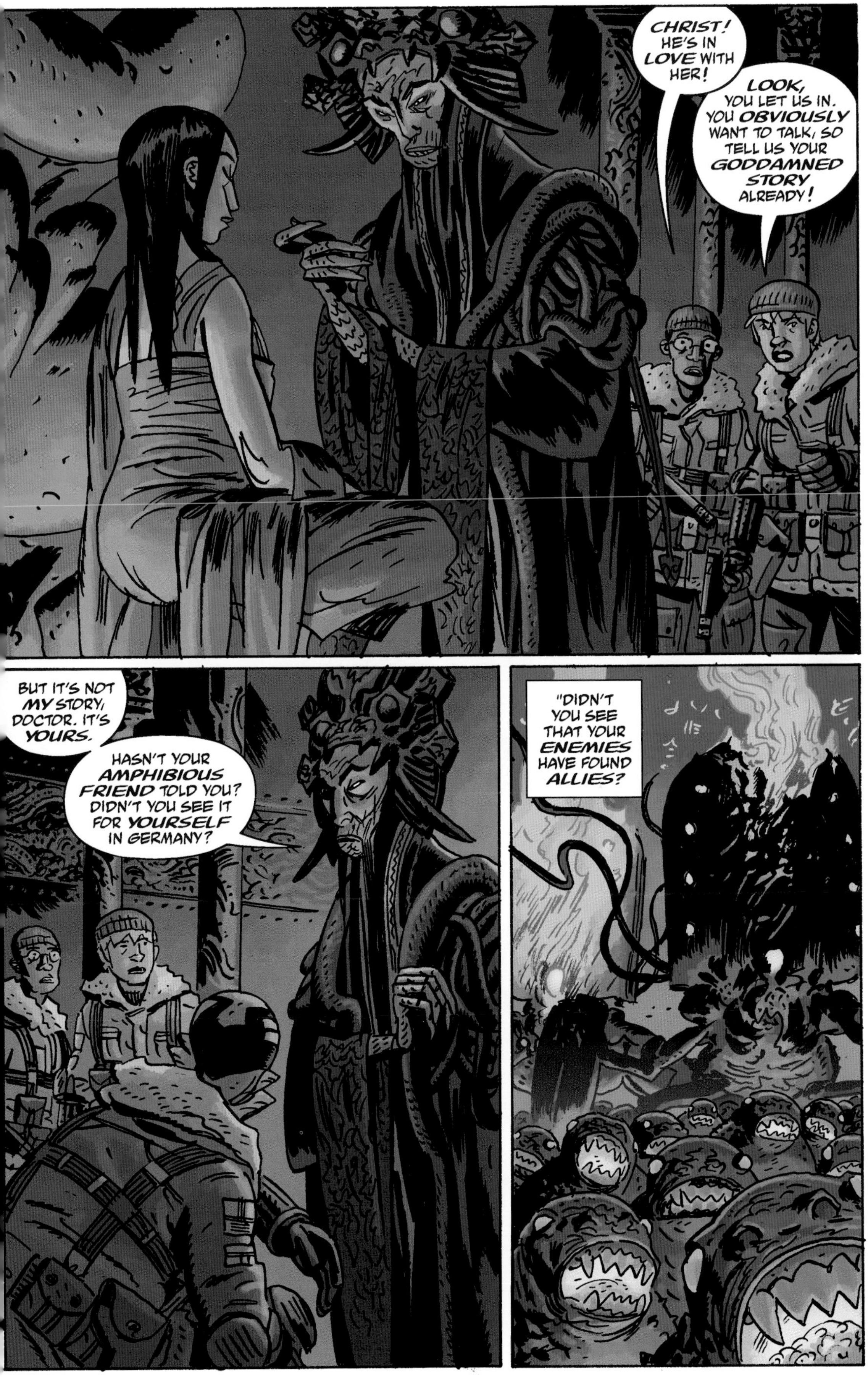
CHRIST! HE'S IN LOVE WITH HER!
LOOK, YOU LET US IN. YOU OBVIOUSLY WANT TO TALK, SO TELL US YOUR GODDAMNED STORY ALREADY!
BUT IT'S NOT MY STORY, DOCTOR. IT'S YOURS.
HASN'T YOUR AMPHIBIOUS FRIEND TOLD YOU? DIDN'T YOU SEE IT FOR YOURSELF IN GERMANY?
"DIDN'T YOU SEE THAT YOUR ENEMIES HAVE FOUND ALLIES?

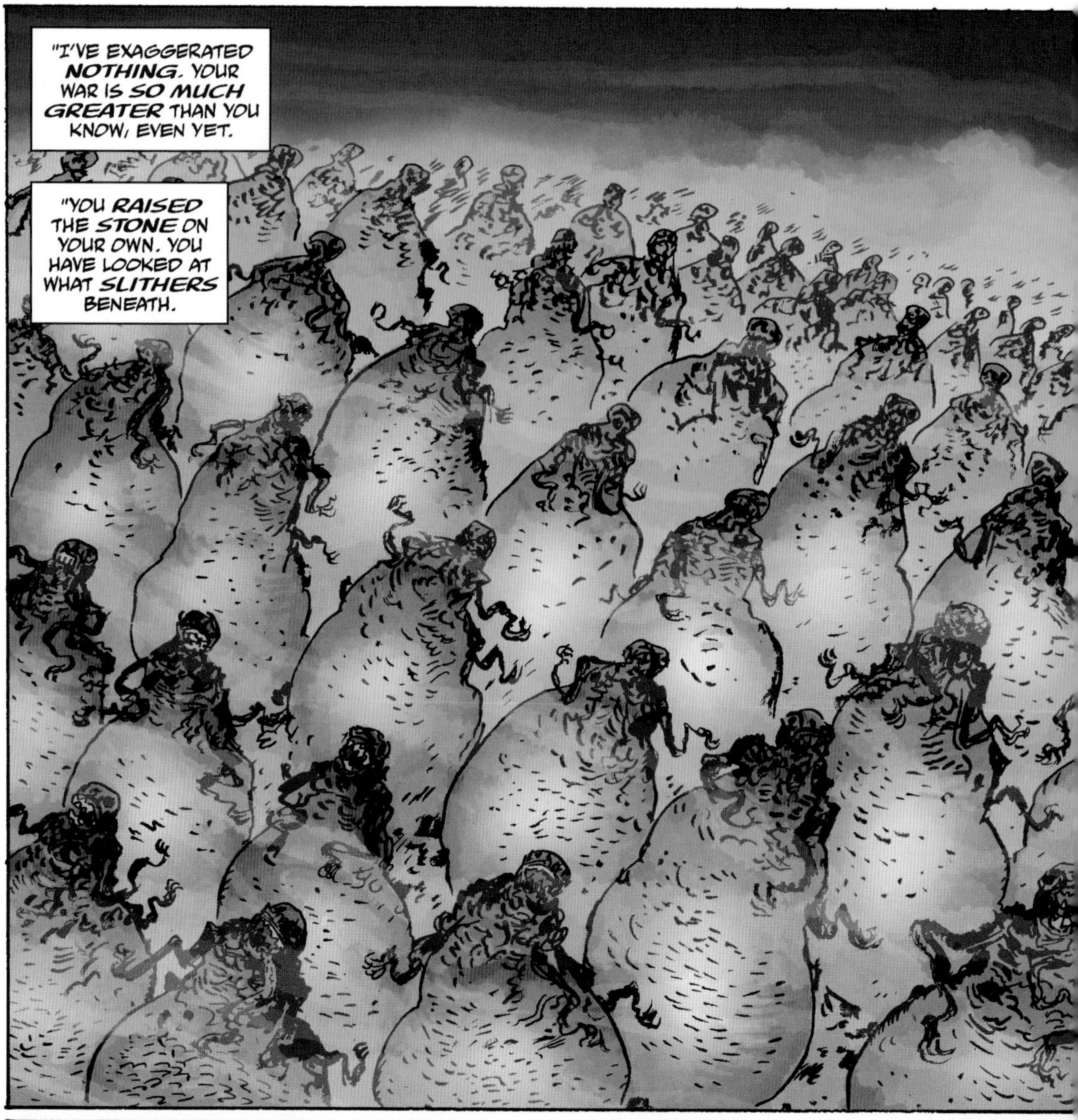
"I'VE EXAGGERATED NOTHING. YOUR WAR IS SO MUCH GREATER THAN YOU KNOW, EVEN YET.
"YOU RAISED THE STONE ON YOUR OWN. YOU HAVE LOOKED AT WHAT SLITHERS BENEATH.

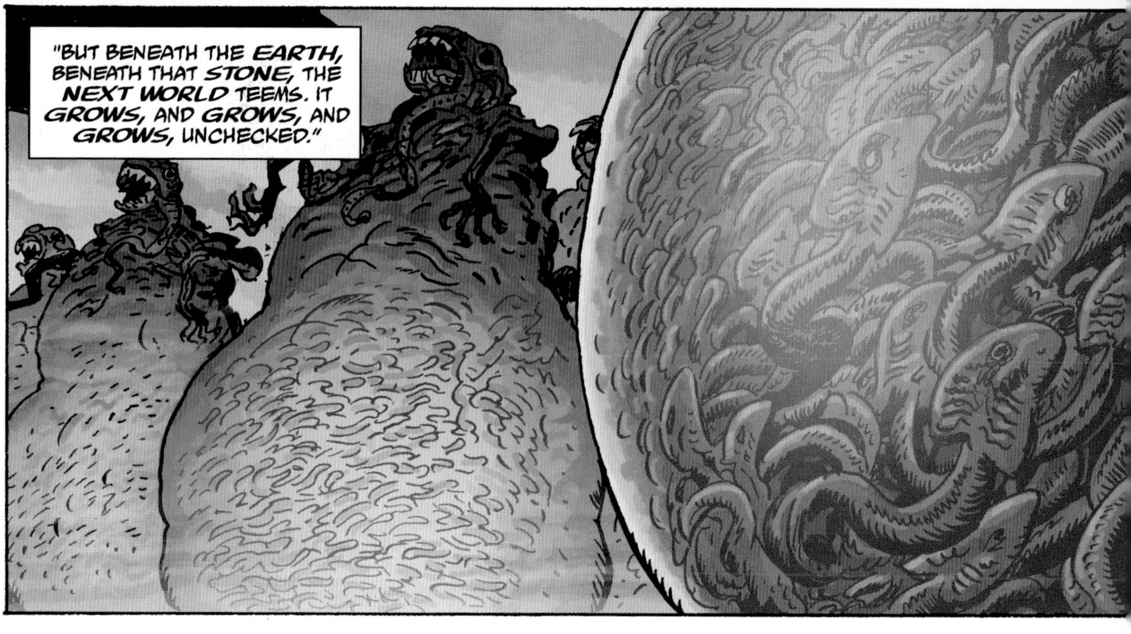
"BUT BENEATH THE EARTH, BENEATH THAT STONE, THE NEXT WORLD TEEMS. IT GROWS, AND GROWS, AND GROWS, UNCHECKED."

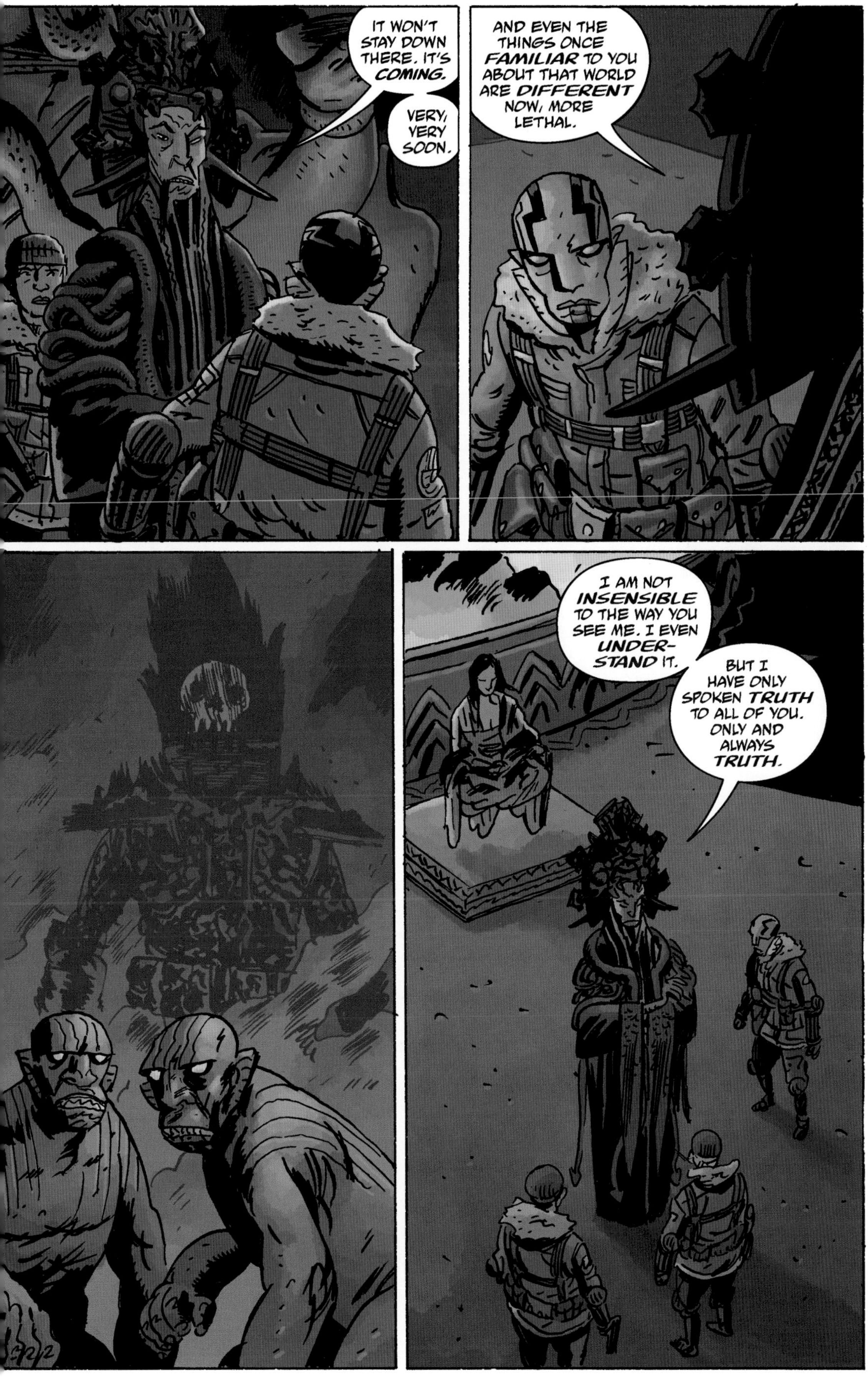
IT WON'T STAY DOWN THERE. IT'S *COMING.*
VERY, VERY SOON.
AND EVEN THE THINGS ONCE *FAMILIAR* TO YOU ABOUT THAT WORLD ARE *DIFFERENT* NOW, MORE LETHAL.
I AM NOT *INSENSIBLE* TO THE WAY YOU SEE ME. I EVEN *UNDER-STAND* IT.
BUT I HAVE ONLY SPOKEN *TRUTH* TO ALL OF YOU. ONLY AND ALWAYS *TRUTH.*

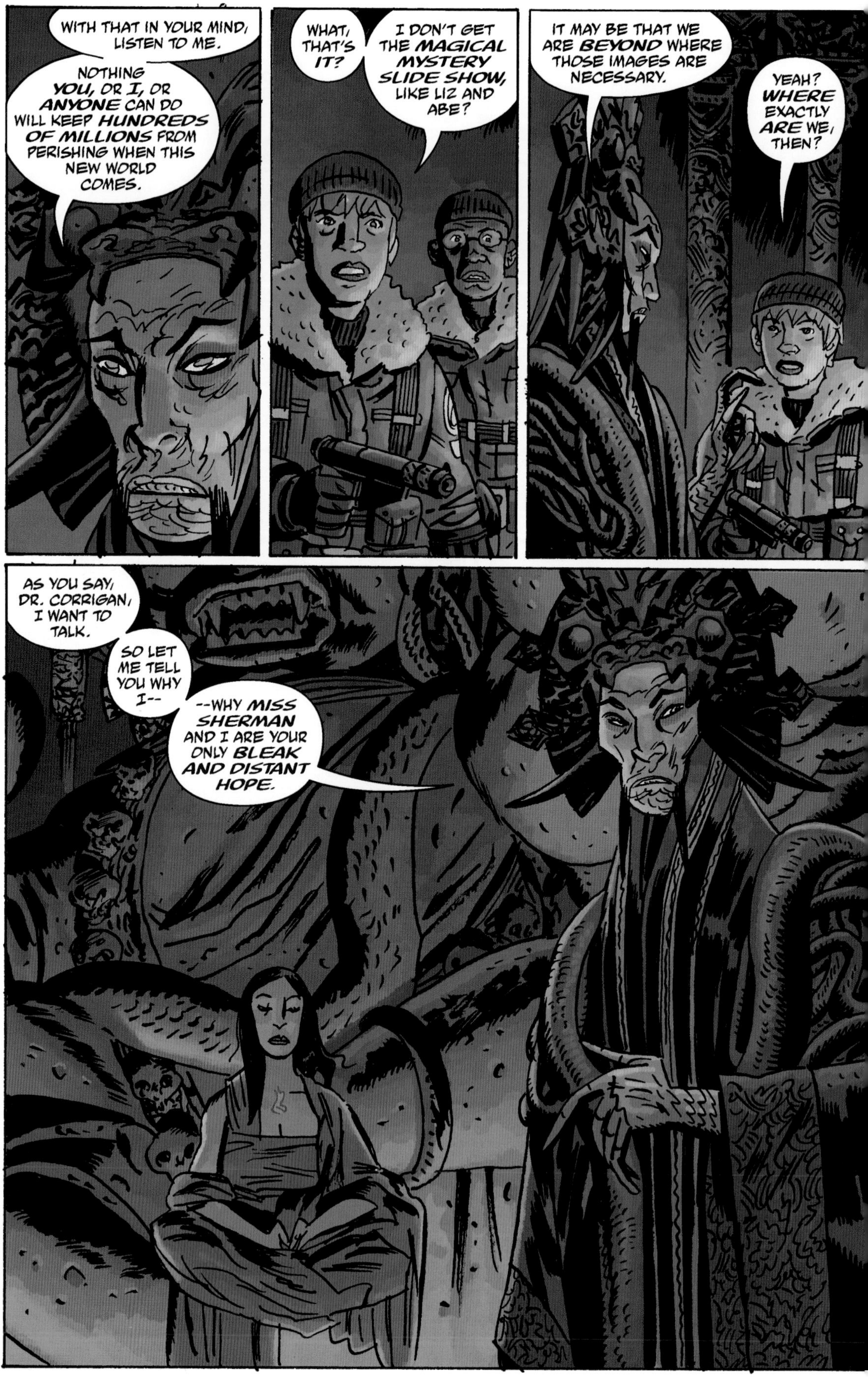

WITH THAT IN YOUR MIND, LISTEN TO ME.
NOTHING YOU, OR I, OR ANYONE CAN DO WILL KEEP HUNDREDS OF MILLIONS FROM PERISHING WHEN THIS NEW WORLD COMES.
WHAT, THAT'S IT?
I DON'T GET THE MAGICAL MYSTERY SLIDE SHOW, LIKE LIZ AND ABE?
IT MAY BE THAT WE ARE BEYOND WHERE THOSE IMAGES ARE NECESSARY.
YEAH? WHERE EXACTLY ARE WE, THEN?
AS YOU SAY, DR. CORRIGAN, I WANT TO TALK.
SO LET ME TELL YOU WHY I--
--WHY MISS SHERMAN AND I ARE YOUR ONLY BLEAK AND DISTANT HOPE.

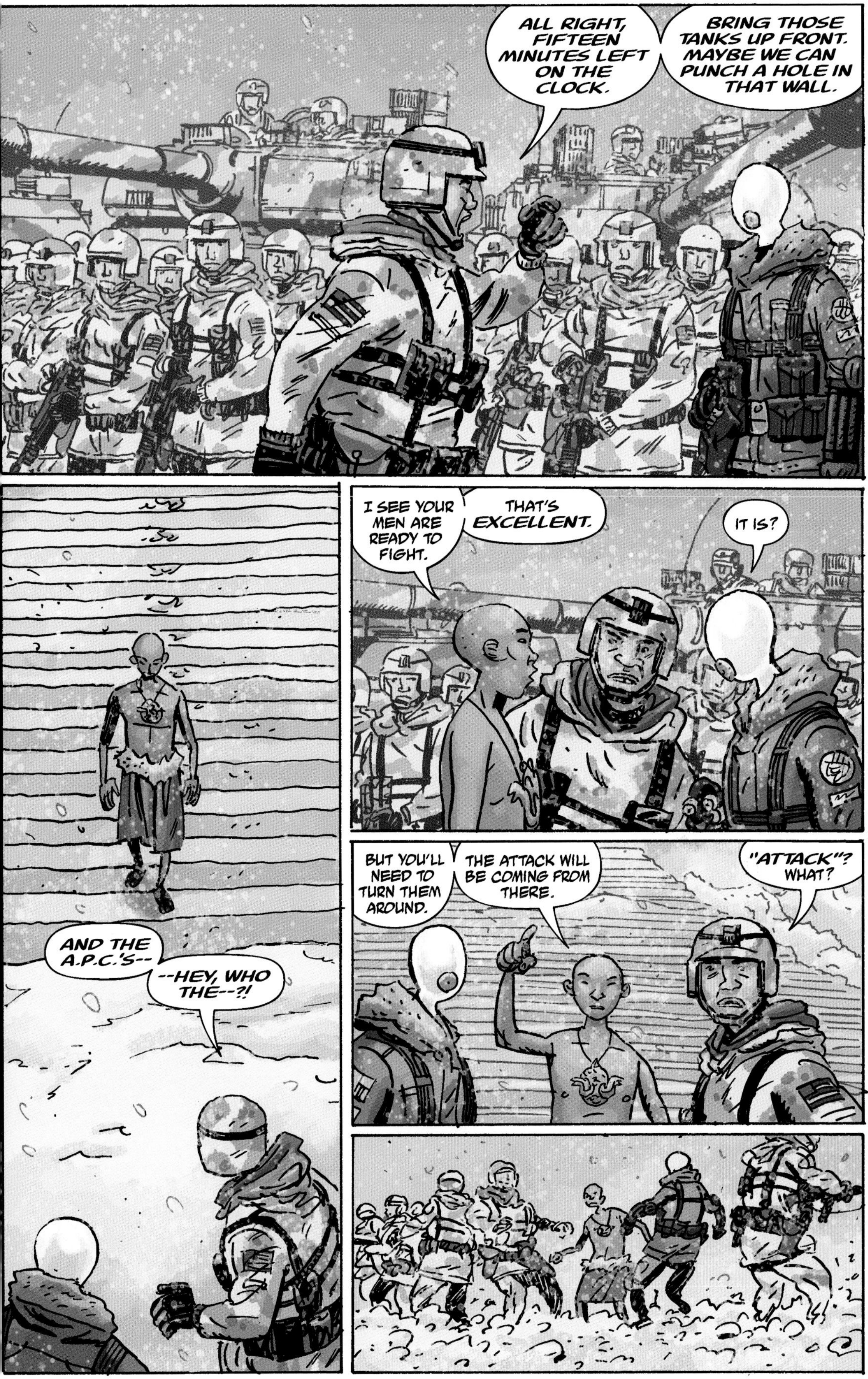
ALL RIGHT, FIFTEEN MINUTES LEFT ON THE CLOCK.
BRING THOSE TANKS UP FRONT. MAYBE WE CAN PUNCH A HOLE IN THAT WALL.
AND THE A.P.C.'S--
--HEY, WHO THE--?!
I SEE YOUR MEN ARE READY TO FIGHT.
THAT'S EXCELLENT.
IT IS?
BUT YOU'LL NEED TO TURN THEM AROUND.
THE ATTACK WILL BE COMING FROM THERE.
"ATTACK"? WHAT?

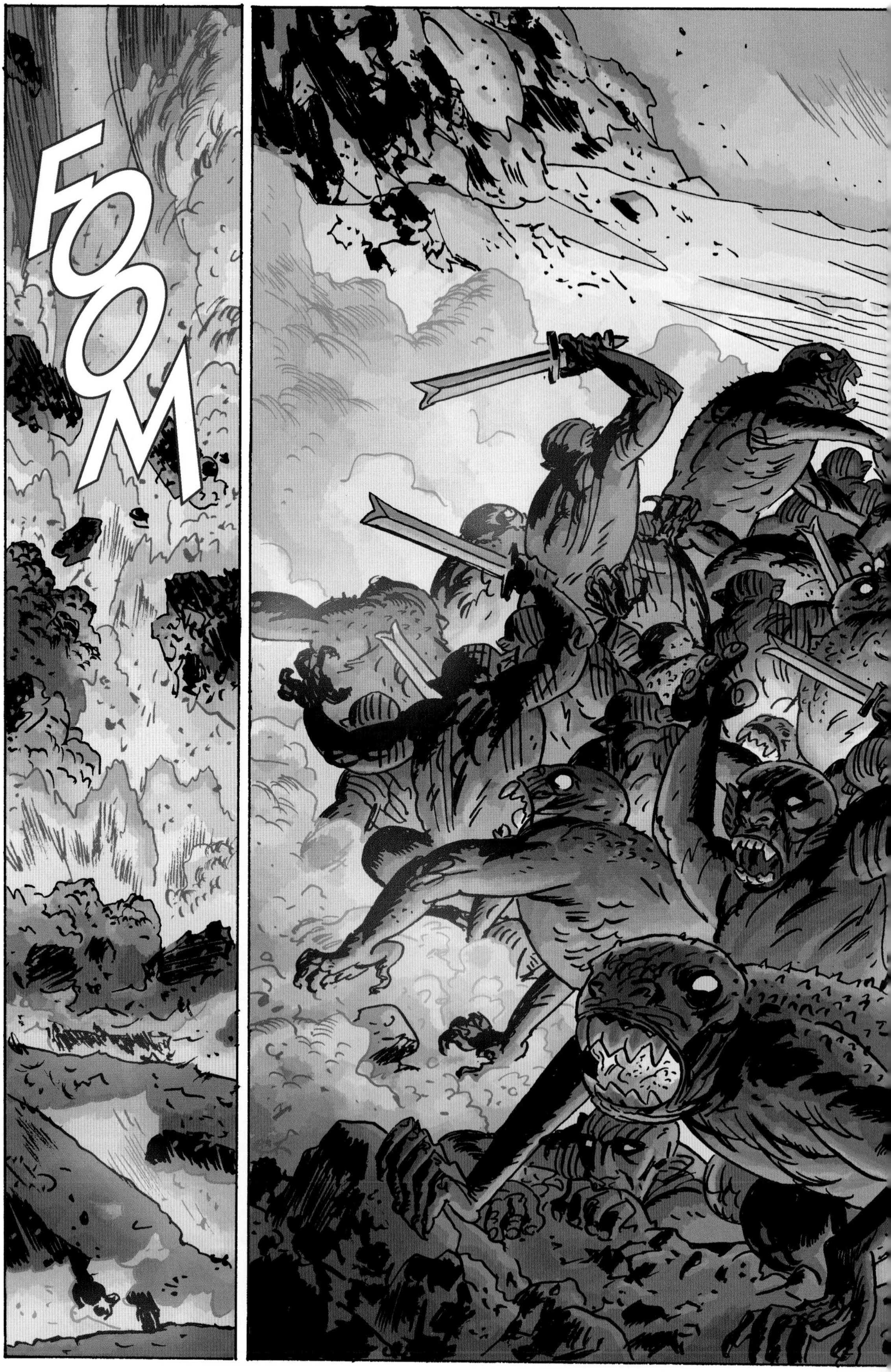
FOOM

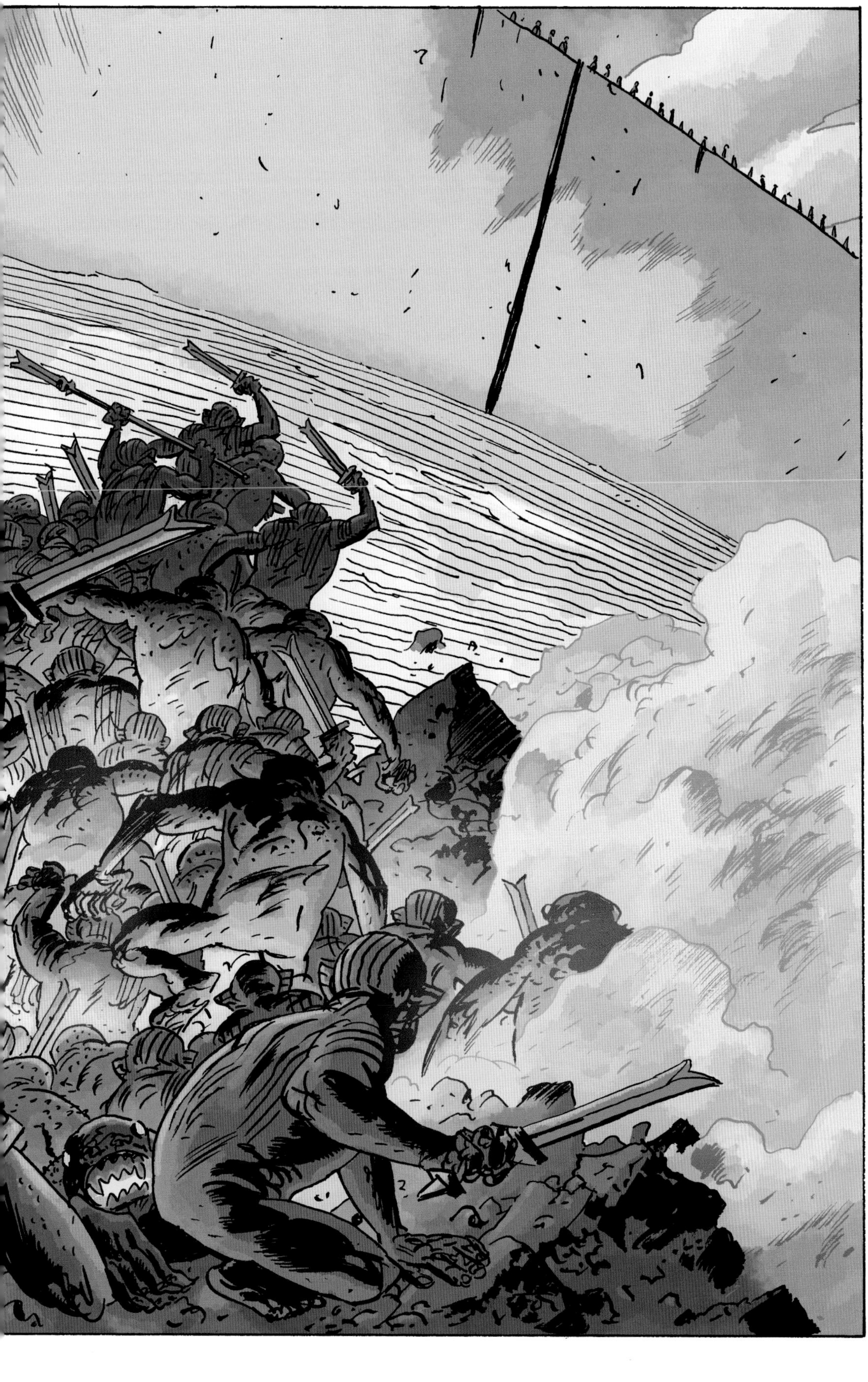

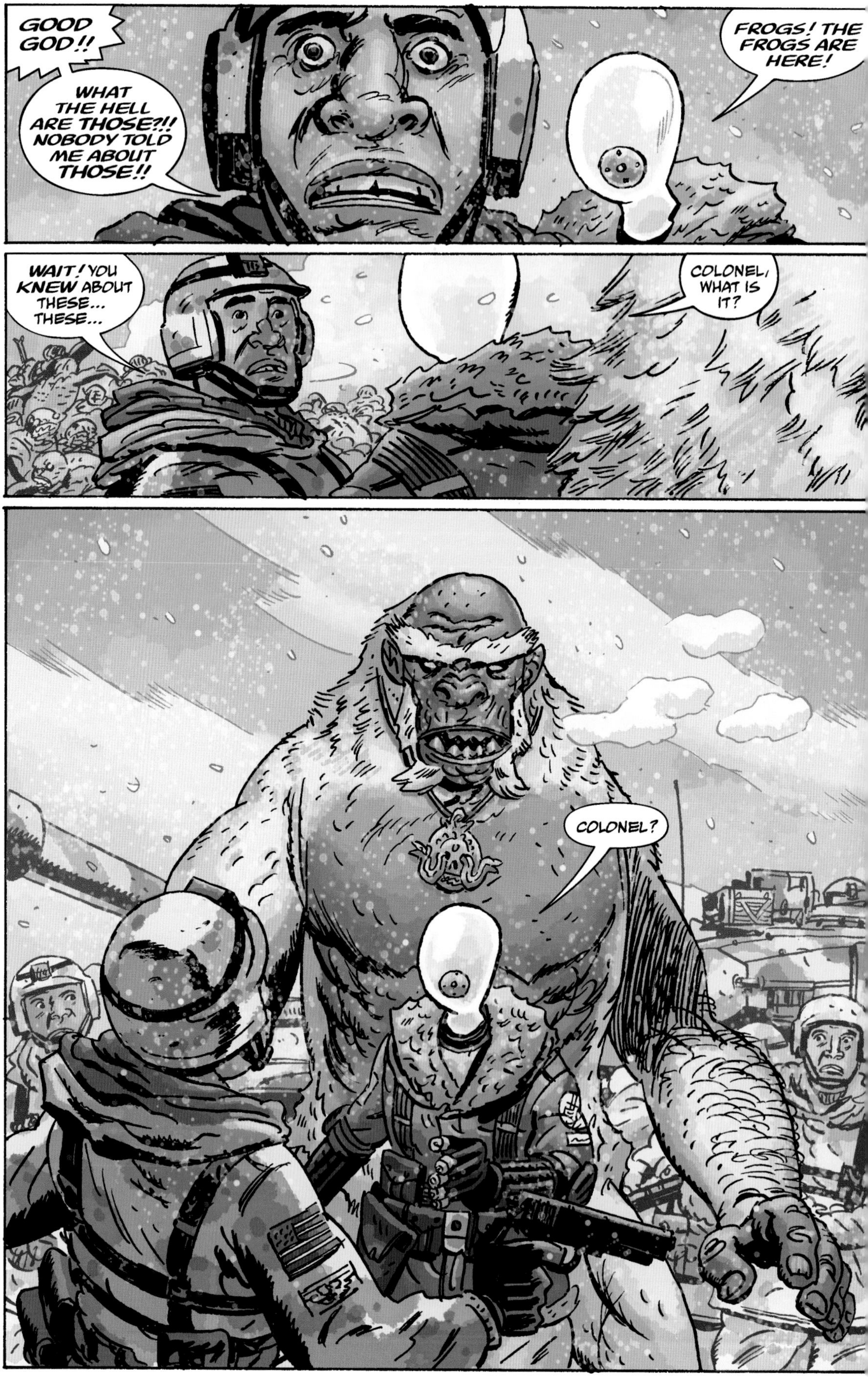
GOOD GOD!!
WHAT THE HELL ARE THOSE?!! NOBODY TOLD ME ABOUT THOSE!!
FROGS! THE FROGS ARE HERE!
WAIT! YOU KNEW ABOUT THESE... THESE...
COLONEL, WHAT IS IT?
COLONEL?

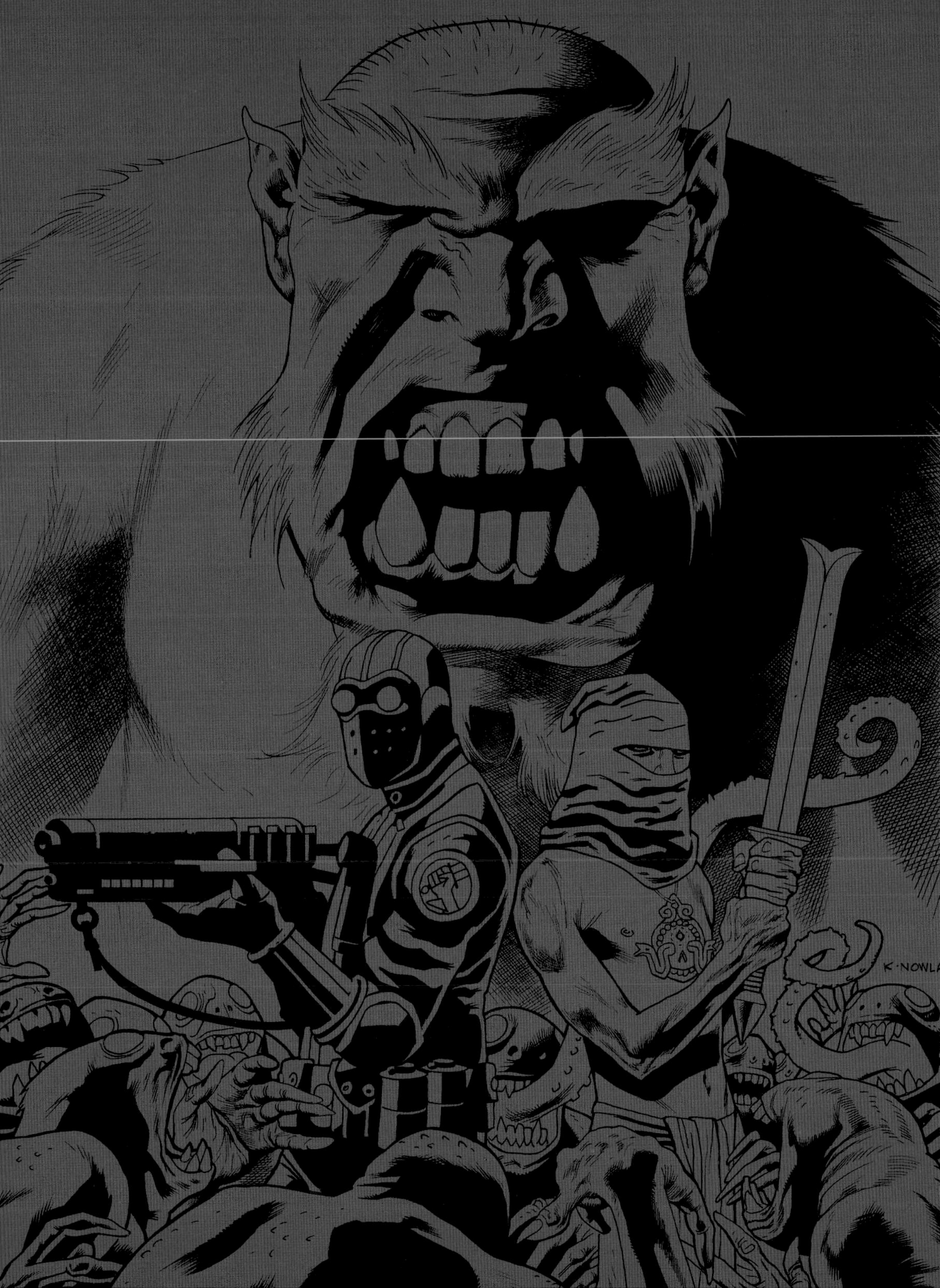

CHAPTER THREE

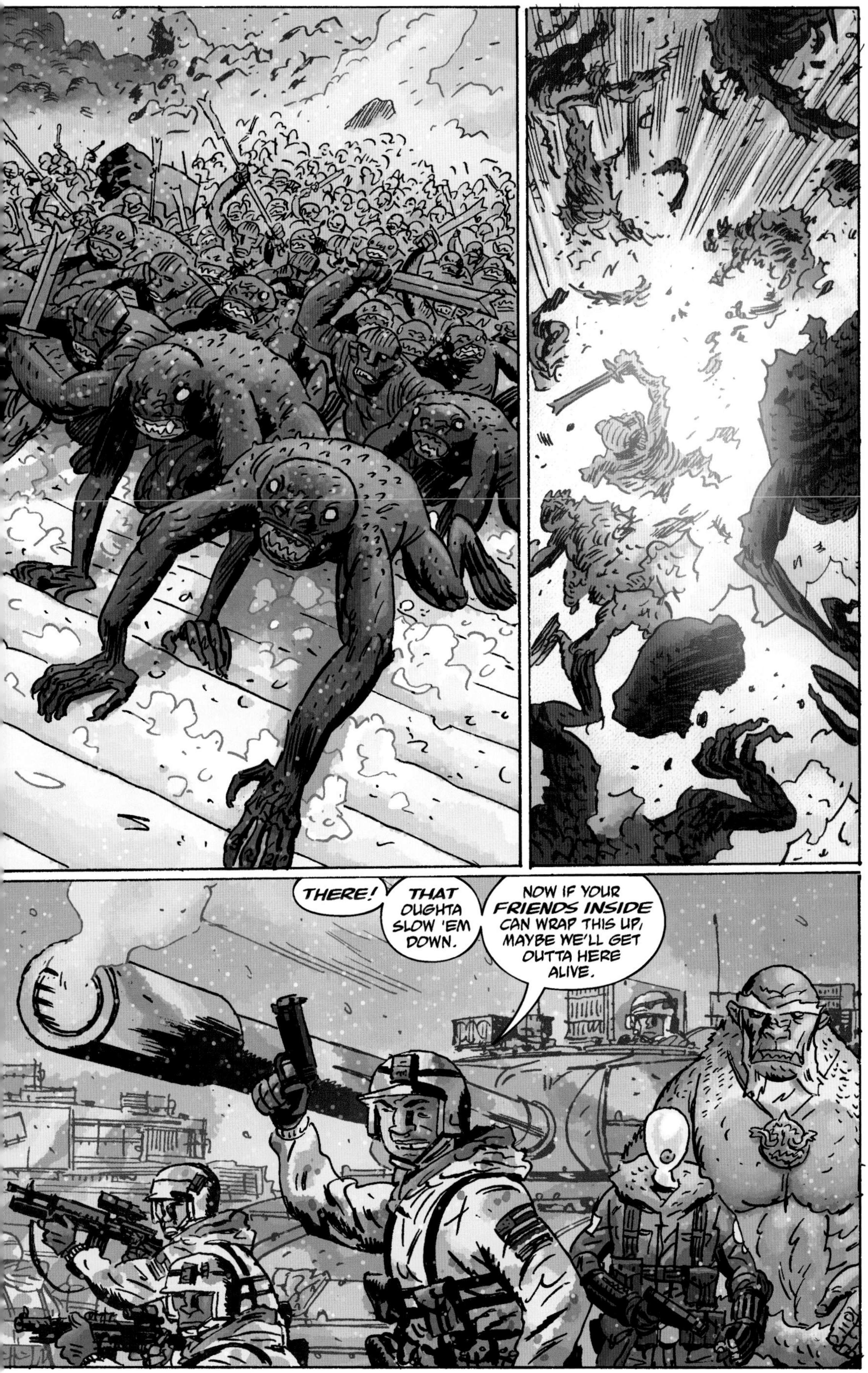
THERE!
THAT OUGHTA SLOW 'EM DOWN.
NOW IF YOUR FRIENDS INSIDE CAN WRAP THIS UP, MAYBE WE'LL GET OUTTA HERE ALIVE.

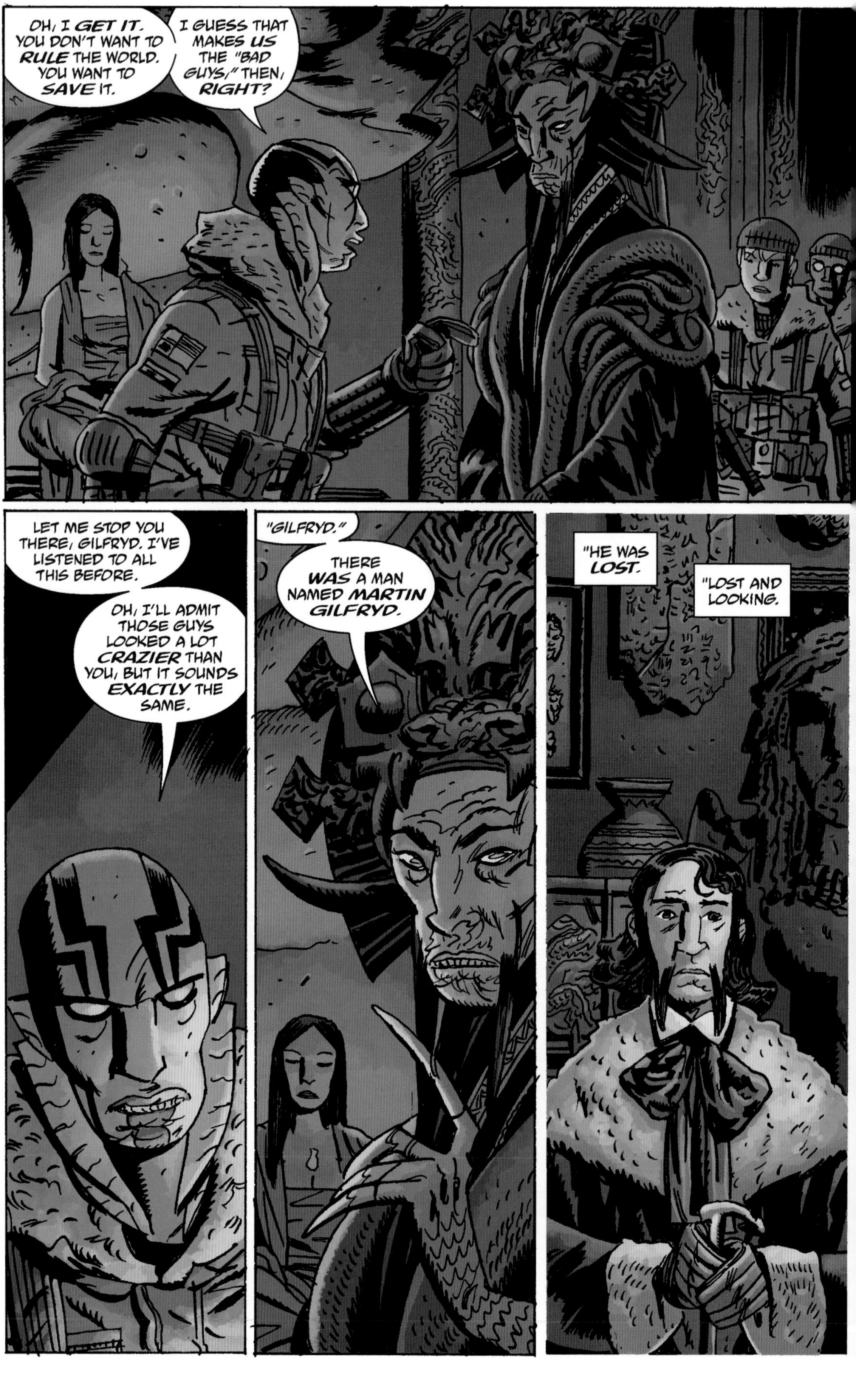
OH, I GET IT. YOU DON'T WANT TO RULE THE WORLD. YOU WANT TO SAVE IT.
I GUESS THAT MAKES US THE "BAD GUYS," THEN, RIGHT?
LET ME STOP YOU THERE, GILFRYD. I'VE LISTENED TO ALL THIS BEFORE.
OH, I'LL ADMIT THOSE GUYS LOOKED A LOT CRAZIER THAN YOU, BUT IT SOUNDS EXACTLY THE SAME.
"GILFRYD."
THERE WAS A MAN NAMED MARTIN GILFRYD.
"HE WAS LOST.
"LOST AND LOOKING.

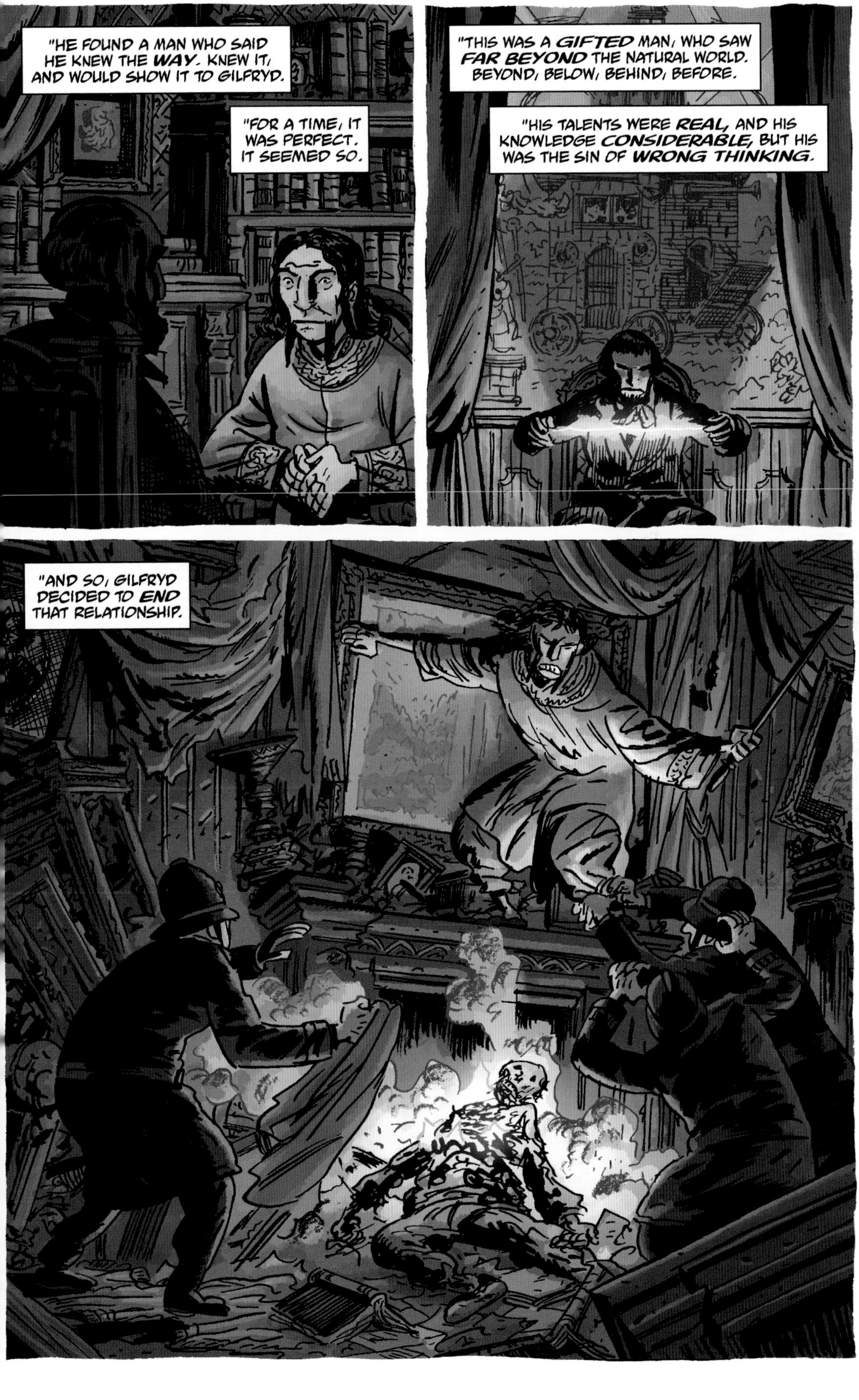
"HE FOUND A MAN WHO SAID HE KNEW THE WAY. KNEW IT, AND WOULD SHOW IT TO GILFRYD.
"FOR A TIME, IT WAS PERFECT. IT SEEMED SO.
"THIS WAS A GIFTED MAN, WHO SAW FAR BEYOND THE NATURAL WORLD. BEYOND, BELOW, BEHIND, BEFORE.
"HIS TALENTS WERE REAL, AND HIS KNOWLEDGE CONSIDERABLE, BUT HIS WAS THE SIN OF WRONG THINKING.
"AND SO, GILFRYD DECIDED TO END THAT RELATIONSHIP.

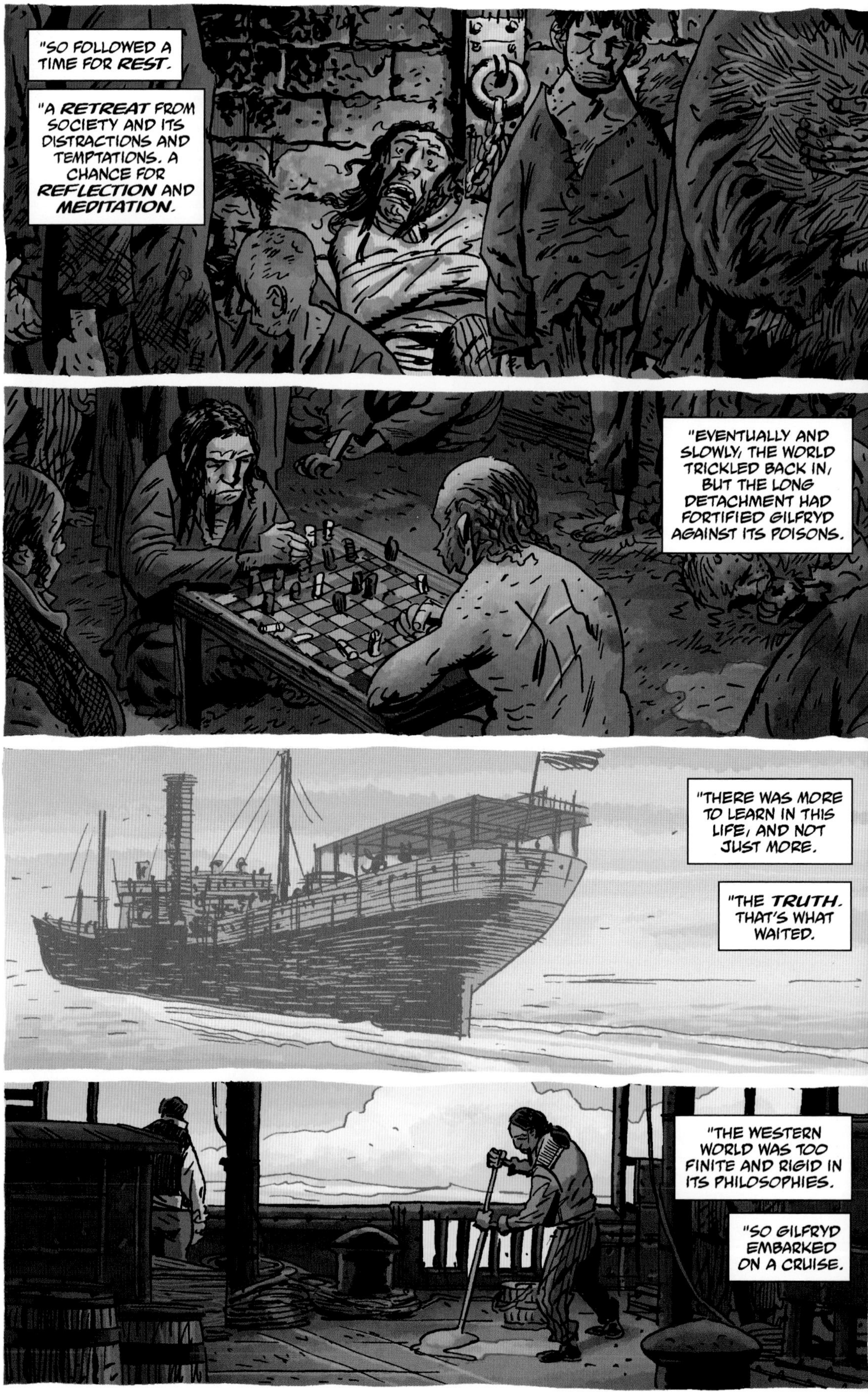
"SO FOLLOWED A TIME FOR REST.
"A RETREAT FROM SOCIETY AND ITS DISTRACTIONS AND TEMPTATIONS. A CHANCE FOR REFLECTION AND MEDITATION.
"EVENTUALLY AND SLOWLY, THE WORLD TRICKLED BACK IN, BUT THE LONG DETACHMENT HAD FORTIFIED GILFRYD AGAINST ITS POISONS.
"THERE WAS MORE TO LEARN IN THIS LIFE, AND NOT JUST MORE.
"THE TRUTH. THAT'S WHAT WAITED.
"THE WESTERN WORLD WAS TOO FINITE AND RIGID IN ITS PHILOSOPHIES.
"SO GILFRYD EMBARKED ON A CRUISE.

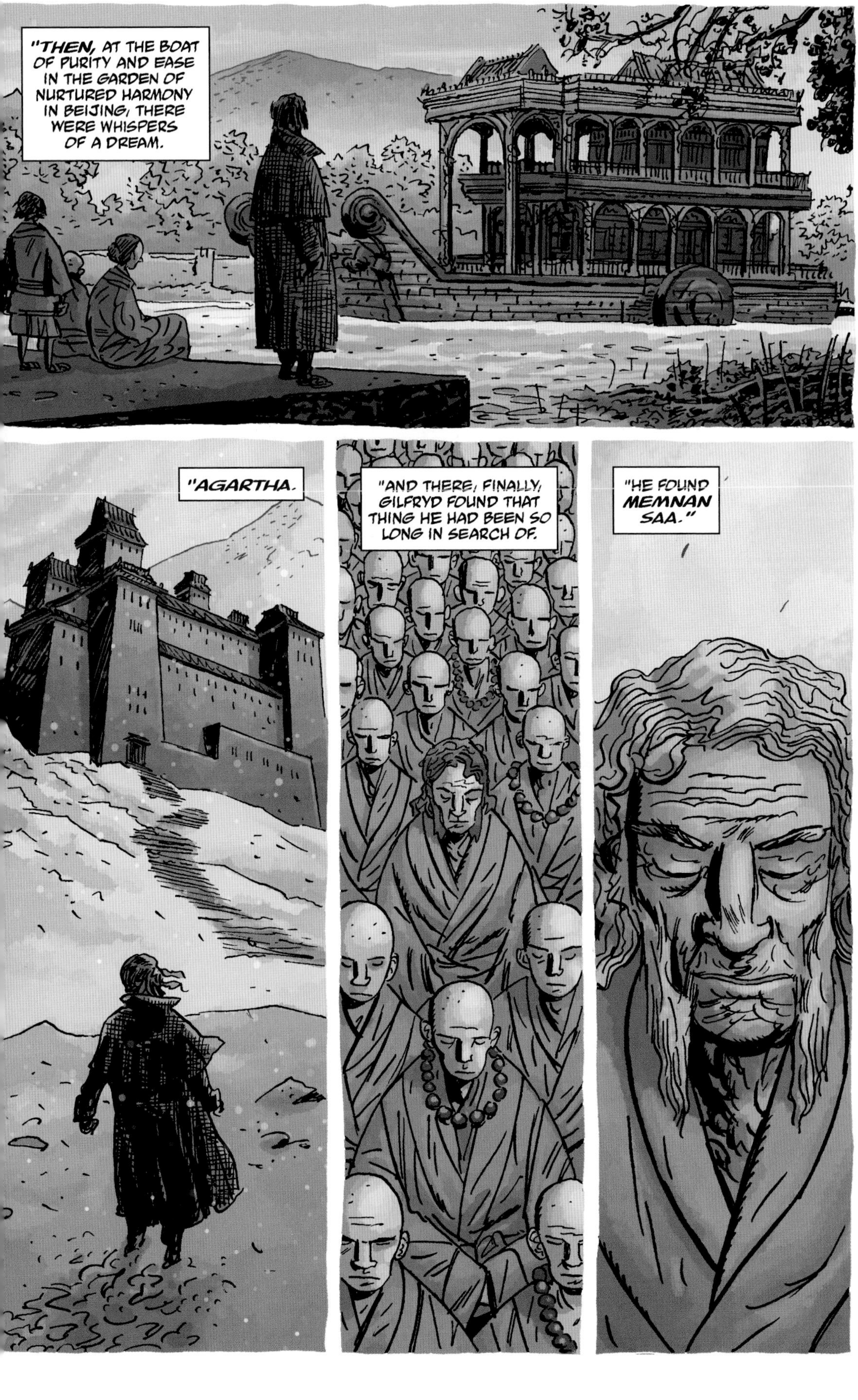
"THEN, AT THE BOAT OF PURITY AND EASE IN THE GARDEN OF NURTURED HARMONY IN BEIJING, THERE WERE WHISPERS OF A DREAM.
"AGARTHA.
"AND THERE, FINALLY, GILFRYD FOUND THAT THING HE HAD BEEN SO LONG IN SEARCH OF.
"HE FOUND MEMNAN SAA."

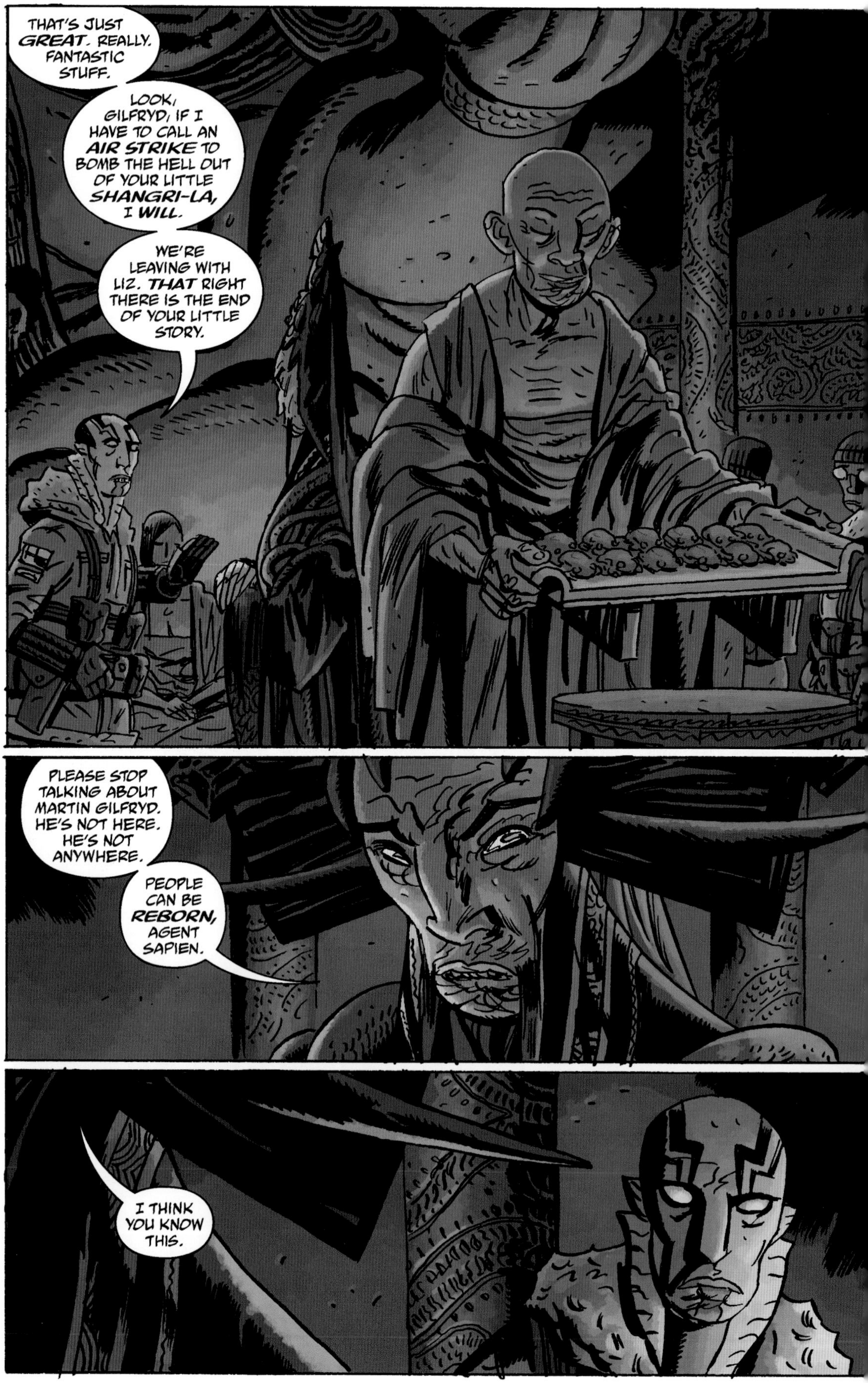
THAT'S JUST GREAT. REALLY. FANTASTIC STUFF.
LOOK, GILFRYD, IF I HAVE TO CALL AN AIR STRIKE TO BOMB THE HELL OUT OF YOUR LITTLE SHANGRI-LA, I WILL.
WE'RE LEAVING WITH LIZ. THAT RIGHT THERE IS THE END OF YOUR LITTLE STORY.
PLEASE STOP TALKING ABOUT MARTIN GILFRYD. HE'S NOT HERE. HE'S NOT ANYWHERE.
PEOPLE CAN BE REBORN, AGENT SAPIEN.
I THINK YOU KNOW THIS.

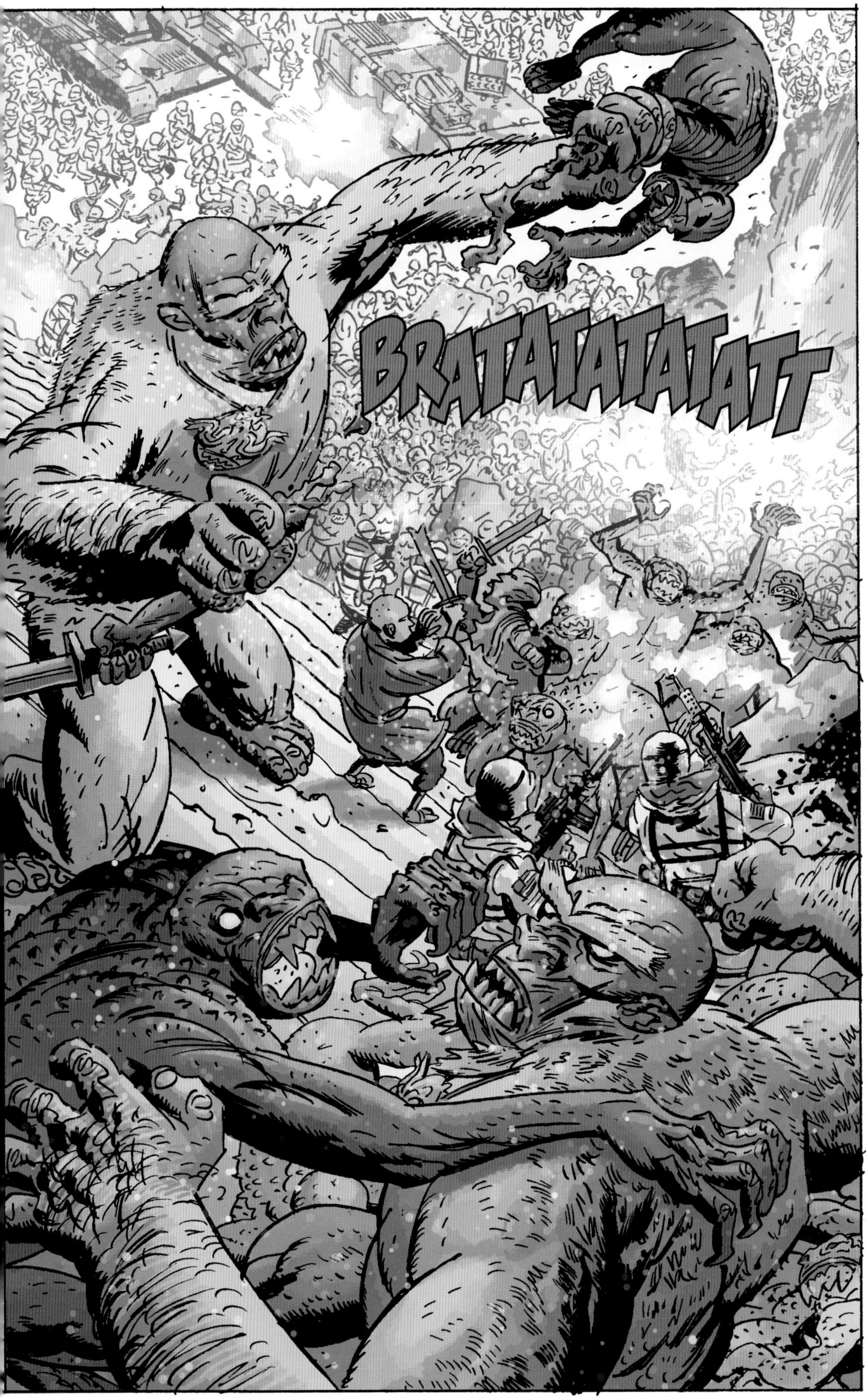
BRATATATATATT

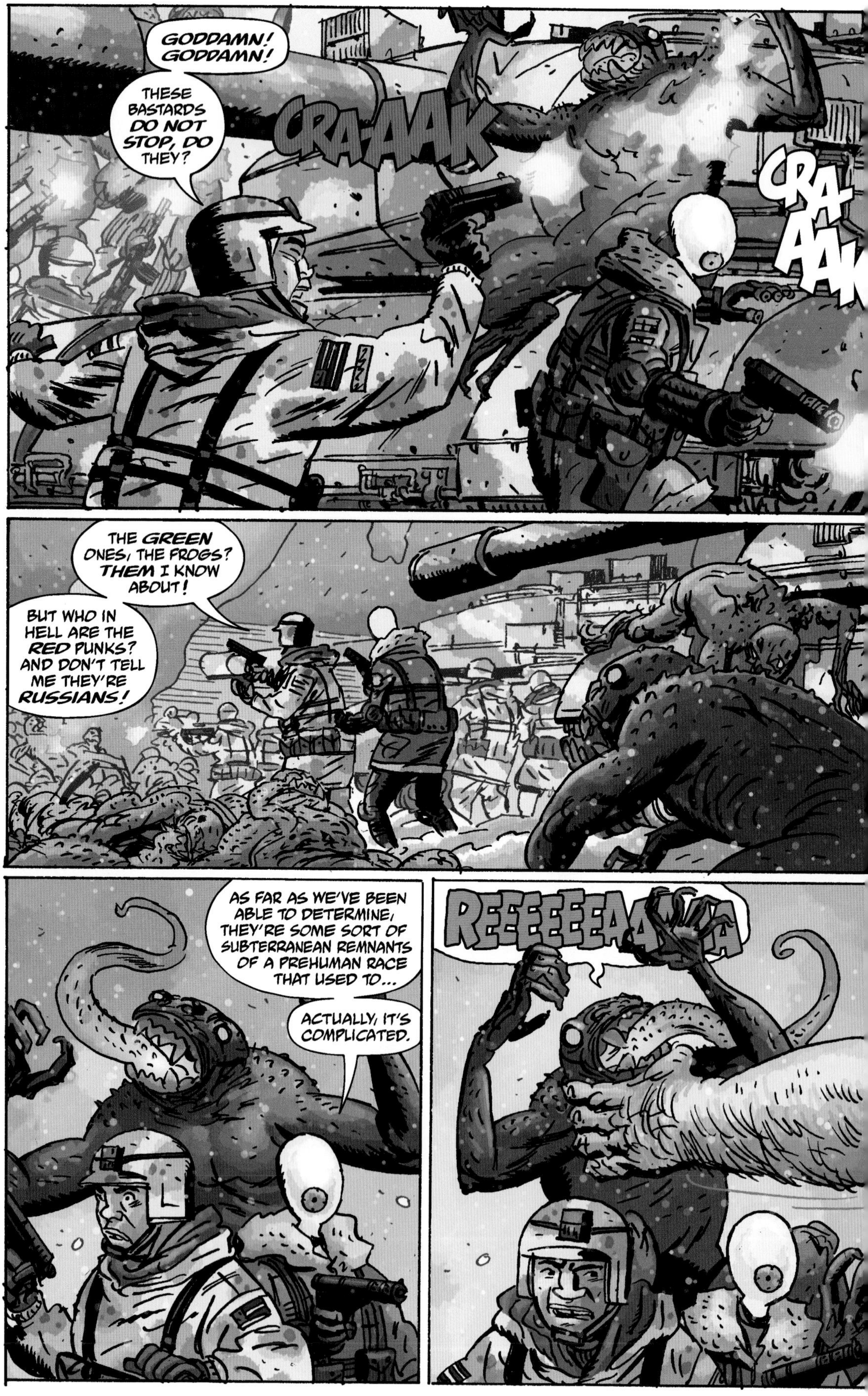
GODDAMN! GODDAMN!
THESE BASTARDS DO NOT STOP, DO THEY?
CRA-AAK
CRA-AAK
THE GREEN ONES, THE FROGS? THEM I KNOW ABOUT!
BUT WHO IN HELL ARE THE RED PUNKS? AND DON'T TELL ME THEY'RE RUSSIANS!
AS FAR AS WE'VE BEEN ABLE TO DETERMINE, THEY'RE SOME SORT OF SUBTERRANEAN REMNANTS OF A PREHUMAN RACE THAT USED TO...
ACTUALLY, IT'S COMPLICATED.
REEEEEEEAAAAA

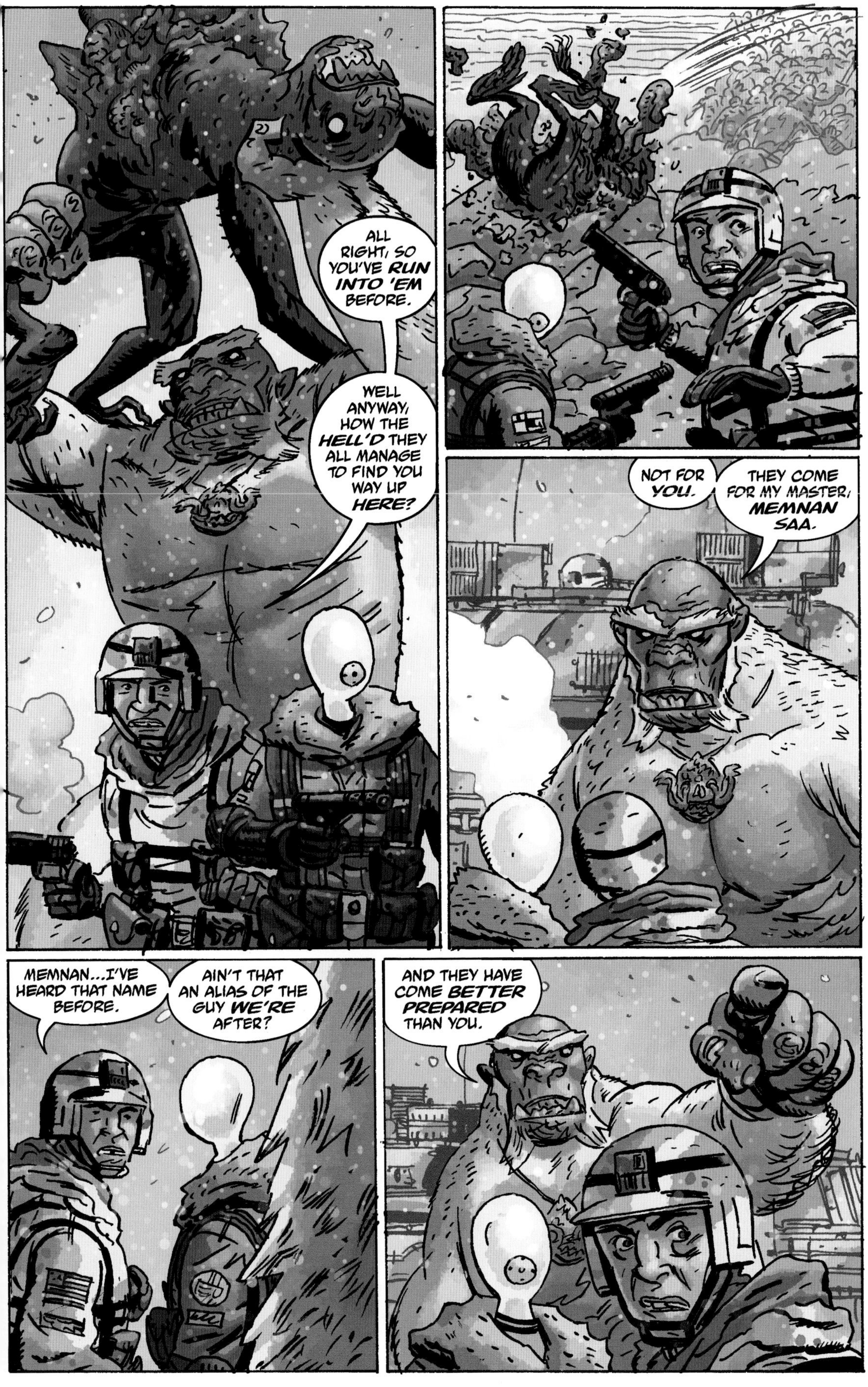
ALL RIGHT, SO YOU'VE RUN INTO 'EM BEFORE.
WELL ANYWAY, HOW THE HELL'D THEY ALL MANAGE TO FIND YOU WAY UP HERE?
NOT FOR YOU.
THEY COME FOR MY MASTER, MEMNAN SAA.
MEMNAN...I'VE HEARD THAT NAME BEFORE.
AIN'T THAT AN ALIAS OF THE GUY WE'RE AFTER?
AND THEY HAVE COME BETTER PREPARED THAN YOU.

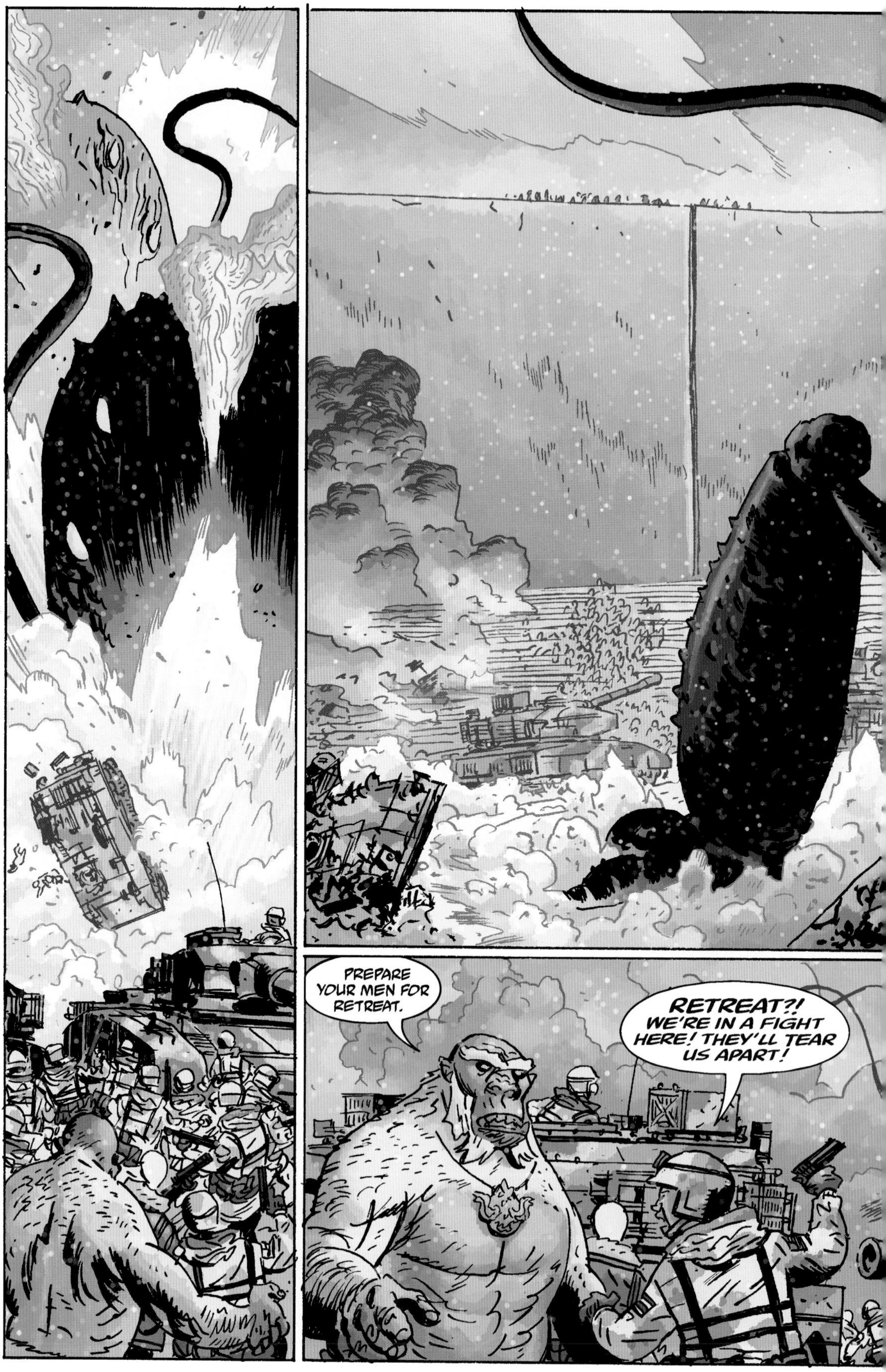
PREPARE YOUR MEN FOR RETREAT.
RETREAT?! WE'RE IN A FIGHT HERE! THEY'LL TEAR US APART!

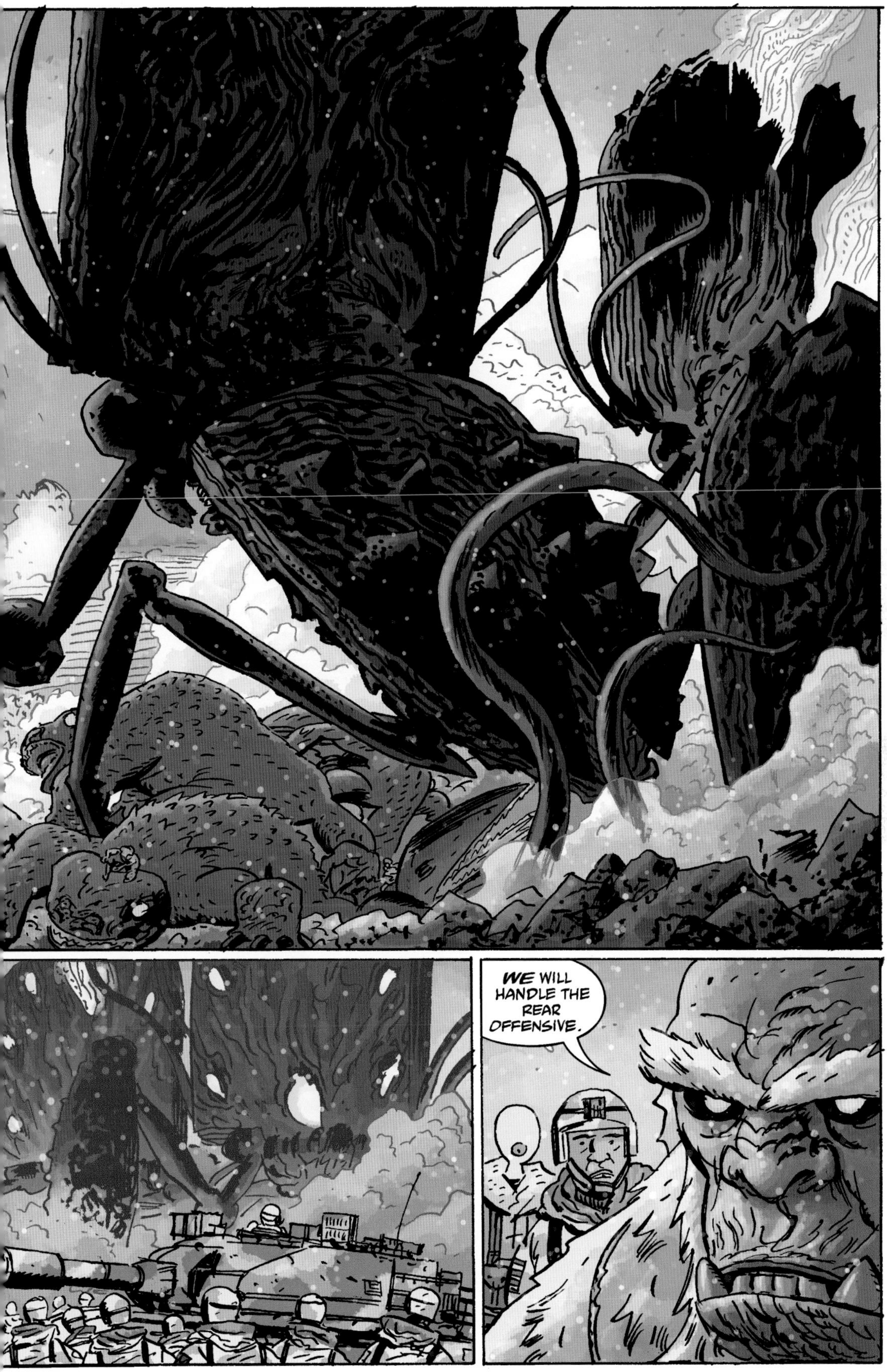
WE WILL HANDLE THE REAR OFFENSIVE.

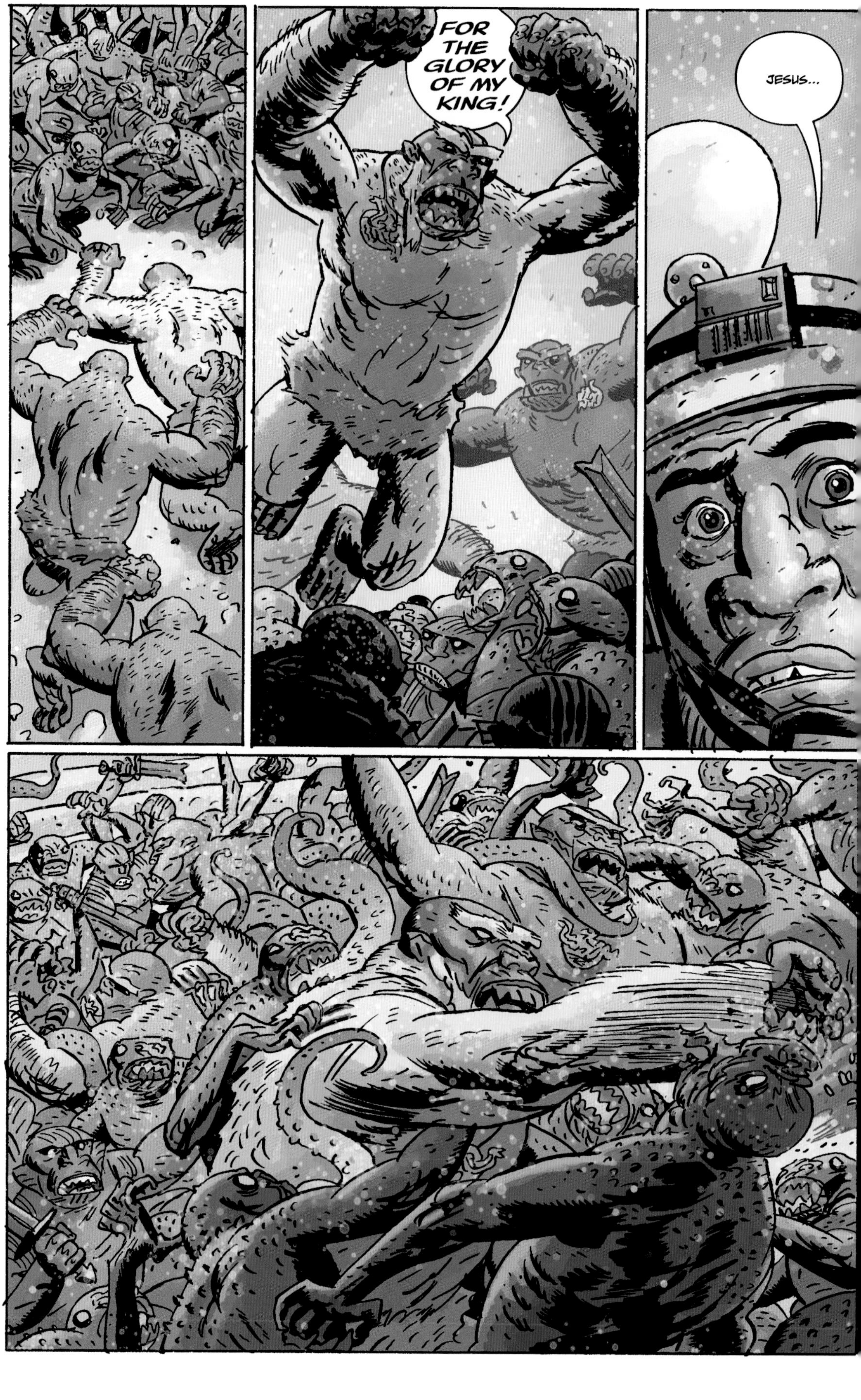
FOR THE GLORY OF MY KING!
JESUS...

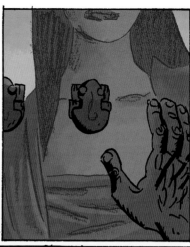

NO. YOU HAVEN'T BROUGHT LIZ BACK TO THE MONKS OF *AGARTHA*. THEY WERE ALL *KILLED*. SO WHAT *IS* THIS?

THAT'S *RIGHT*, DR. CORRIGAN. *YOU* ARE THE *CURIOUS* ONE. YOU WANT TO *UNDERSTAND*.

AND NOW I WOULD *PREFER* YOU UNDER-STAND.

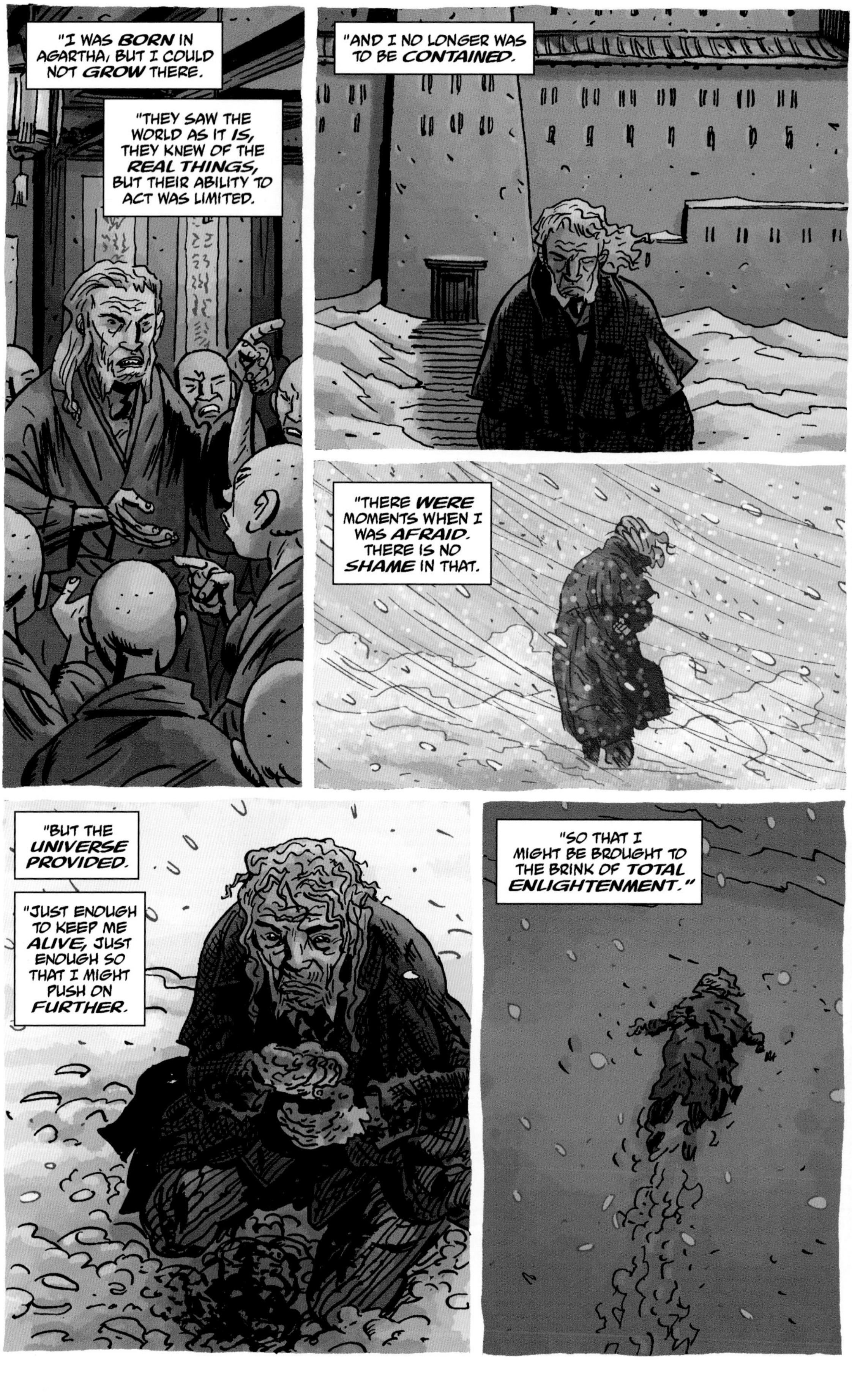
"I WAS BORN IN AGARTHA, BUT I COULD NOT GROW THERE.
"THEY SAW THE WORLD AS IT IS, THEY KNEW OF THE REAL THINGS, BUT THEIR ABILITY TO ACT WAS LIMITED.
"AND I NO LONGER WAS TO BE CONTAINED.
"THERE WERE MOMENTS WHEN I WAS AFRAID. THERE IS NO SHAME IN THAT.
"BUT THE UNIVERSE PROVIDED.
"JUST ENOUGH TO KEEP ME ALIVE, JUST ENOUGH SO THAT I MIGHT PUSH ON FURTHER.
"SO THAT I MIGHT BE BROUGHT TO THE BRINK OF TOTAL ENLIGHTENMENT."

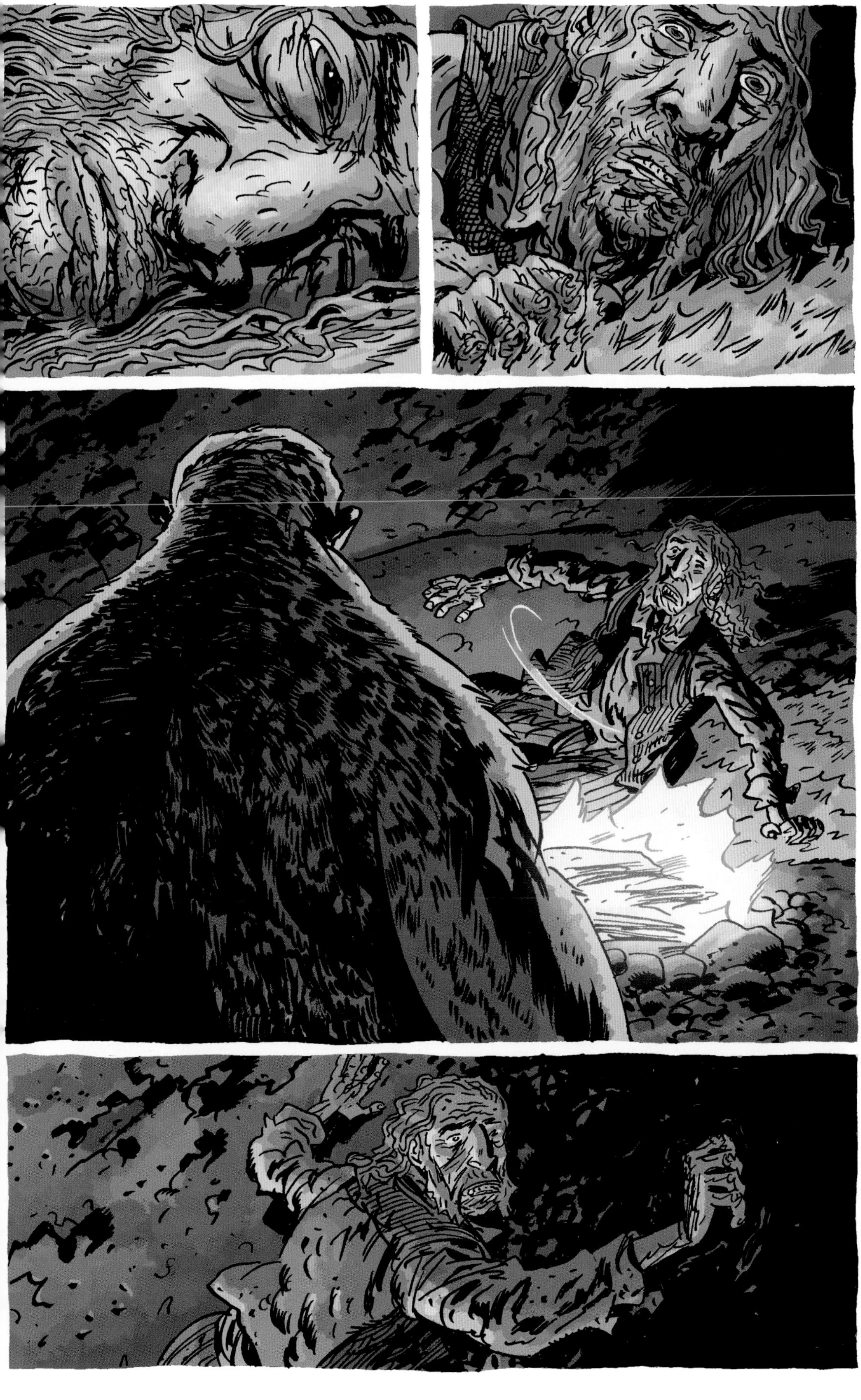

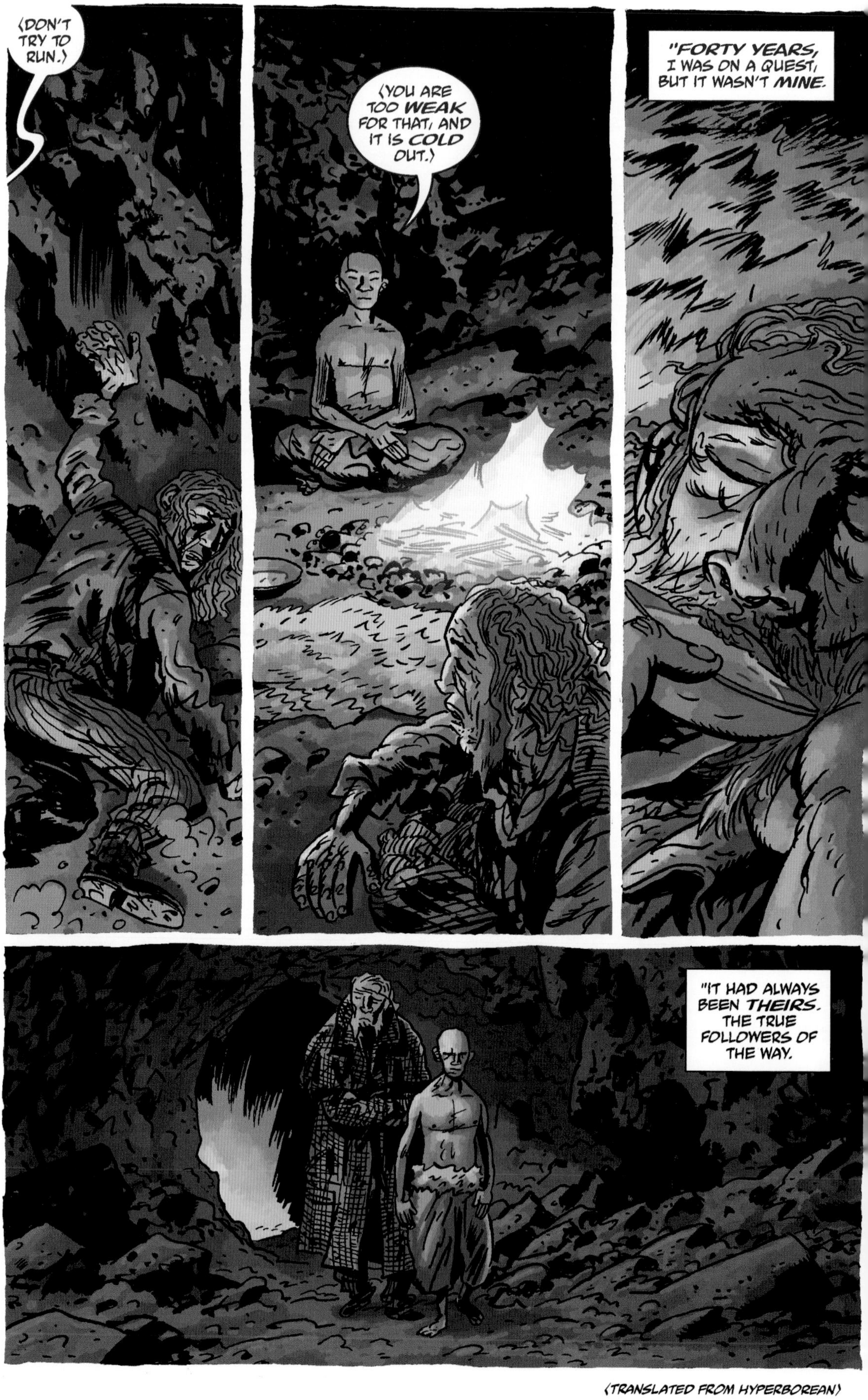

(DON'T TRY TO RUN.)
(YOU ARE TOO WEAK FOR THAT, AND IT IS COLD OUT.)
"FORTY YEARS, I WAS ON A QUEST, BUT IT WASN'T MINE.
"IT HAD ALWAYS BEEN THEIRS. THE TRUE FOLLOWERS OF THE WAY.

(TRANSLATED FROM HYPERBOREAN)

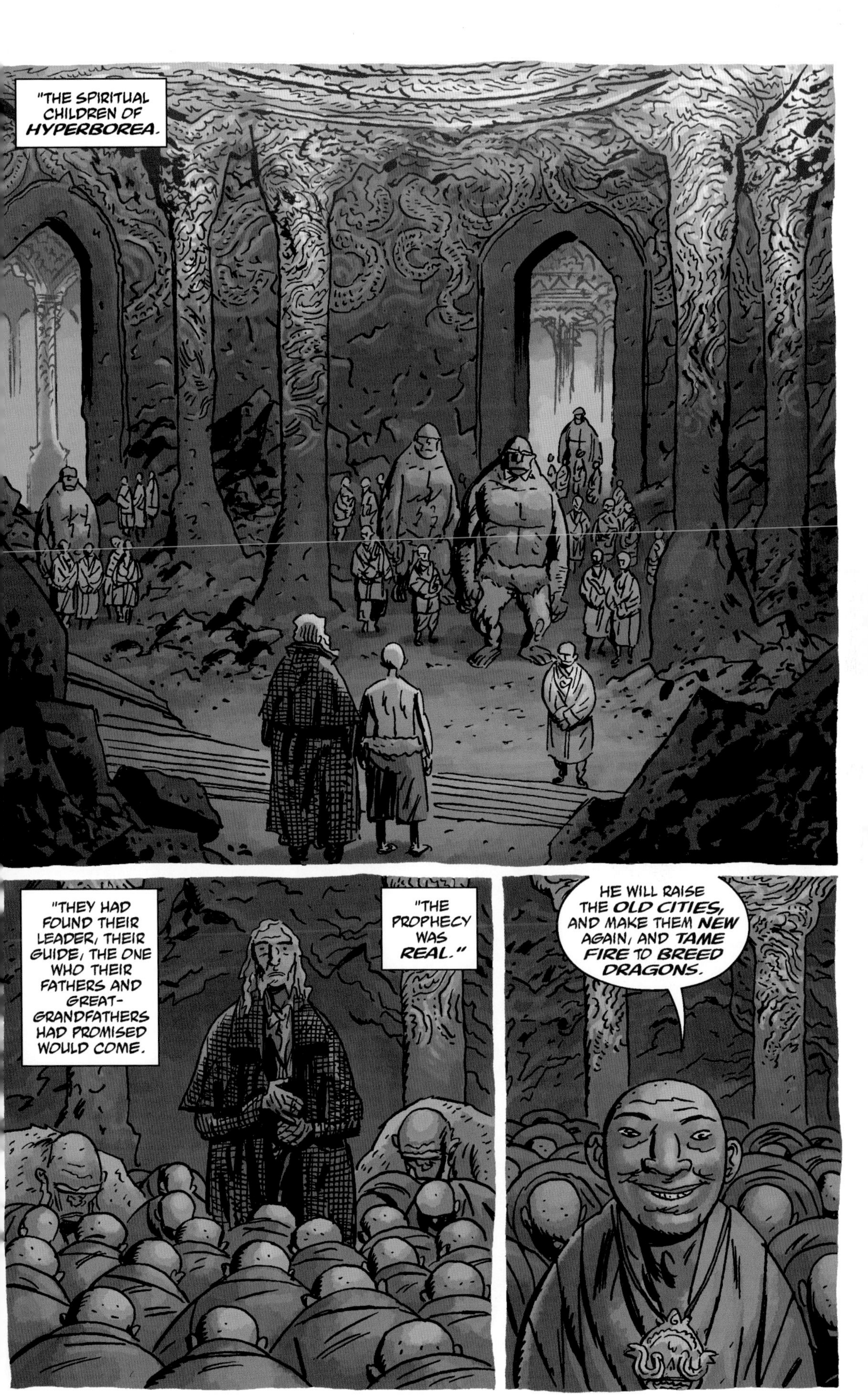
"THE SPIRITUAL CHILDREN OF HYPERBOREA.
"THEY HAD FOUND THEIR LEADER, THEIR GUIDE, THE ONE WHO THEIR FATHERS AND GREAT-GRANDFATHERS HAD PROMISED WOULD COME.
"THE PROPHECY WAS REAL."
HE WILL RAISE THE OLD CITIES, AND MAKE THEM NEW AGAIN, AND TAME FIRE TO BREED DRAGONS.

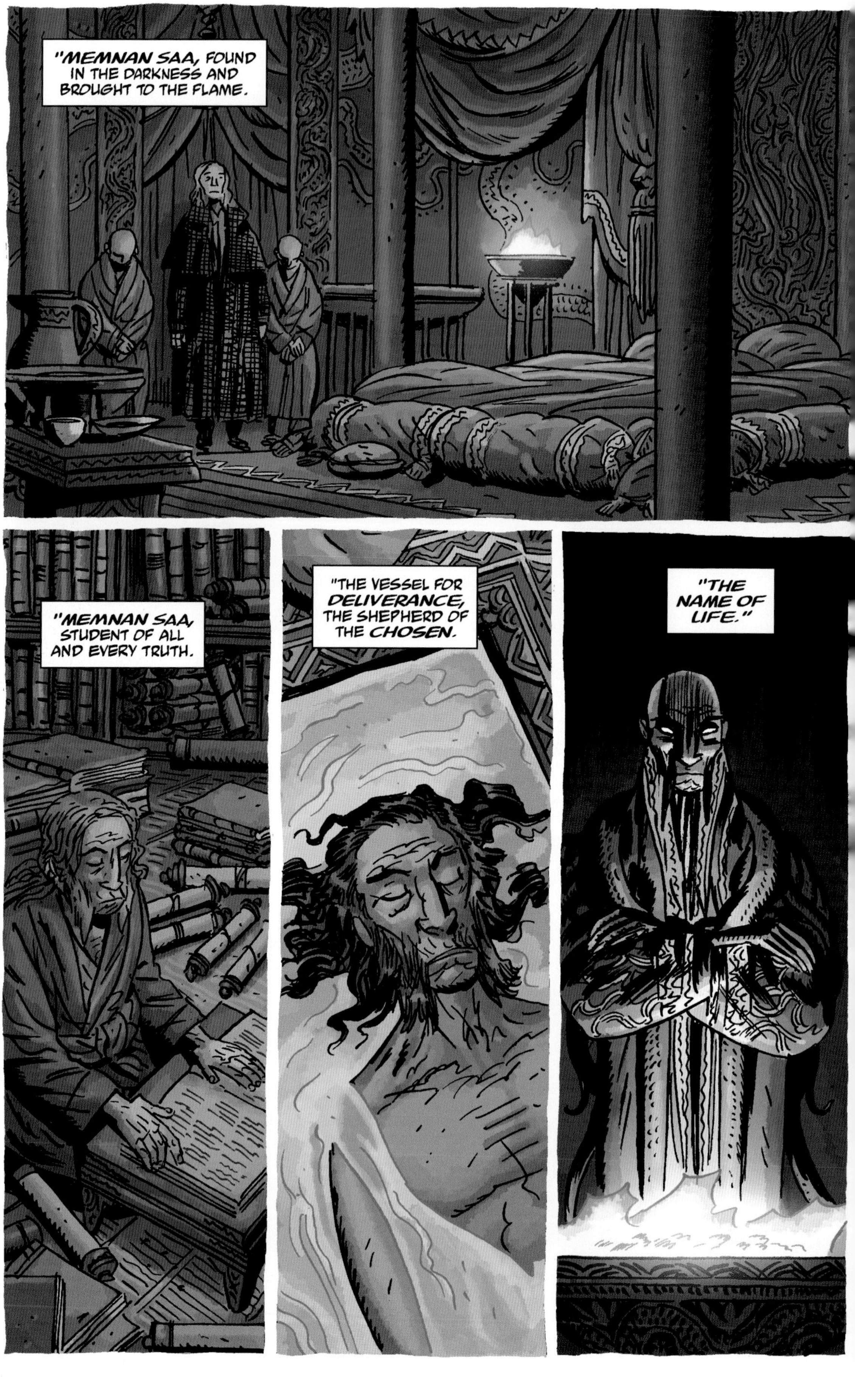
"MEMNAN SAA, FOUND IN THE DARKNESS AND BROUGHT TO THE FLAME.
"MEMNAN SAA, STUDENT OF ALL AND EVERY TRUTH.
"THE VESSEL FOR DELIVERANCE, THE SHEPHERD OF THE CHOSEN.
"THE NAME OF LIFE."

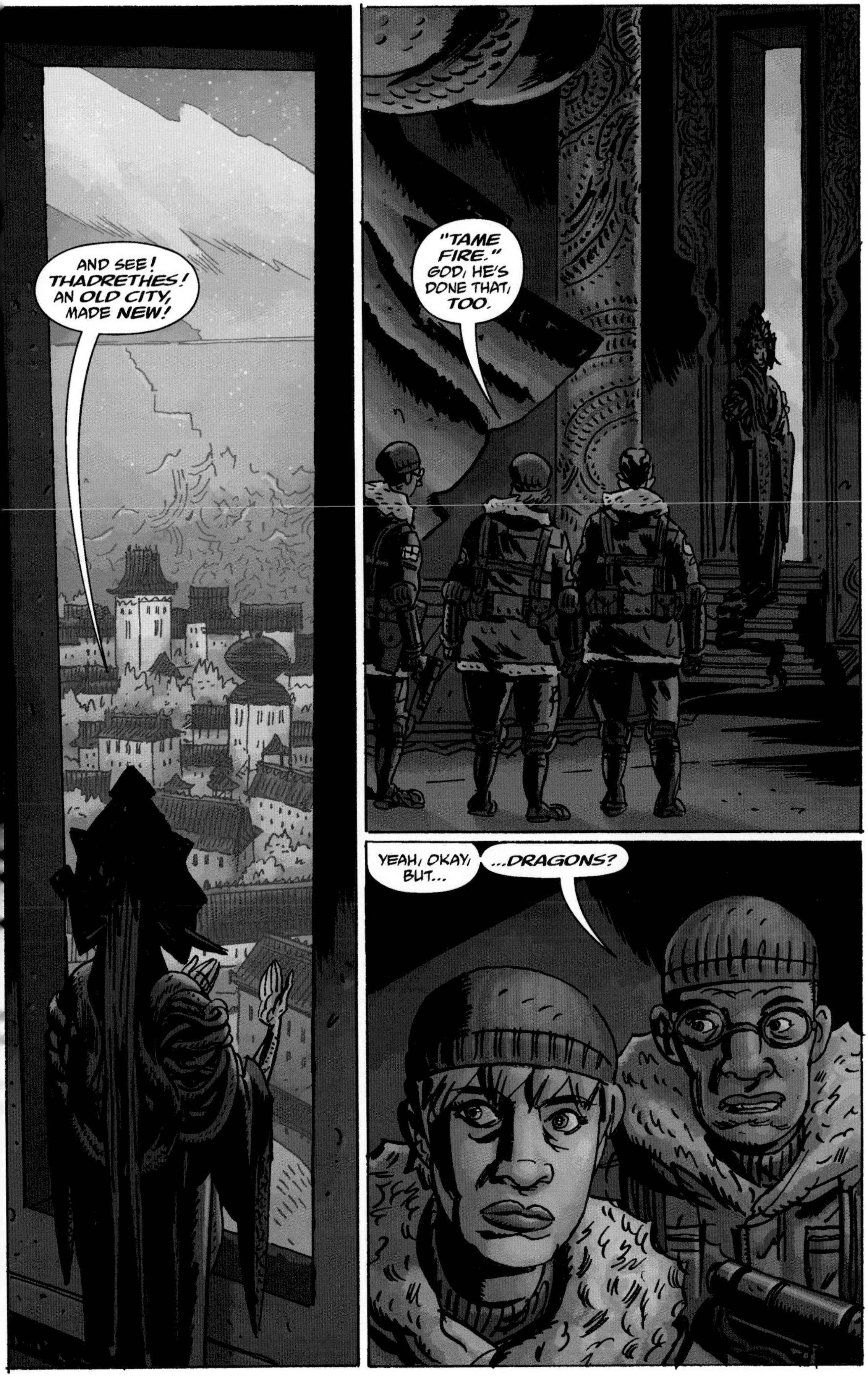
AND SEE! THADRETHES! AN OLD CITY, MADE NEW!
"TAME FIRE." GOD, HE'S DONE THAT, TOO.
YEAH, OKAY, BUT...
...DRAGONS?

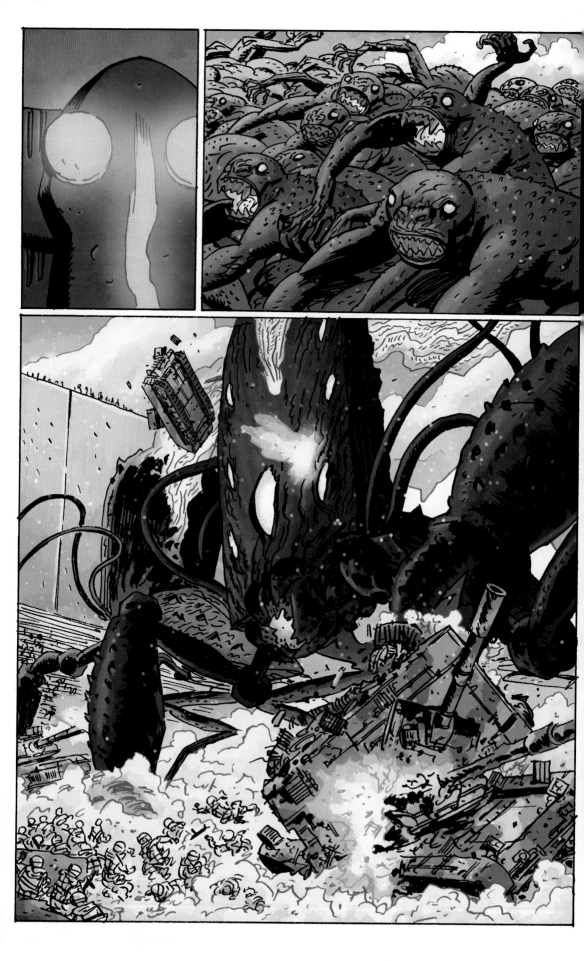

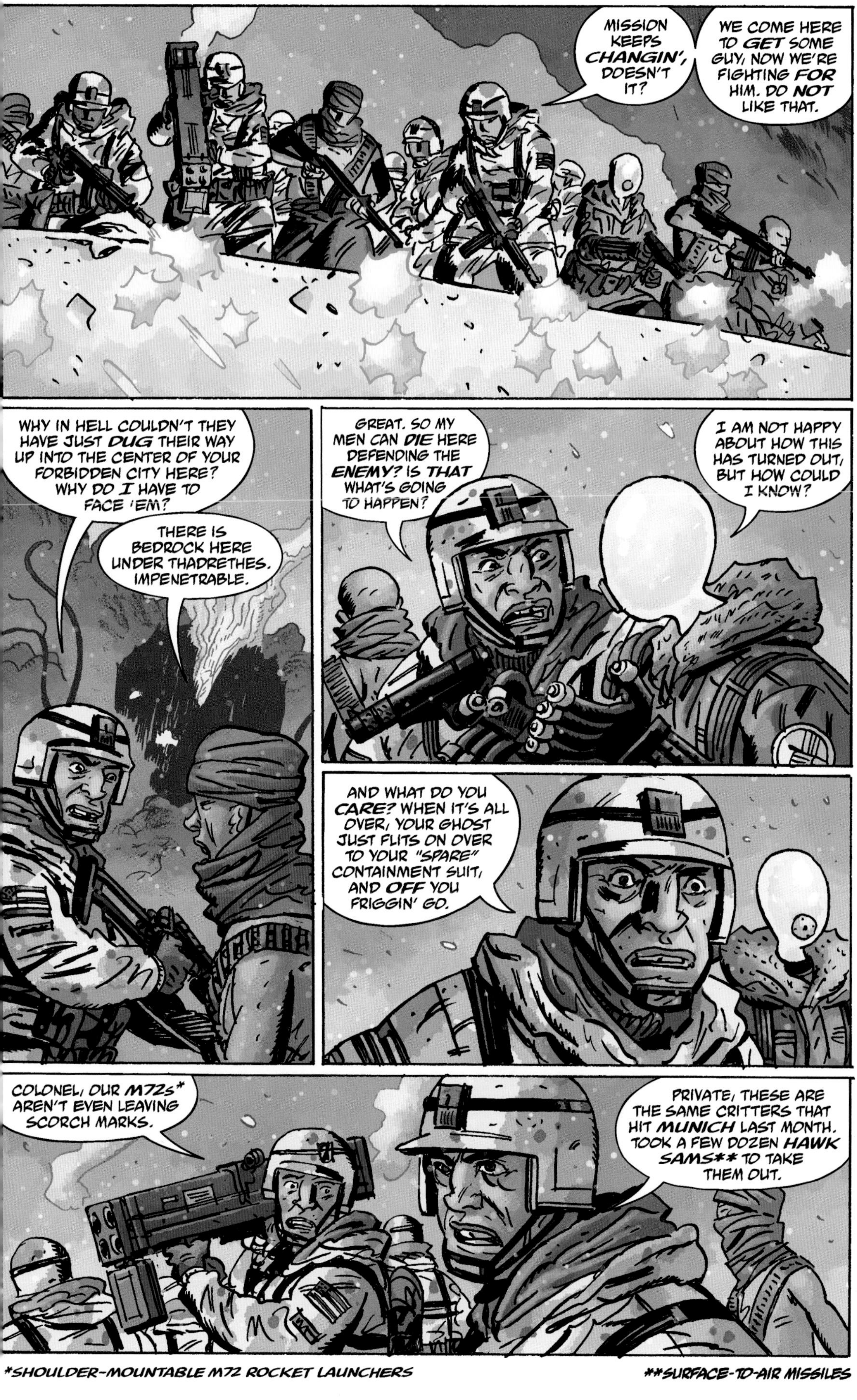
MISSION KEEPS CHANGIN', DOESN'T IT?
WE COME HERE TO GET SOME GUY, NOW WE'RE FIGHTING FOR HIM. DO NOT LIKE THAT.
WHY IN HELL COULDN'T THEY HAVE JUST DUG THEIR WAY UP INTO THE CENTER OF YOUR FORBIDDEN CITY HERE? WHY DO I HAVE TO FACE 'EM?
THERE IS BEDROCK HERE UNDER THADRETHES. IMPENETRABLE.
GREAT. SO MY MEN CAN DIE HERE DEFENDING THE ENEMY? IS THAT WHAT'S GOING TO HAPPEN?
I AM NOT HAPPY ABOUT HOW THIS HAS TURNED OUT, BUT HOW COULD I KNOW?
AND WHAT DO YOU CARE? WHEN IT'S ALL OVER, YOUR GHOST JUST FLITS ON OVER TO YOUR "SPARE" CONTAINMENT SUIT, AND OFF YOU FRIGGIN' GO.
COLONEL, OUR M72s* AREN'T EVEN LEAVING SCORCH MARKS.
PRIVATE, THESE ARE THE SAME CRITTERS THAT HIT MUNICH LAST MONTH. TOOK A FEW DOZEN HAWK SAMS** TO TAKE THEM OUT.

*SHOULDER-MOUNTABLE M72 ROCKET LAUNCHERS

**SURFACE-TO-AIR MISSILES

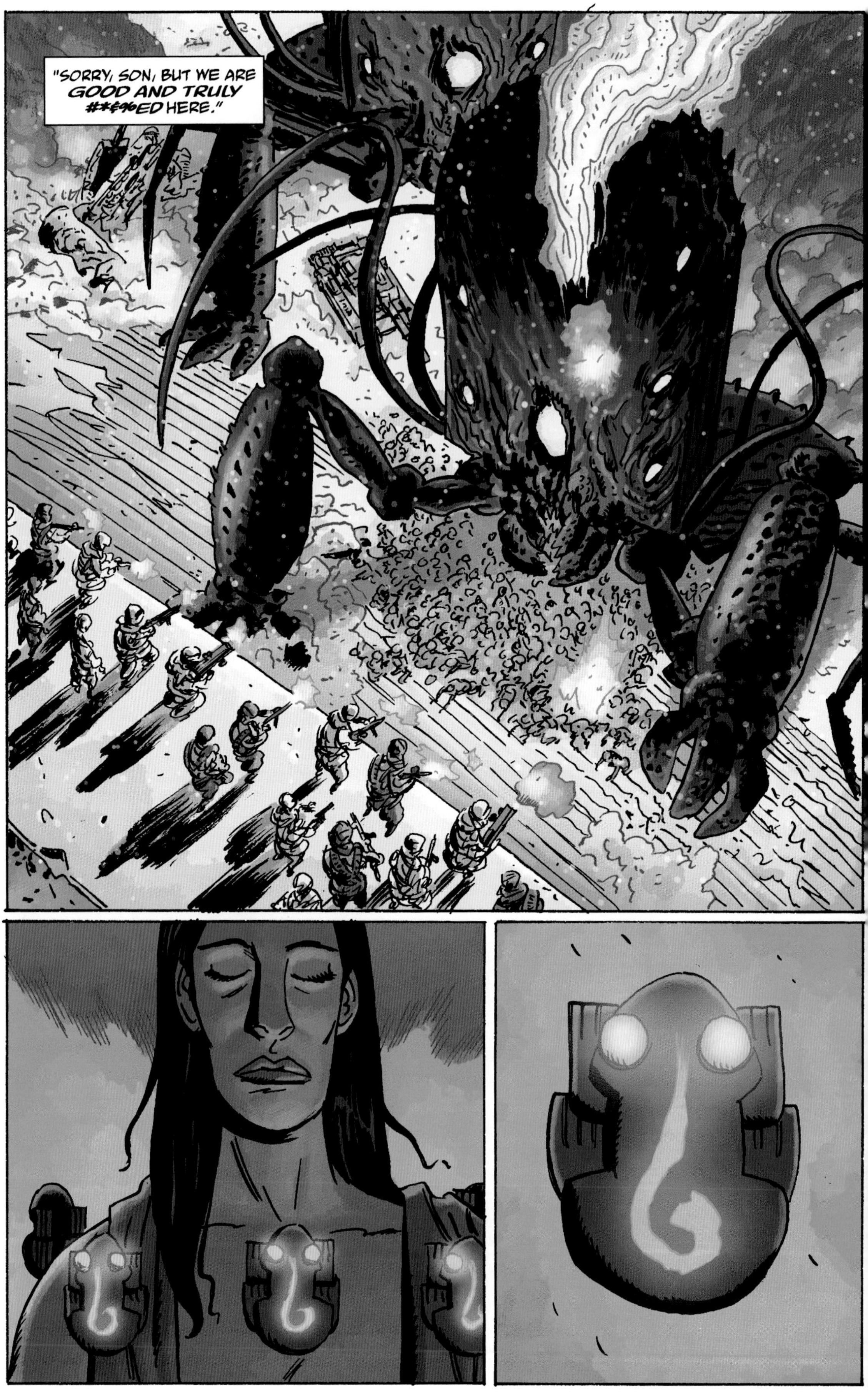
"SORRY, SON, BUT WE ARE GOOD AND TRULY #*$%ED HERE."

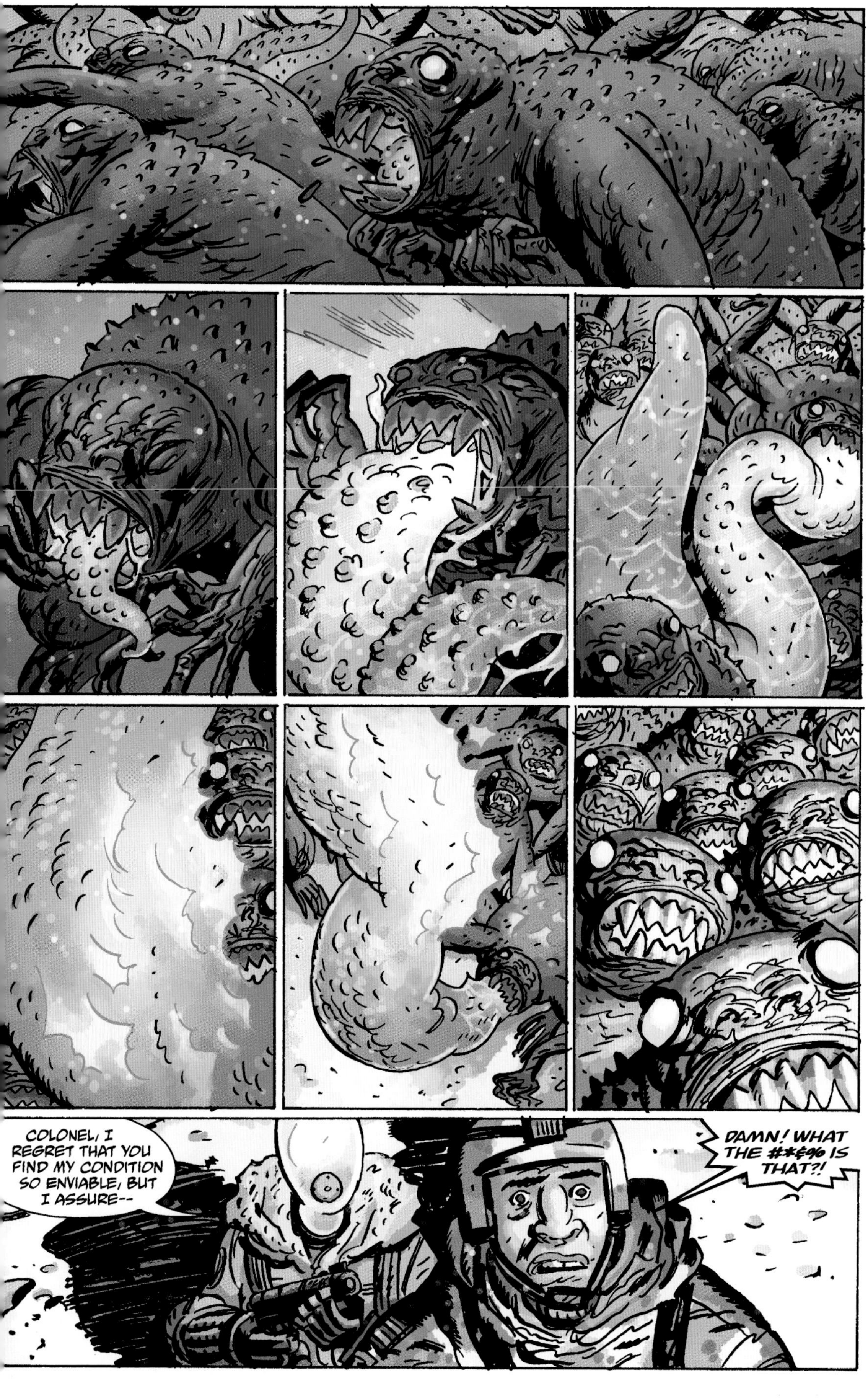
COLONEL, I REGRET THAT YOU FIND MY CONDITION SO ENVIABLE, BUT I ASSURE--
DAMN! WHAT THE ##*$%% IS THAT?!

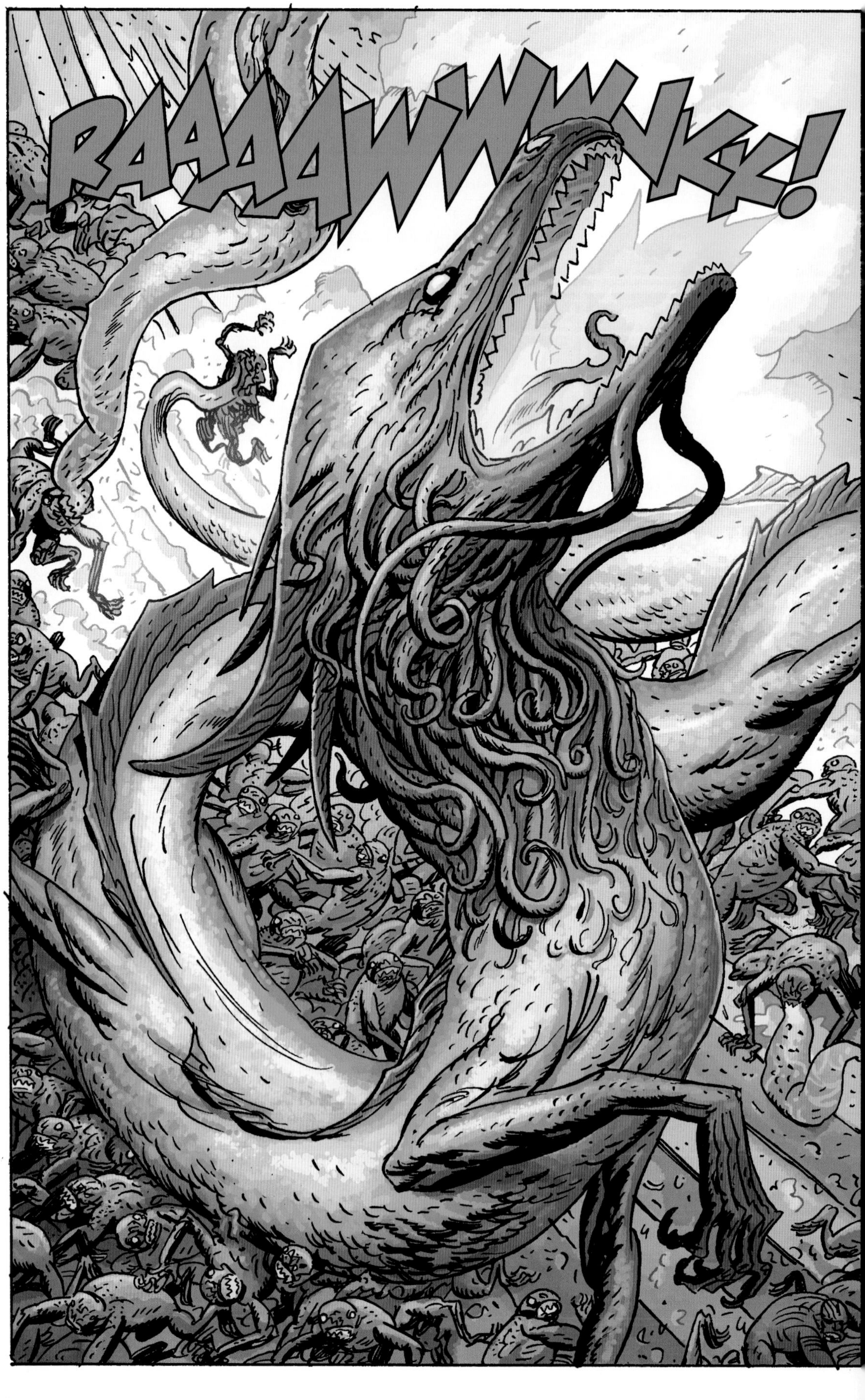
RAAAAWWWNKK!

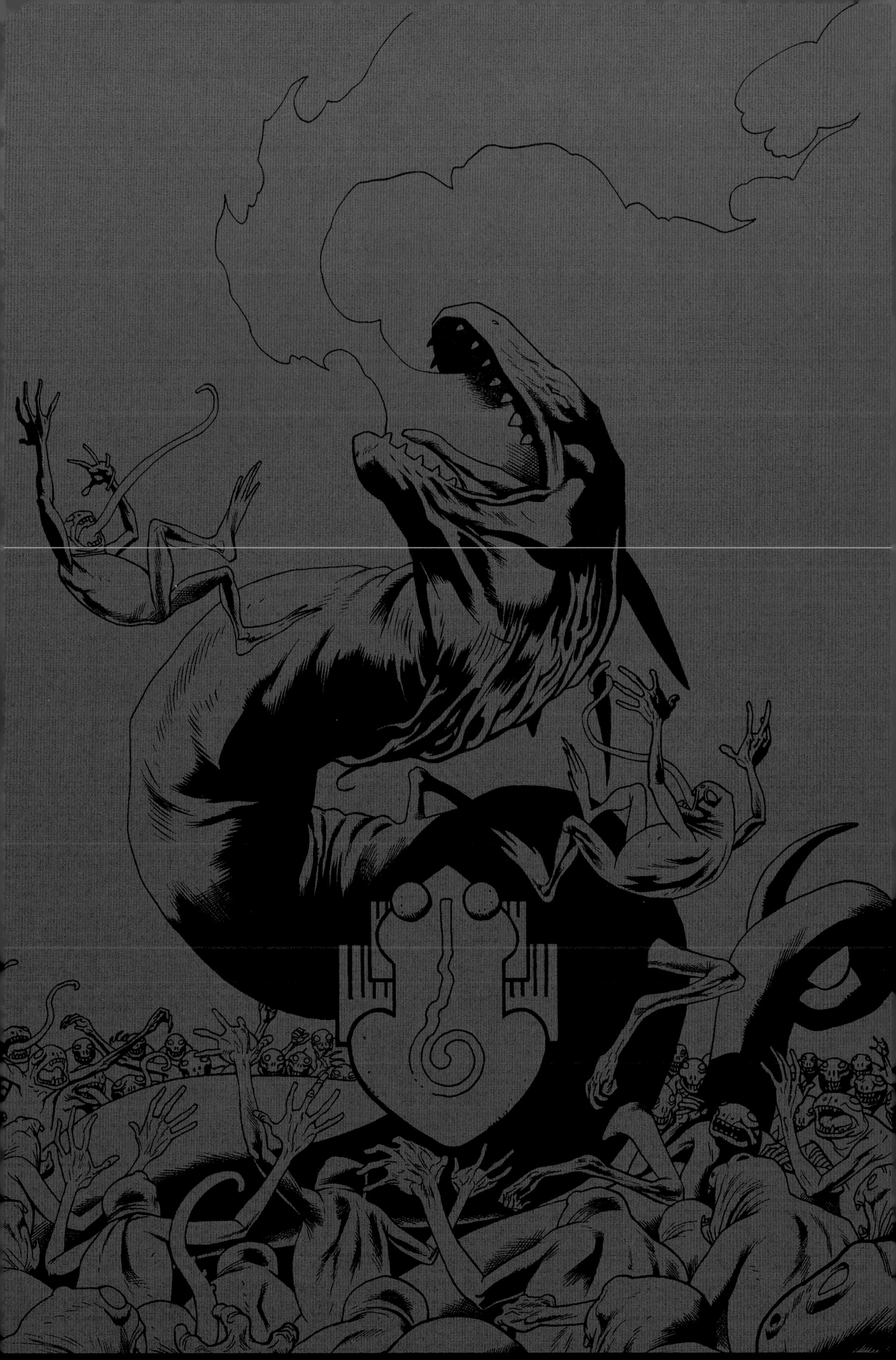

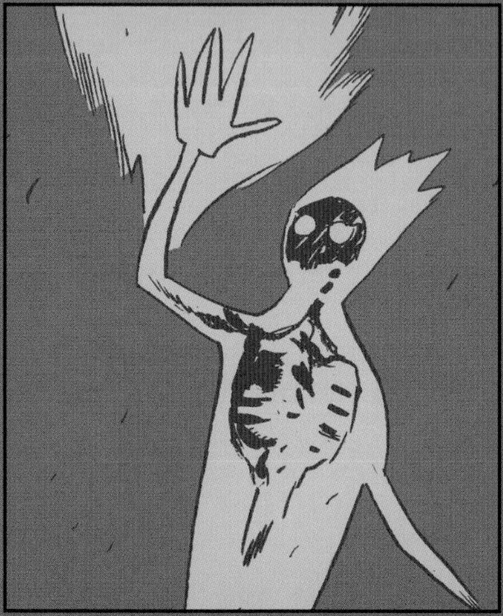

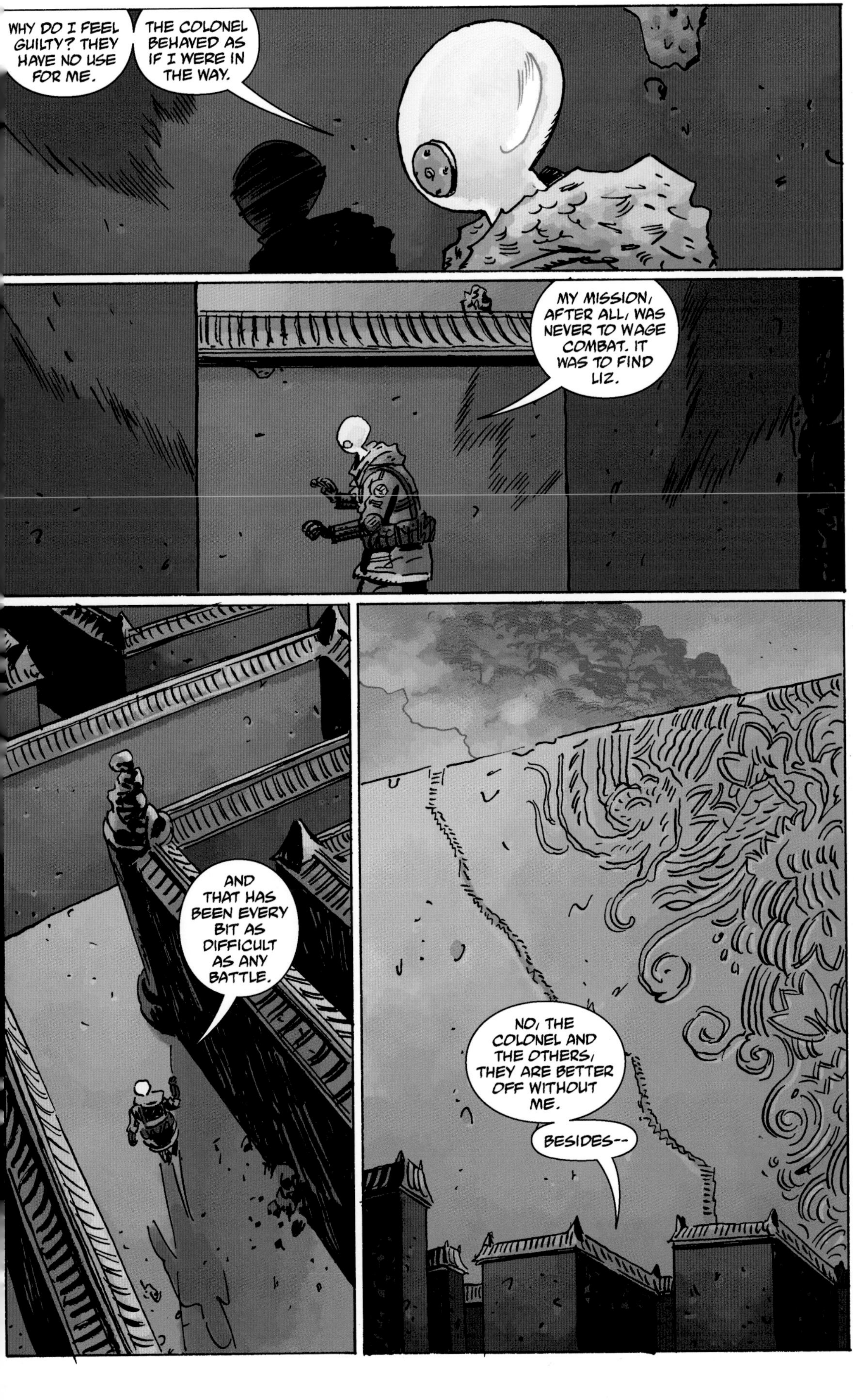
WHY DO I FEEL GUILTY? THEY HAVE NO USE FOR ME.
THE COLONEL BEHAVED AS IF I WERE IN THE WAY.
MY MISSION, AFTER ALL, WAS NEVER TO WAGE COMBAT. IT WAS TO FIND LIZ.
AND THAT HAS BEEN EVERY BIT AS DIFFICULT AS ANY BATTLE.
NO, THE COLONEL AND THE OTHERS, THEY ARE BETTER OFF WITHOUT ME.
BESIDES--

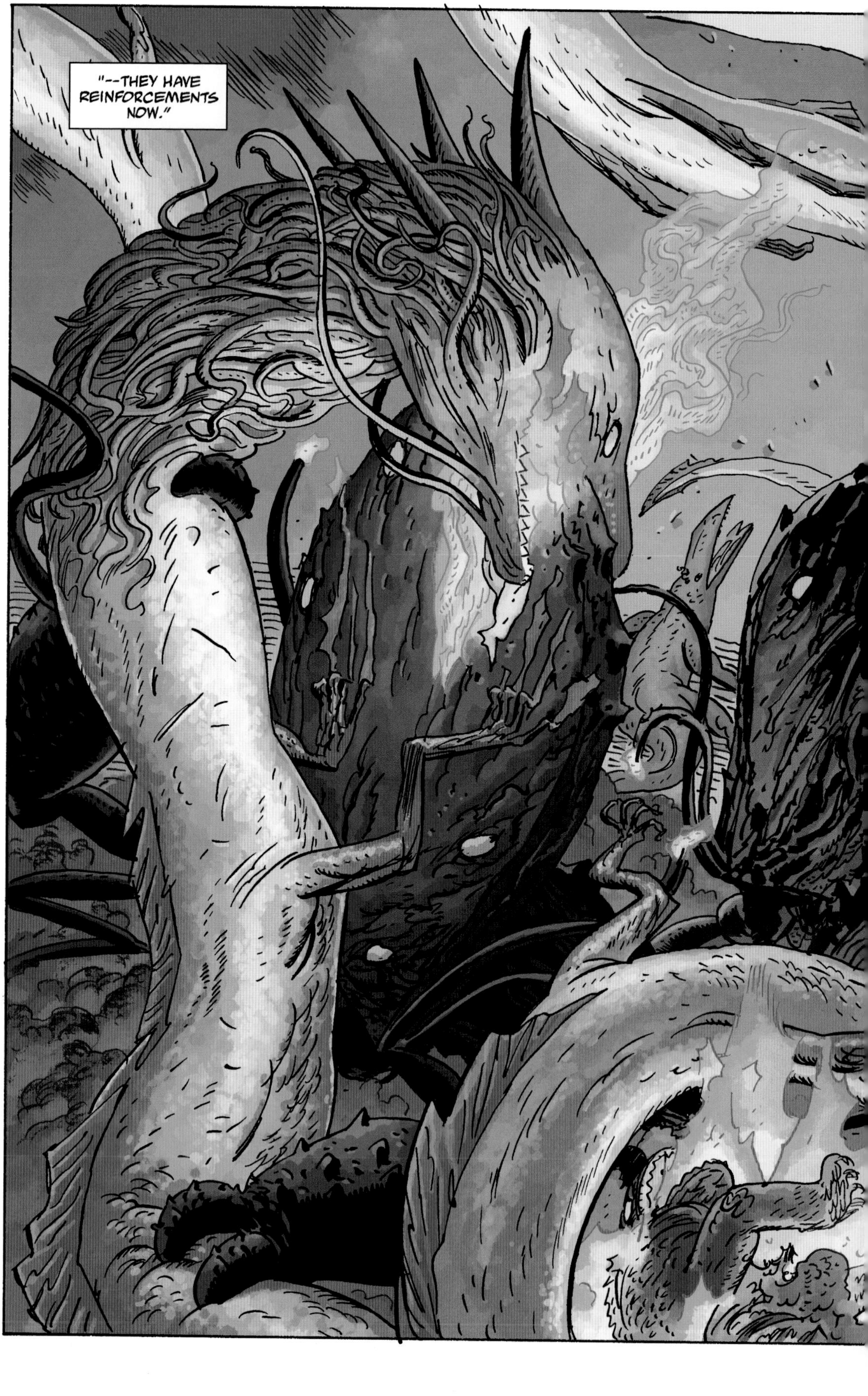
"--THEY HAVE REINFORCEMENTS NOW."

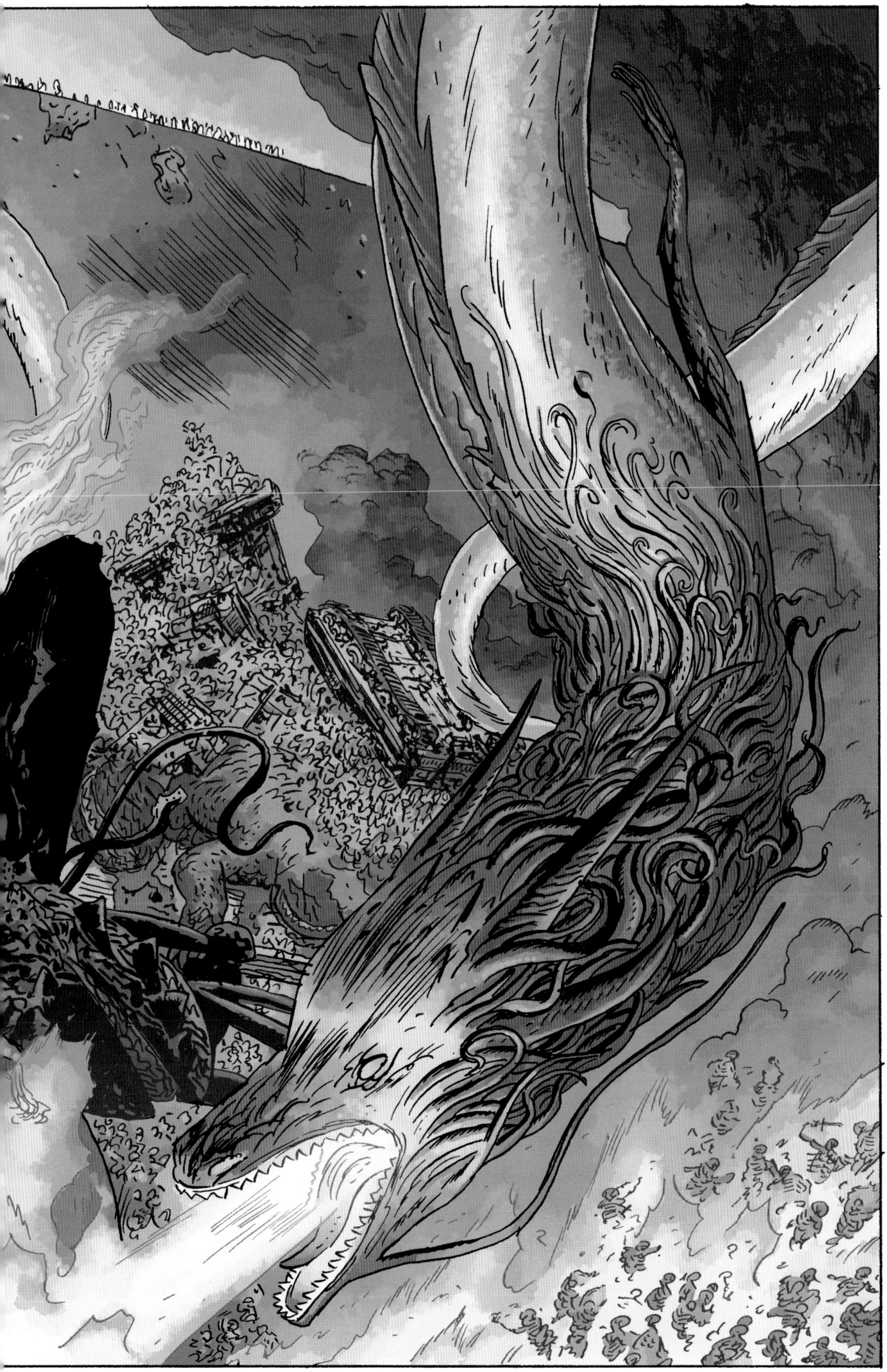

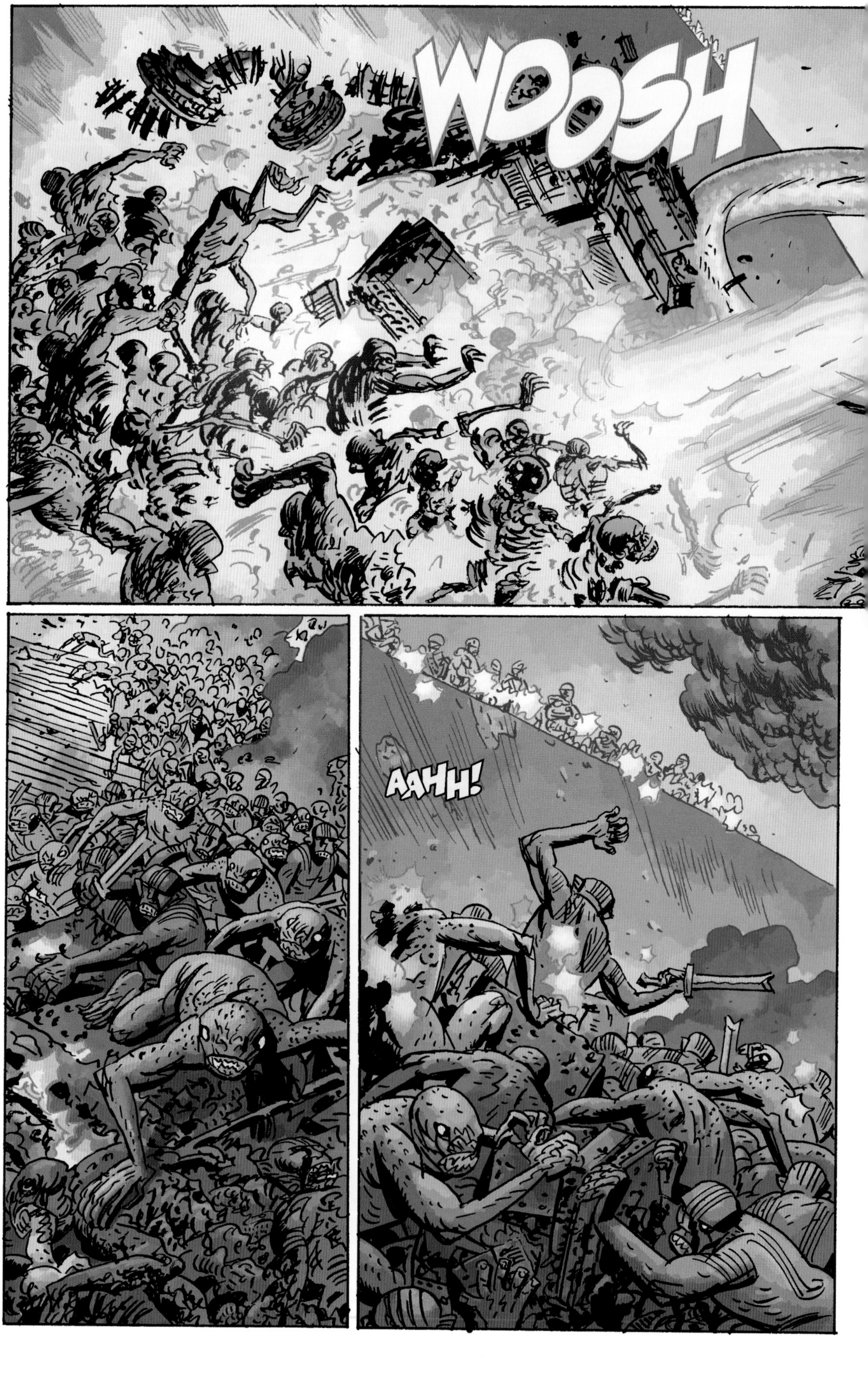
WOOSH
AAHH!

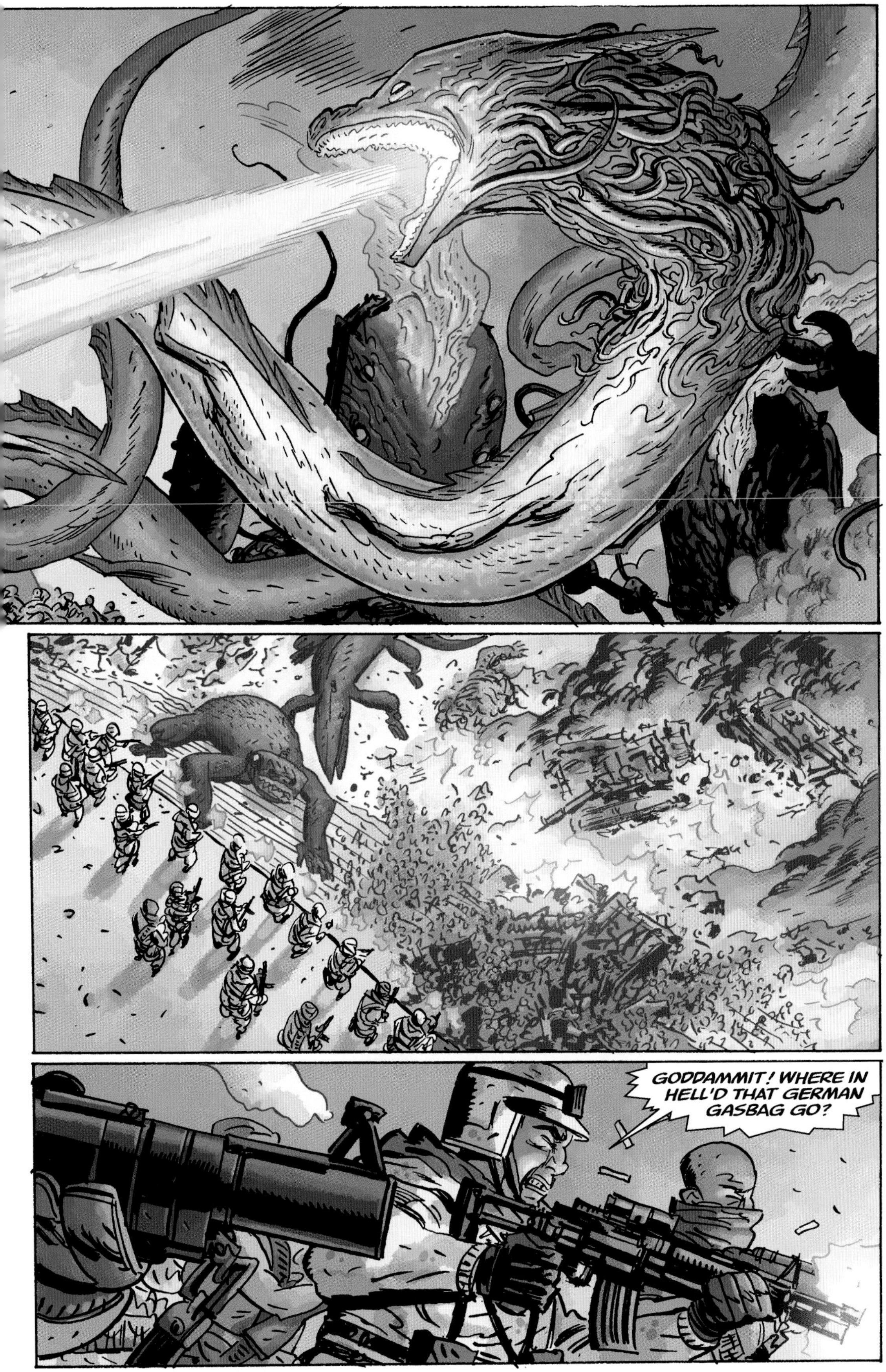
GODDAMMIT! WHERE IN HELL'D THAT GERMAN GASBAG GO?

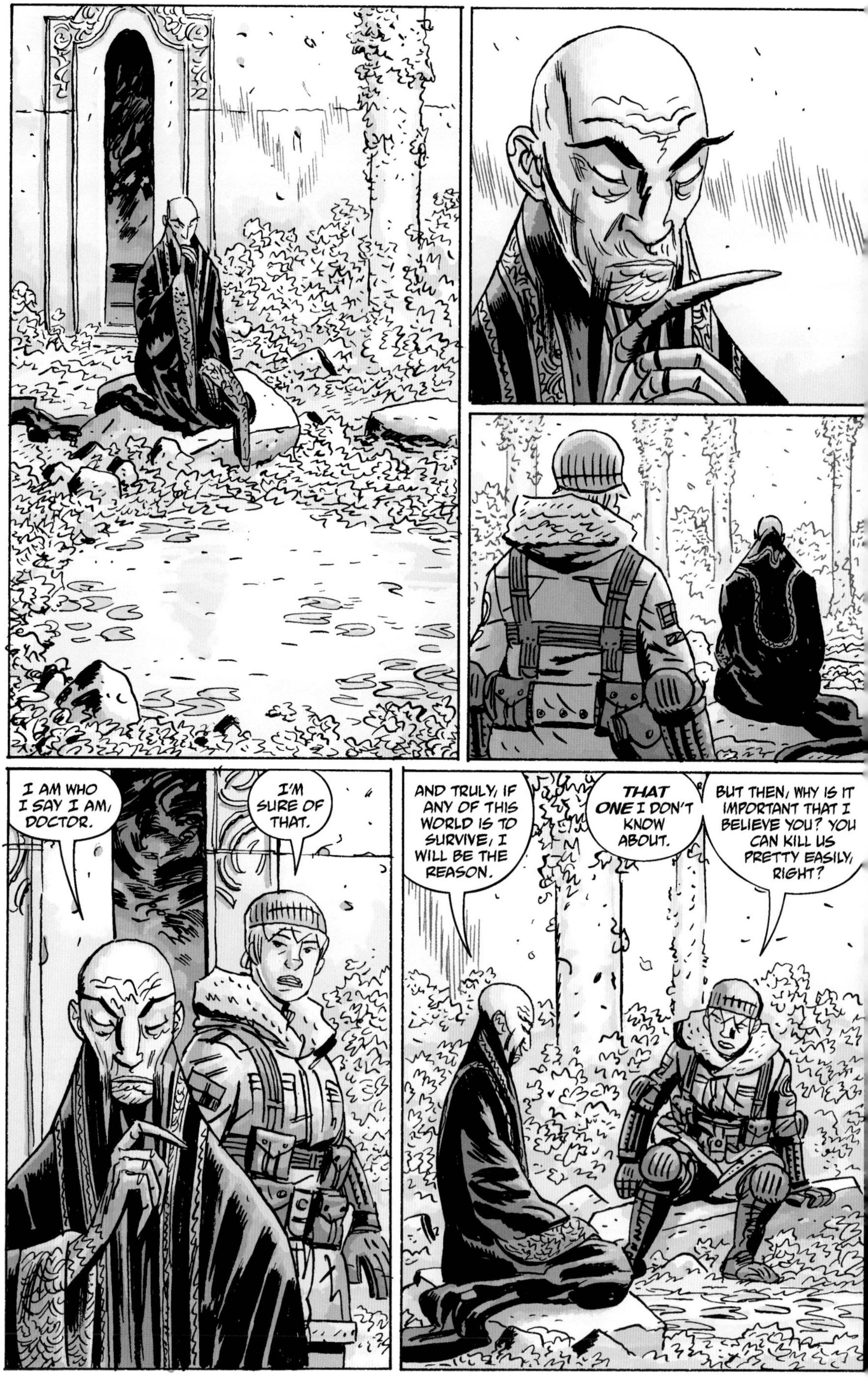
I AM WHO I SAY I AM, DOCTOR.
I'M SURE OF THAT.
AND TRULY, IF ANY OF THIS WORLD IS TO SURVIVE, I WILL BE THE REASON.
THAT ONE I DON'T KNOW ABOUT.
BUT THEN, WHY IS IT IMPORTANT THAT I BELIEVE YOU? YOU CAN KILL US PRETTY EASILY, RIGHT?

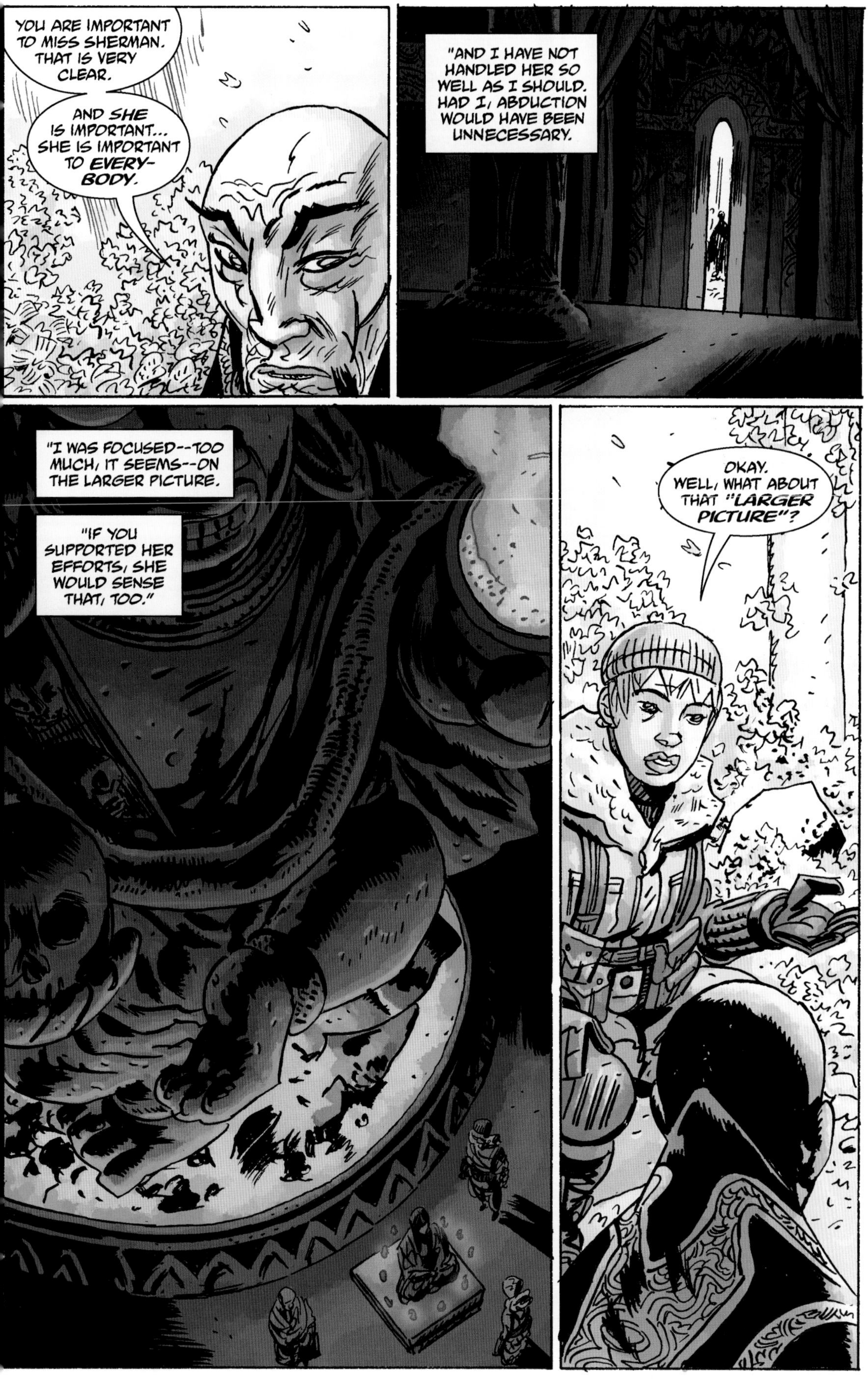
YOU ARE IMPORTANT TO MISS SHERMAN. THAT IS VERY CLEAR.
AND SHE IS IMPORTANT... SHE IS IMPORTANT TO EVERY-BODY.
"AND I HAVE NOT HANDLED HER SO WELL AS I SHOULD. HAD I, ABDUCTION WOULD HAVE BEEN UNNECESSARY.
"I WAS FOCUSED--TOO MUCH, IT SEEMS--ON THE LARGER PICTURE.
"IF YOU SUPPORTED HER EFFORTS, SHE WOULD SENSE THAT, TOO."
OKAY. WELL, WHAT ABOUT THAT "LARGER PICTURE"?

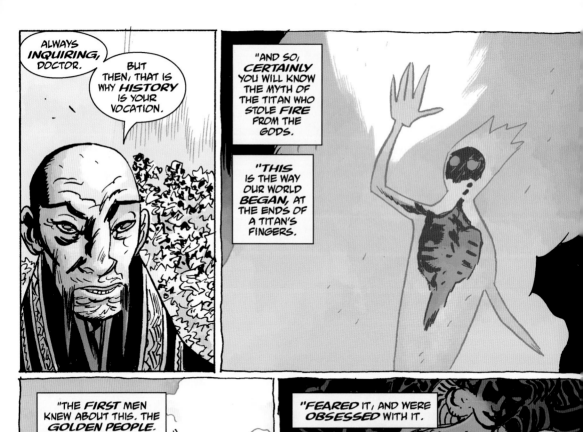

ALWAYS *INQUIRING*, DOCTOR.

BUT THEN, THAT IS WHY *HISTORY* IS YOUR VOCATION.

"AND SO, *CERTAINLY* YOU WILL KNOW THE MYTH OF THE TITAN WHO STOLE *FIRE* FROM THE GODS.

"*THIS* IS THE WAY OUR WORLD *BEGAN*, AT THE ENDS OF A TITAN'S FINGERS.

"THE *FIRST* MEN KNEW ABOUT THIS. THE *GOLDEN PEOPLE.*

"A *GRAND RACE* THAT FEARED FEW THINGS FEARED THAT *STOLEN FIRE* FOR TEN THOUSAND YEARS.

"*FEARED* IT, AND WERE *OBSESSED* WITH IT.

"WHY *ELSE* WOULD KING THOTH HAVE HELD ITS SECRET *SO CLOSE?*

"IN HIS OWN PRIVATE GARDEN, IN THE MINDS OF *THREE FALLEN TITANS.*

"*WATCHERS*, HE CALLED THEM. *ANGELS.*

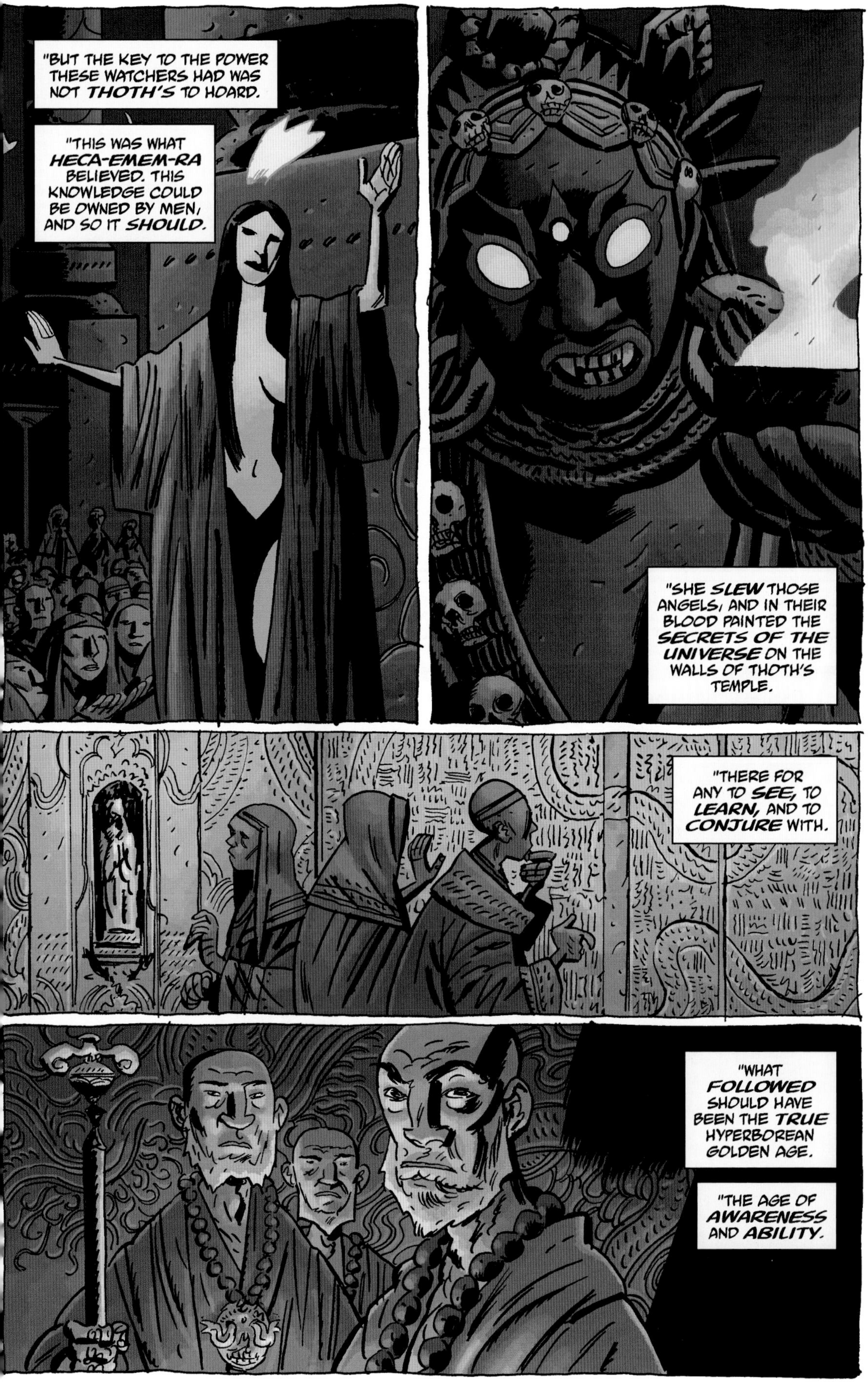
"BUT THE KEY TO THE POWER THESE WATCHERS HAD WAS NOT THOTH'S TO HOARD.
"THIS WAS WHAT HECA-EMEM-RA BELIEVED. THIS KNOWLEDGE COULD BE OWNED BY MEN, AND SO IT SHOULD.
"SHE SLEW THOSE ANGELS, AND IN THEIR BLOOD PAINTED THE SECRETS OF THE UNIVERSE ON THE WALLS OF THOTH'S TEMPLE.
"THERE FOR ANY TO SEE, TO LEARN, AND TO CONJURE WITH.
"WHAT FOLLOWED SHOULD HAVE BEEN THE TRUE HYPERBOREAN GOLDEN AGE.
"THE AGE OF AWARENESS AND ABILITY.

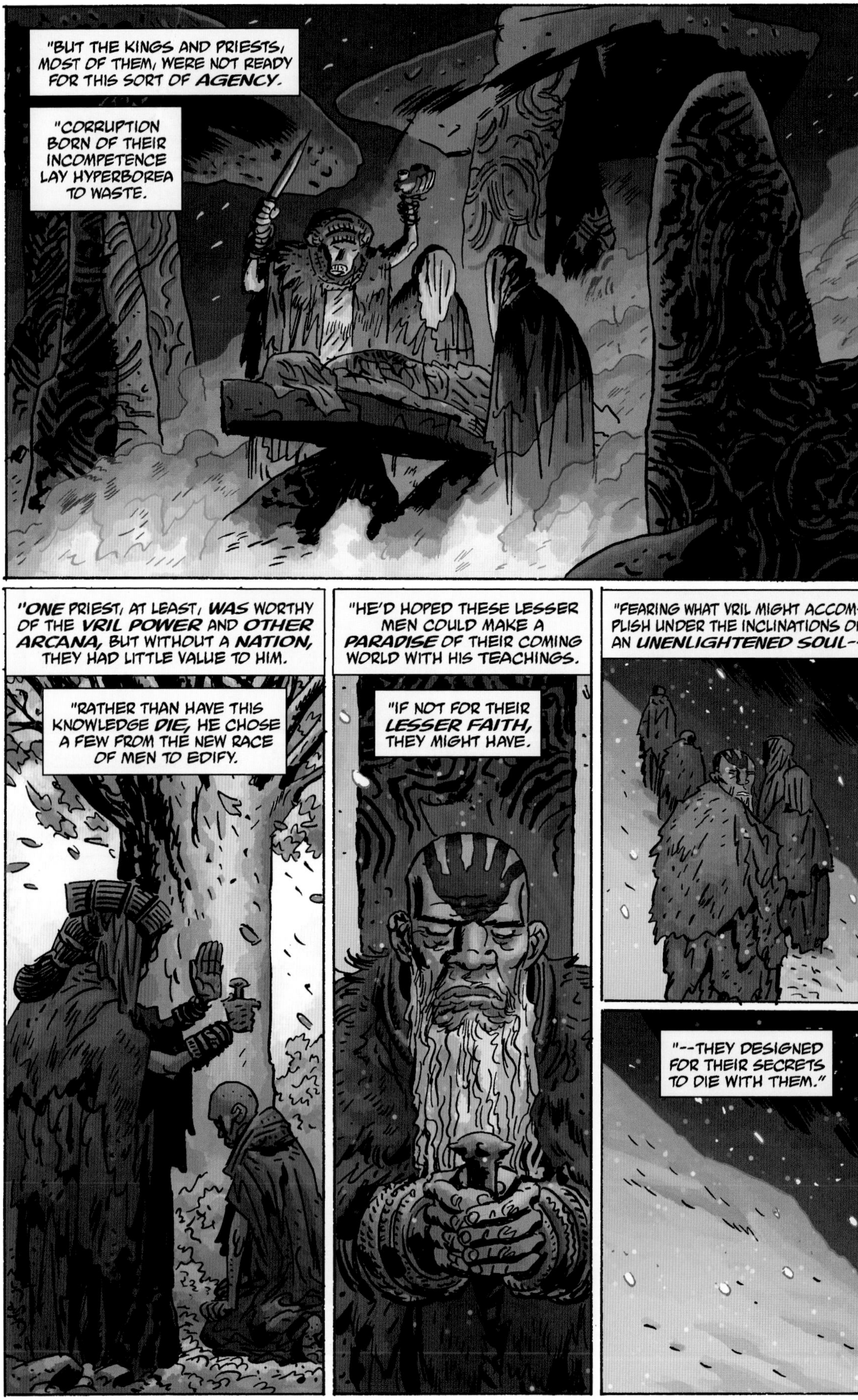
"BUT THE KINGS AND PRIESTS, MOST OF THEM, WERE NOT READY FOR THIS SORT OF AGENCY.
"CORRUPTION BORN OF THEIR INCOMPETENCE LAY HYPERBOREA TO WASTE.
"ONE PRIEST, AT LEAST, WAS WORTHY OF THE VRIL POWER AND OTHER ARCANA, BUT WITHOUT A NATION, THEY HAD LITTLE VALUE TO HIM.
"RATHER THAN HAVE THIS KNOWLEDGE DIE, HE CHOSE A FEW FROM THE NEW RACE OF MEN TO EDIFY.
"HE'D HOPED THESE LESSER MEN COULD MAKE A PARADISE OF THEIR COMING WORLD WITH HIS TEACHINGS.
"IF NOT FOR THEIR LESSER FAITH, THEY MIGHT HAVE.
"FEARING WHAT VRIL MIGHT ACCOMPLISH UNDER THE INCLINATIONS OF AN UNENLIGHTENED SOUL--
"--THEY DESIGNED FOR THEIR SECRETS TO DIE WITH THEM."

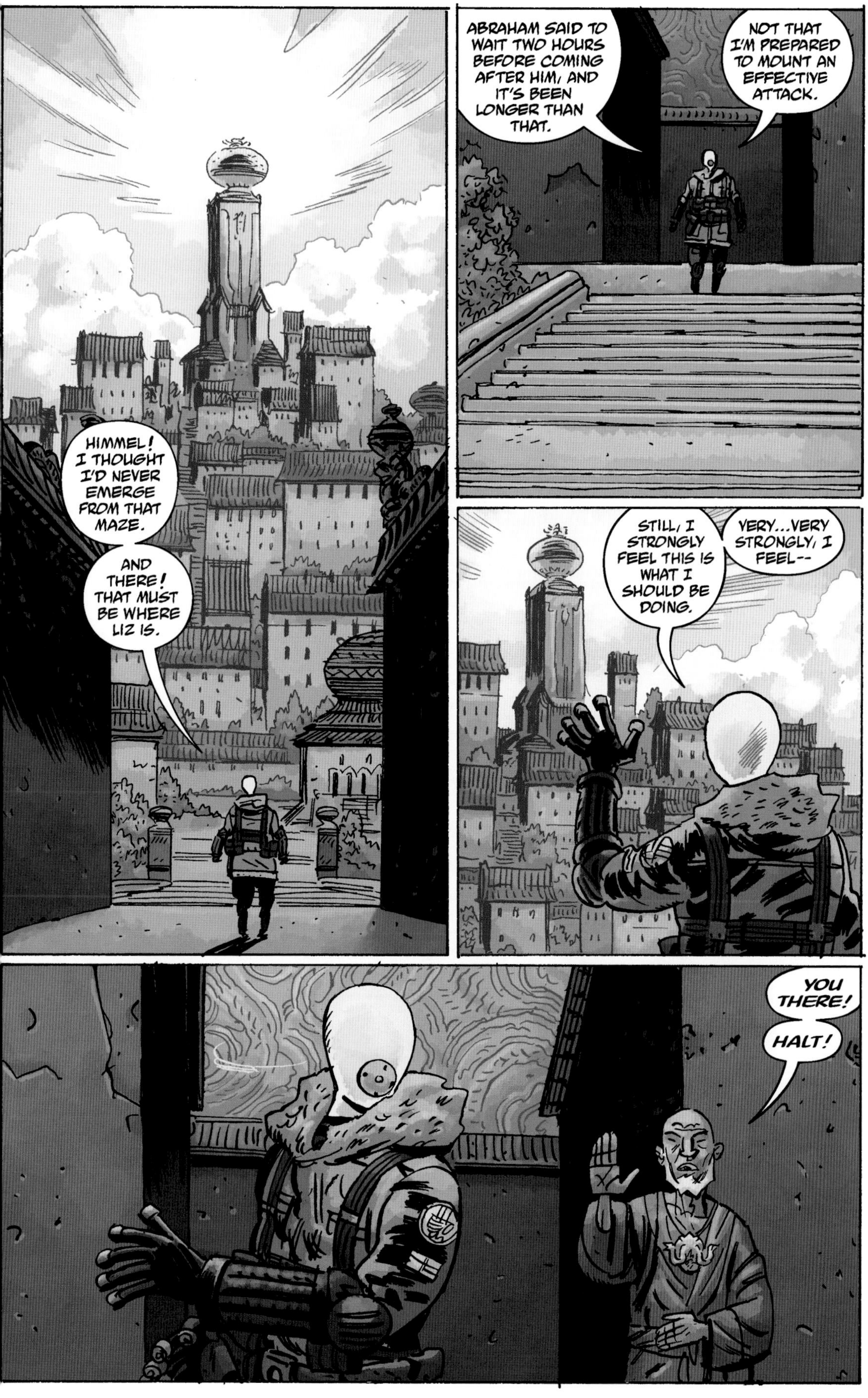
HIMMEL! I THOUGHT I'D NEVER EMERGE FROM THAT MAZE.
AND THERE! THAT MUST BE WHERE LIZ IS.
ABRAHAM SAID TO WAIT TWO HOURS BEFORE COMING AFTER HIM, AND IT'S BEEN LONGER THAN THAT.
NOT THAT I'M PREPARED TO MOUNT AN EFFECTIVE ATTACK.
STILL, I STRONGLY FEEL THIS IS WHAT I SHOULD BE DOING.
VERY...VERY STRONGLY, I FEEL--
YOU THERE!
HALT!

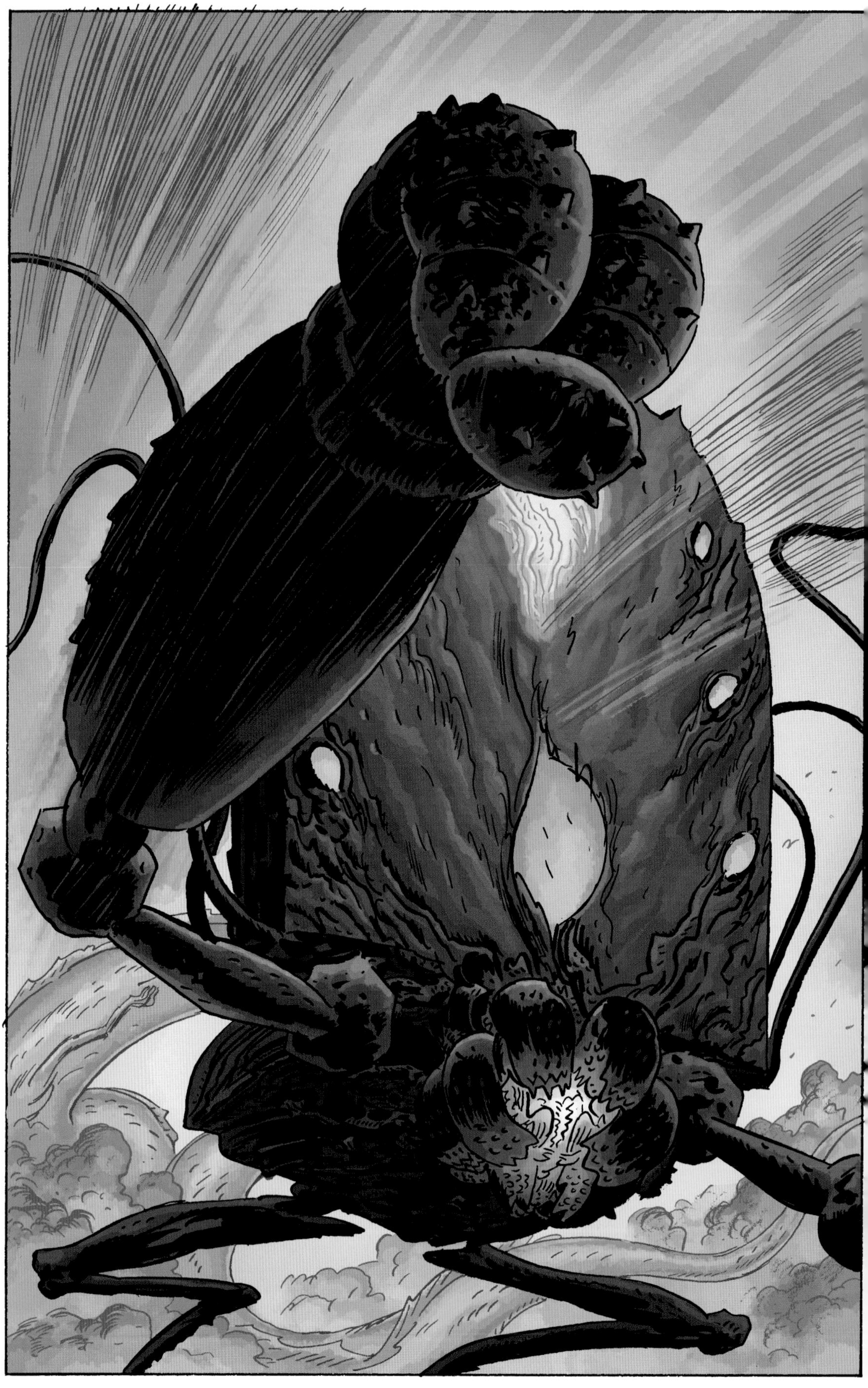

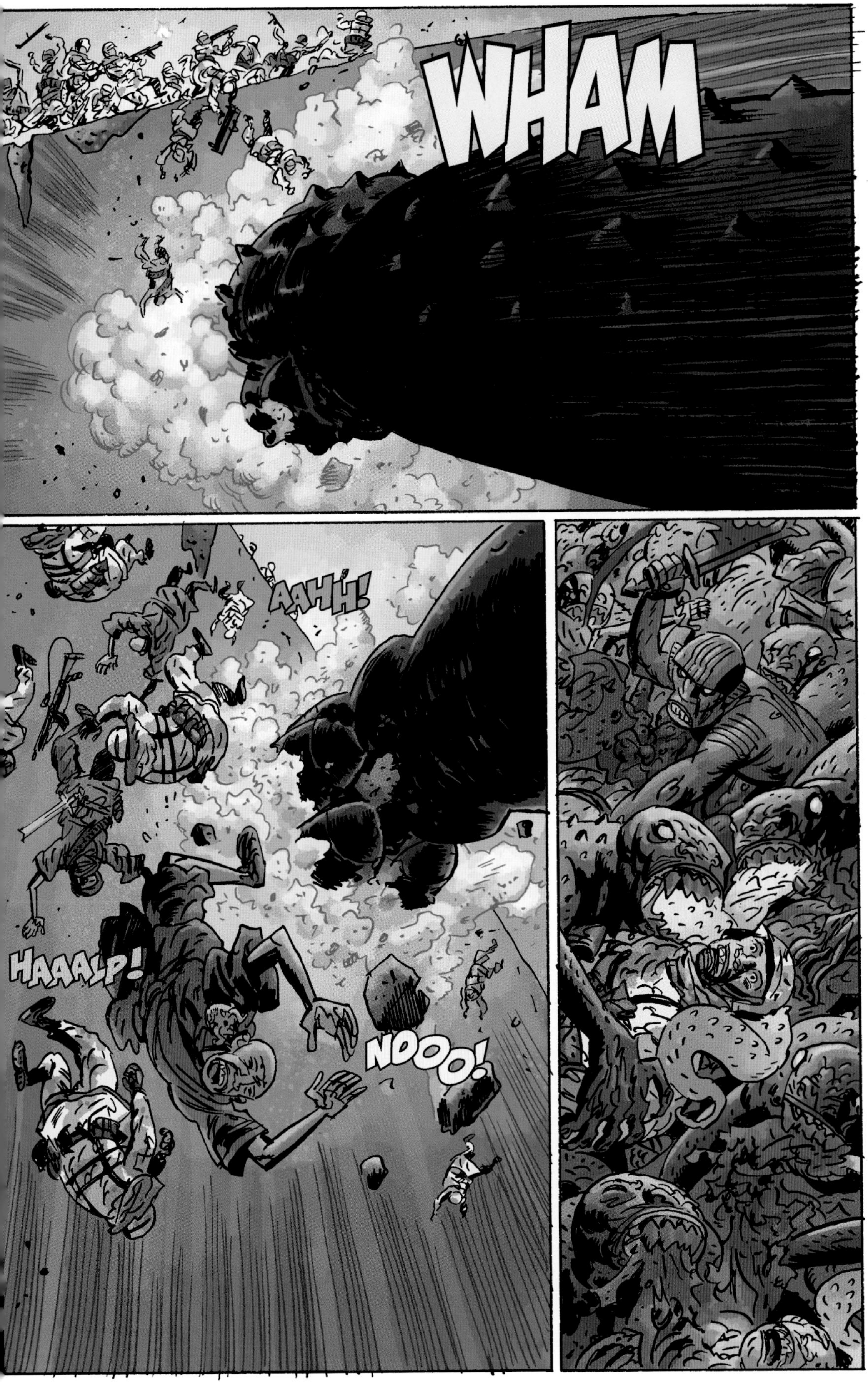
WHAM
AAHH!
HAAALP!
NOOO!

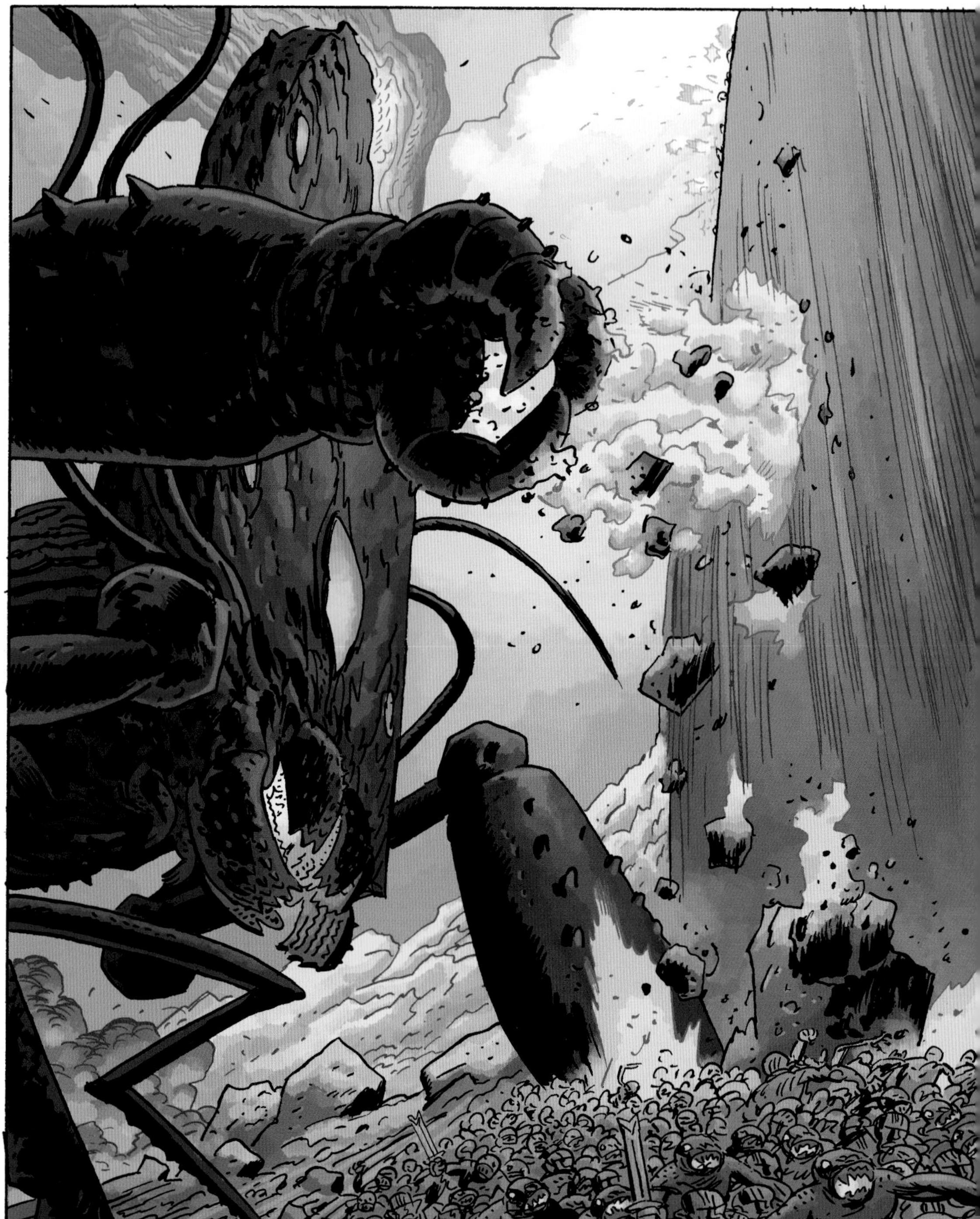
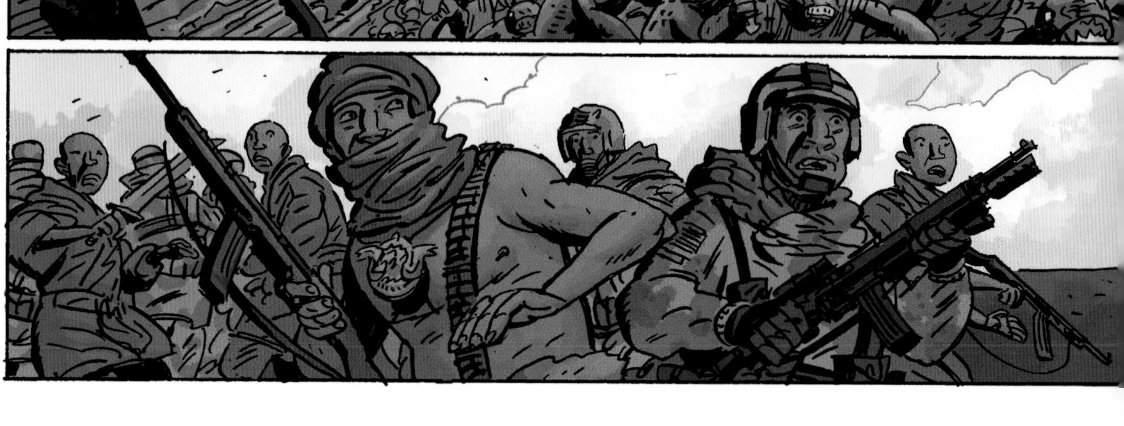

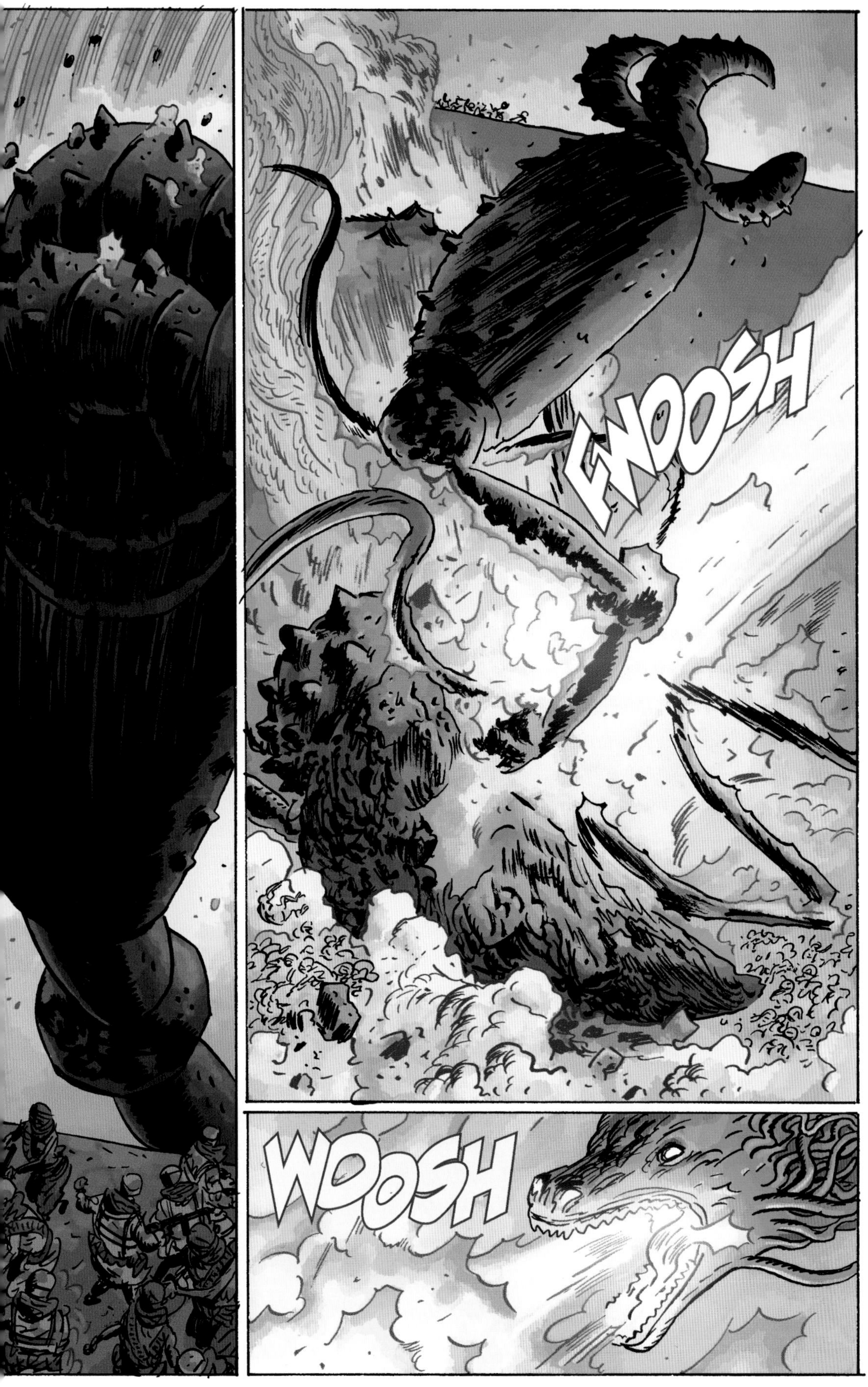
FWOOSH
WOOSH

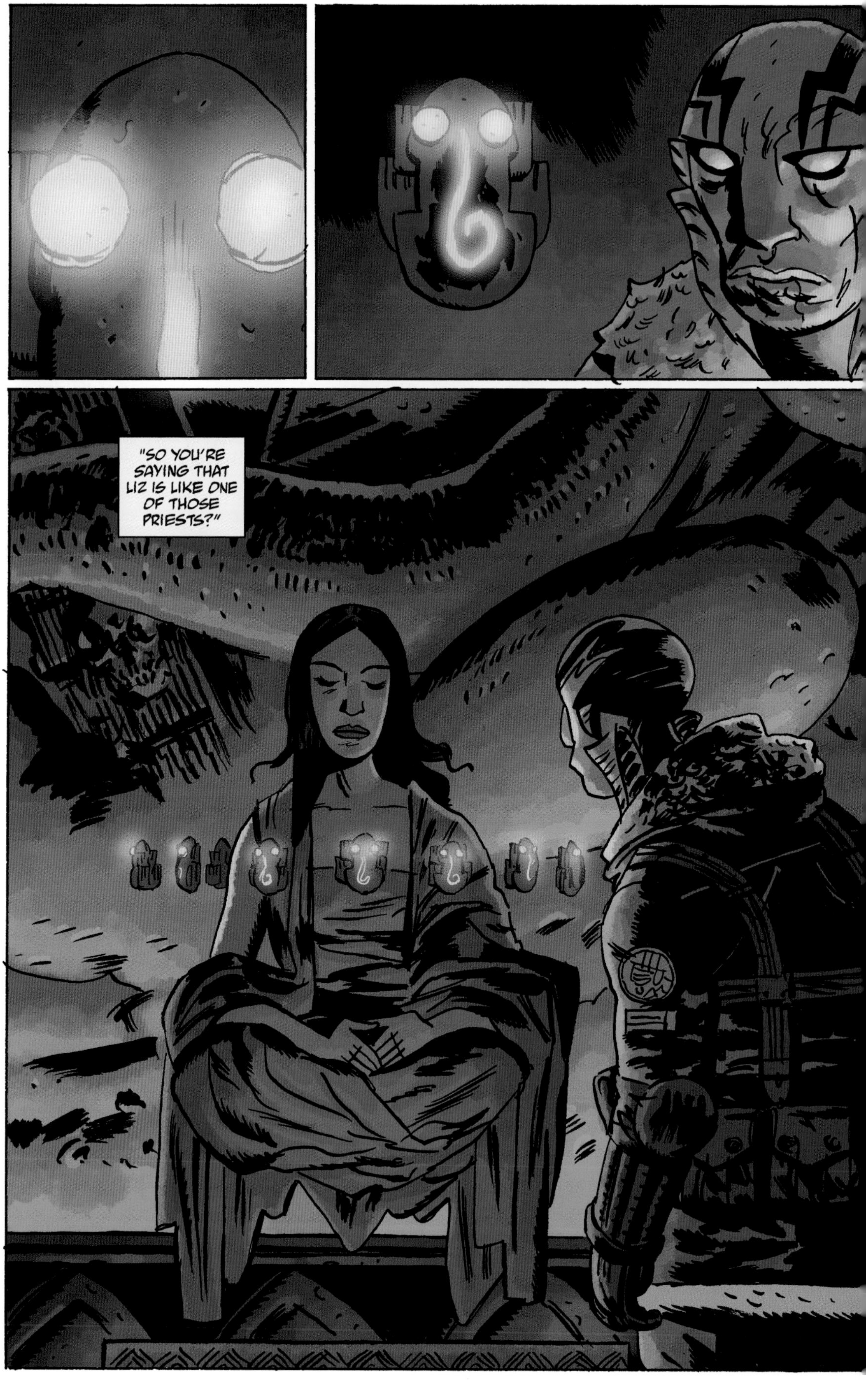
"SO YOU'RE SAYING THAT LIZ IS LIKE ONE OF THOSE PRIESTS?"

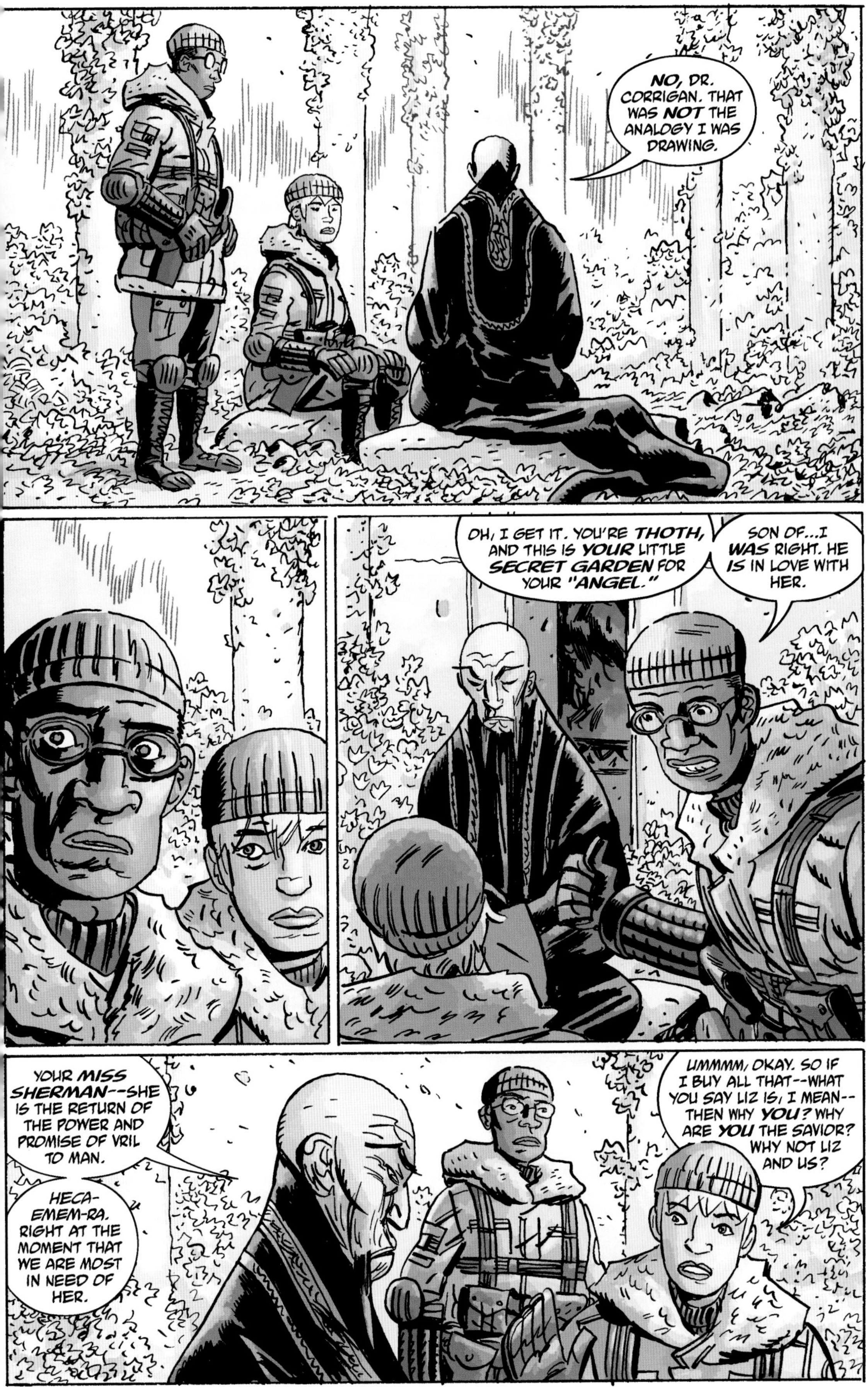
NO, DR. CORRIGAN. THAT WAS NOT THE ANALOGY I WAS DRAWING.
OH, I GET IT. YOU'RE THOTH, AND THIS IS YOUR LITTLE SECRET GARDEN FOR YOUR "ANGEL."
SON OF...I WAS RIGHT. HE IS IN LOVE WITH HER.
YOUR MISS SHERMAN--SHE IS THE RETURN OF THE POWER AND PROMISE OF VRIL TO MAN.
HECA-EMEM-RA. RIGHT AT THE MOMENT THAT WE ARE MOST IN NEED OF HER.
UMMMM, OKAY. SO IF I BUY ALL THAT--WHAT YOU SAY LIZ IS, I MEAN--THEN WHY YOU? WHY ARE YOU THE SAVIOR? WHY NOT LIZ AND US?

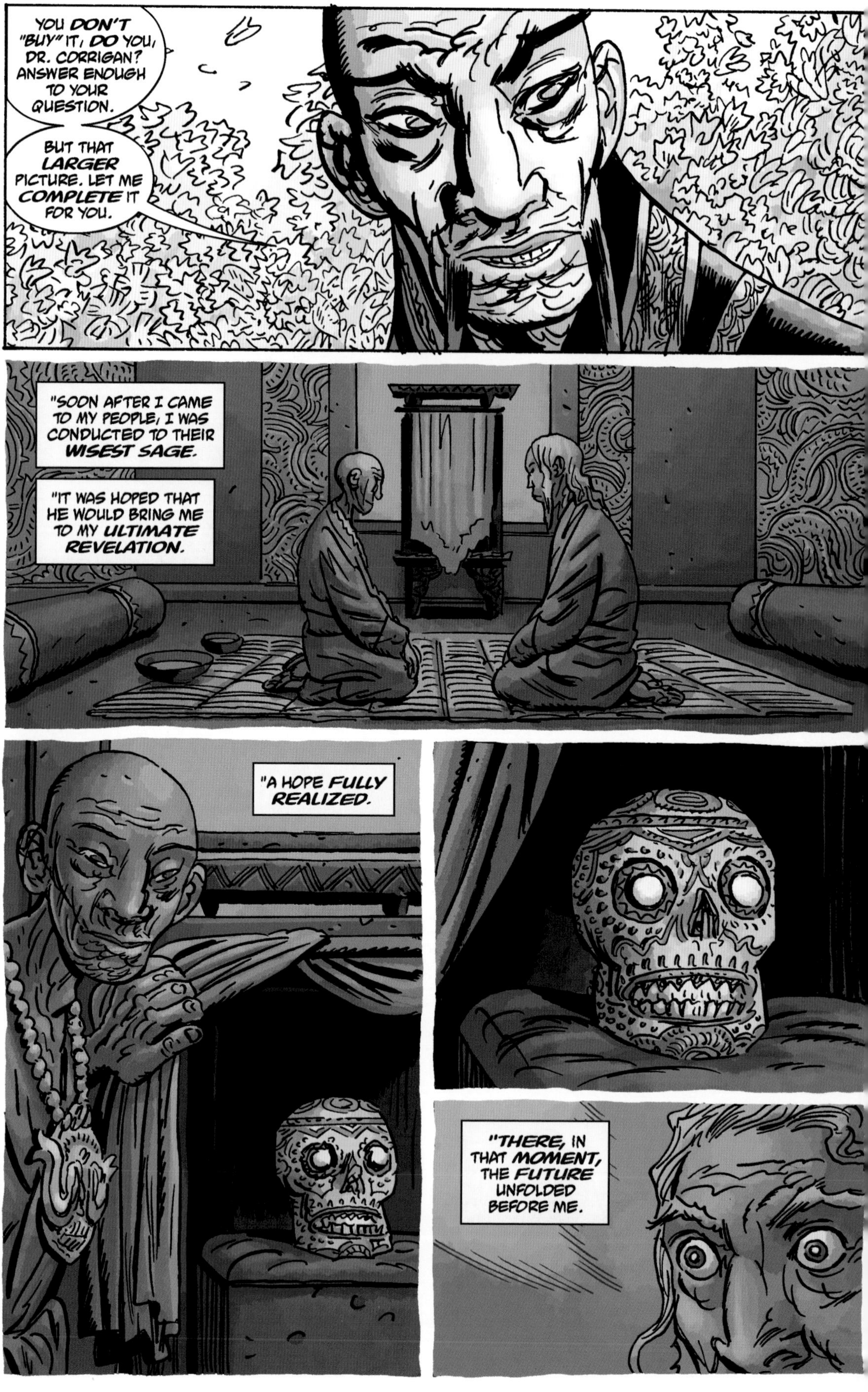
YOU DON'T "BUY" IT, DO YOU, DR. CORRIGAN? ANSWER ENOUGH TO YOUR QUESTION.
BUT THAT LARGER PICTURE. LET ME COMPLETE IT FOR YOU.
"SOON AFTER I CAME TO MY PEOPLE, I WAS CONDUCTED TO THEIR WISEST SAGE.
"IT WAS HOPED THAT HE WOULD BRING ME TO MY ULTIMATE REVELATION.
"A HOPE FULLY REALIZED.
"THERE, IN THAT MOMENT, THE FUTURE UNFOLDED BEFORE ME.

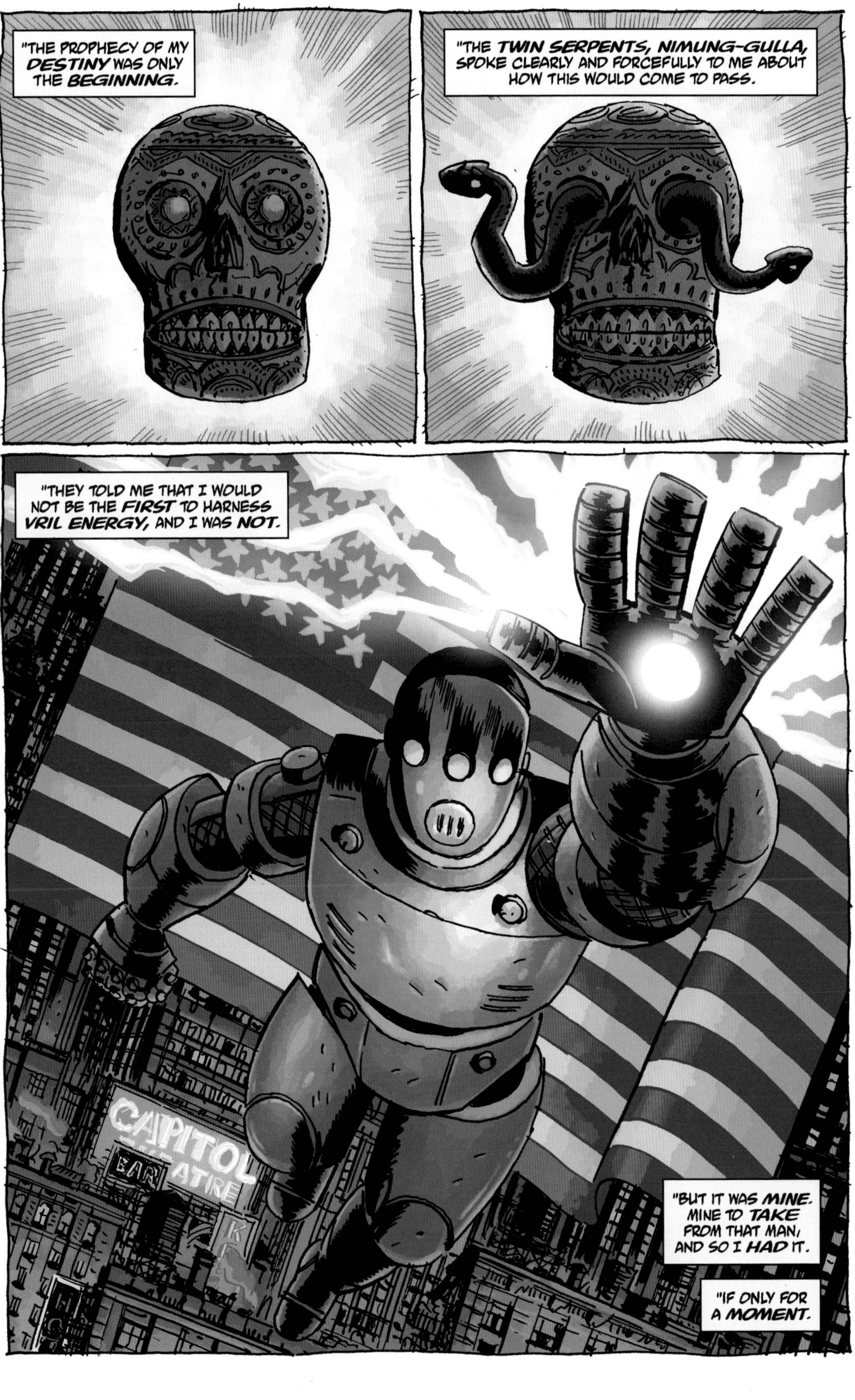
"THE PROPHECY OF MY DESTINY WAS ONLY THE BEGINNING.
"THE TWIN SERPENTS, NIMUNG-GULLA, SPOKE CLEARLY AND FORCEFULLY TO ME ABOUT HOW THIS WOULD COME TO PASS.
"THEY TOLD ME THAT I WOULD NOT BE THE FIRST TO HARNESS VRIL ENERGY, AND I WAS NOT.
CAPITOL
BAR
"BUT IT WAS MINE. MINE TO TAKE FROM THAT MAN, AND SO I HAD IT.
"IF ONLY FOR A MOMENT.

"THEY STRETCHED OUT THE *CENTURY* BEFORE ME, LIKE THE *INSTRUMENTS* ON A *SURGEON'S* TABLE.

"AND THEY ALLOWED ME MY *FIRST GLIMPSE* OF THE *PRICE OF FAILURE.*

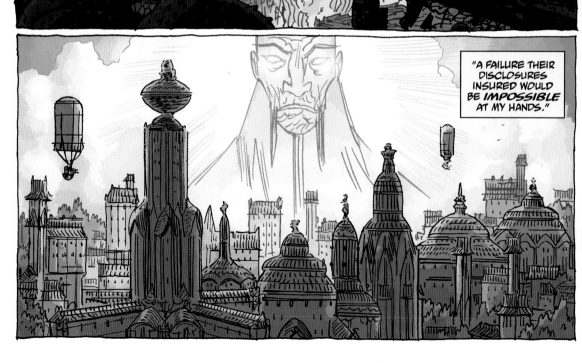

"A FAILURE THEIR *DISCLOSURES* INSURED WOULD BE *IMPOSSIBLE* AT MY HANDS."

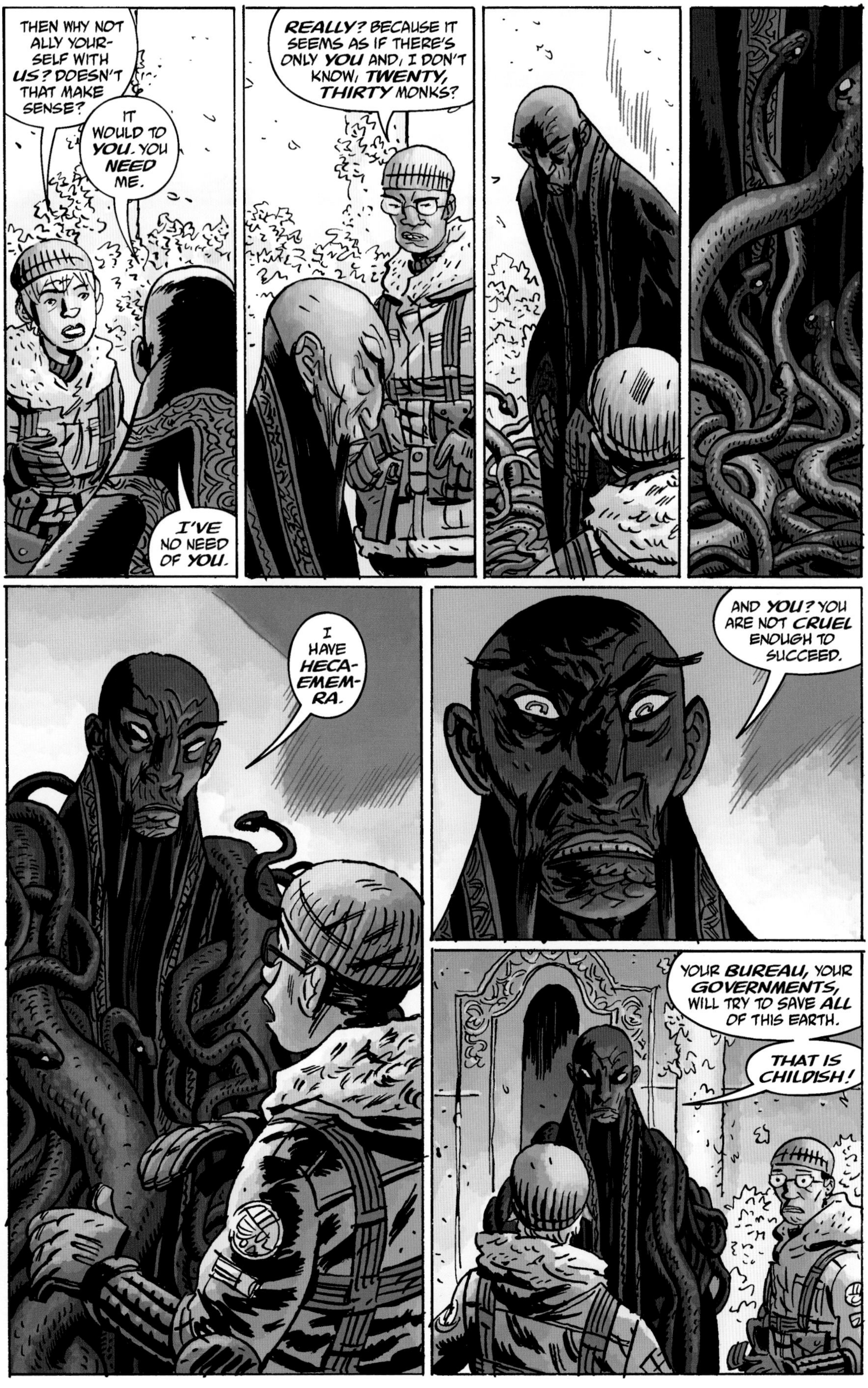
THEN WHY NOT ALLY YOURSELF WITH US? DOESN'T THAT MAKE SENSE?
IT WOULD TO YOU. YOU NEED ME.
I'VE NO NEED OF YOU.
REALLY? BECAUSE IT SEEMS AS IF THERE'S ONLY YOU AND, I DON'T KNOW, TWENTY, THIRTY MONKS?
I HAVE HECAEMEMRA.
AND YOU? YOU ARE NOT CRUEL ENOUGH TO SUCCEED.
YOUR BUREAU, YOUR GOVERNMENTS, WILL TRY TO SAVE ALL OF THIS EARTH.
THAT IS CHILDISH!

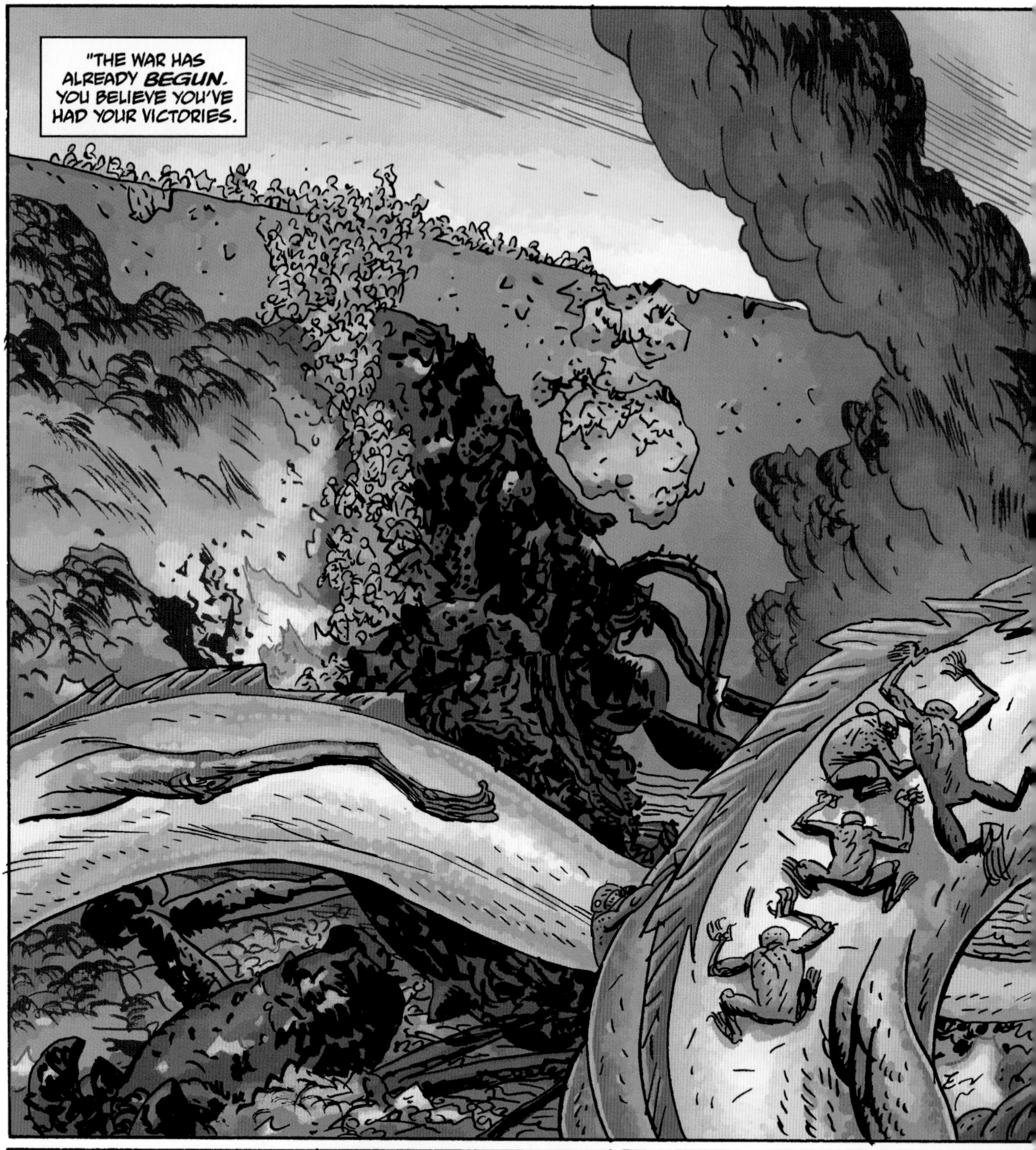
"THE WAR HAS ALREADY BEGUN. YOU BELIEVE YOU'VE HAD YOUR VICTORIES.
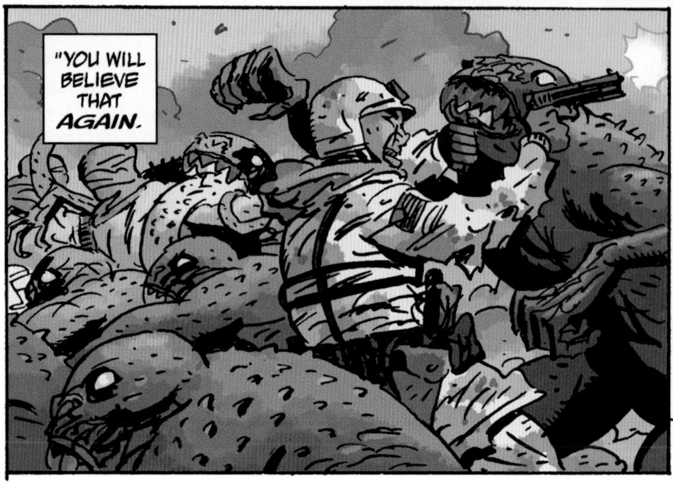
"YOU WILL BELIEVE THAT AGAIN.
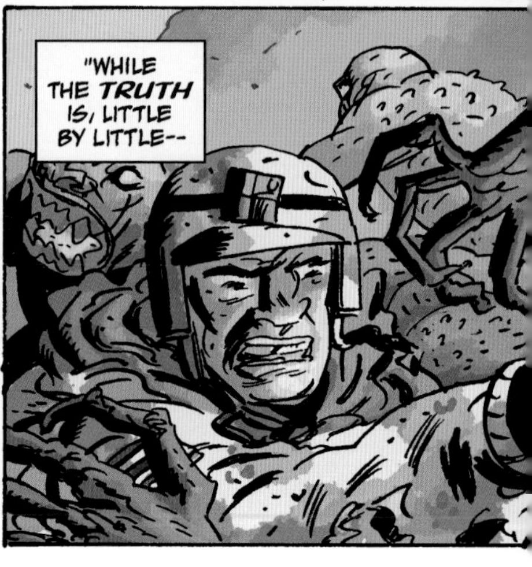
"WHILE THE TRUTH IS, LITTLE BY LITTLE--

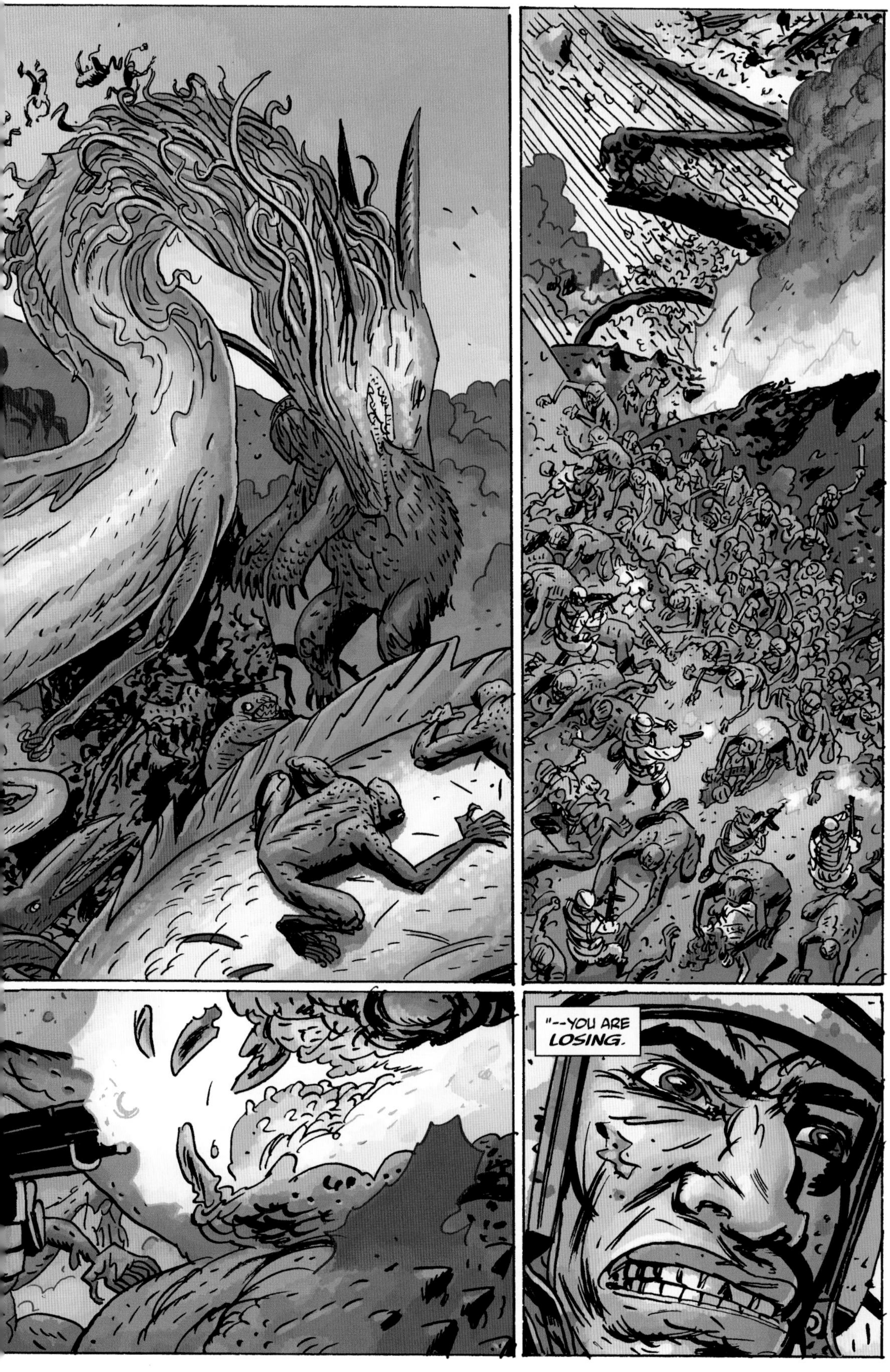
"--YOU ARE LOSING.

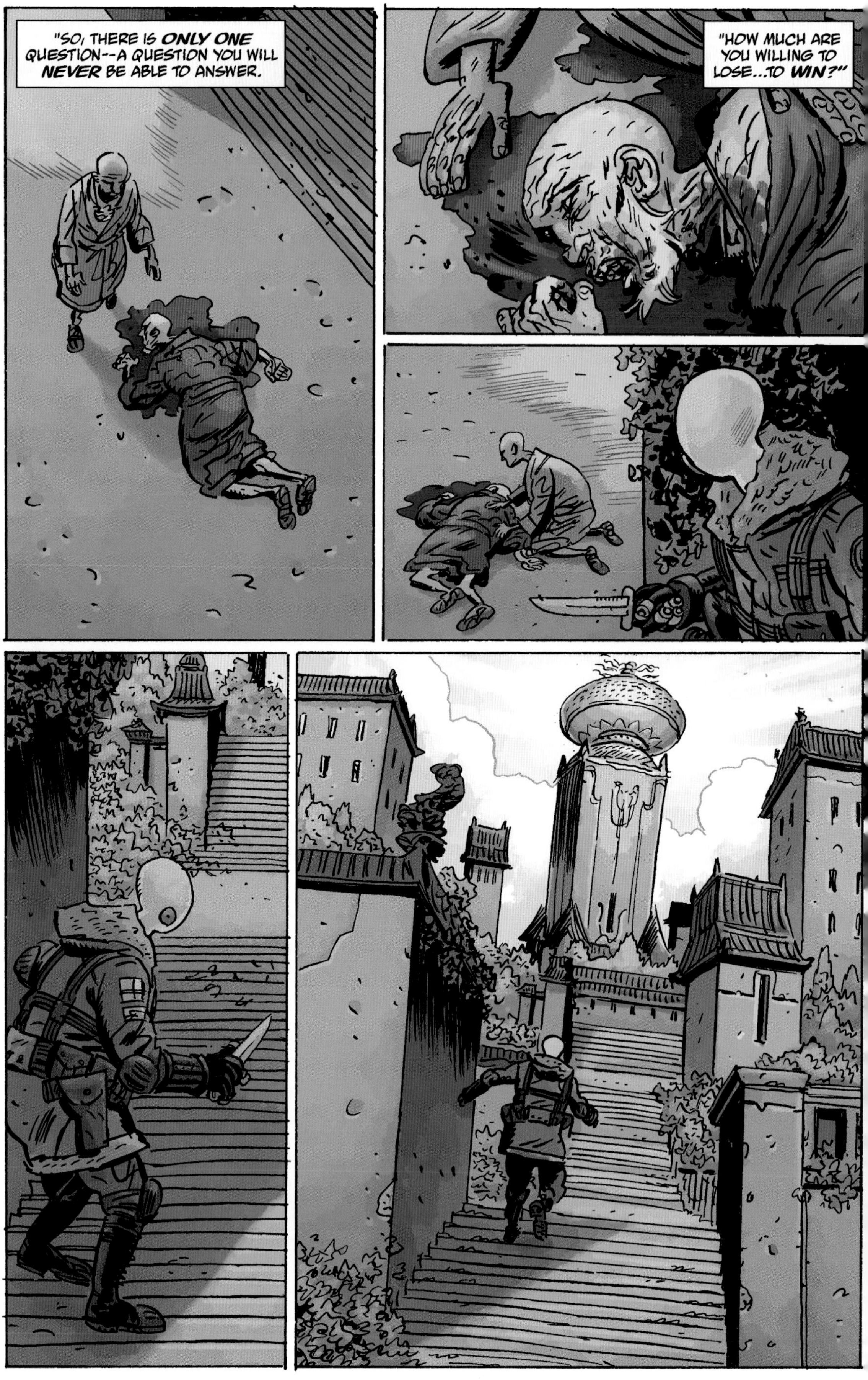
"SO, THERE IS ONLY ONE QUESTION--A QUESTION YOU WILL NEVER BE ABLE TO ANSWER.
"HOW MUCH ARE YOU WILLING TO LOSE...TO WIN?"

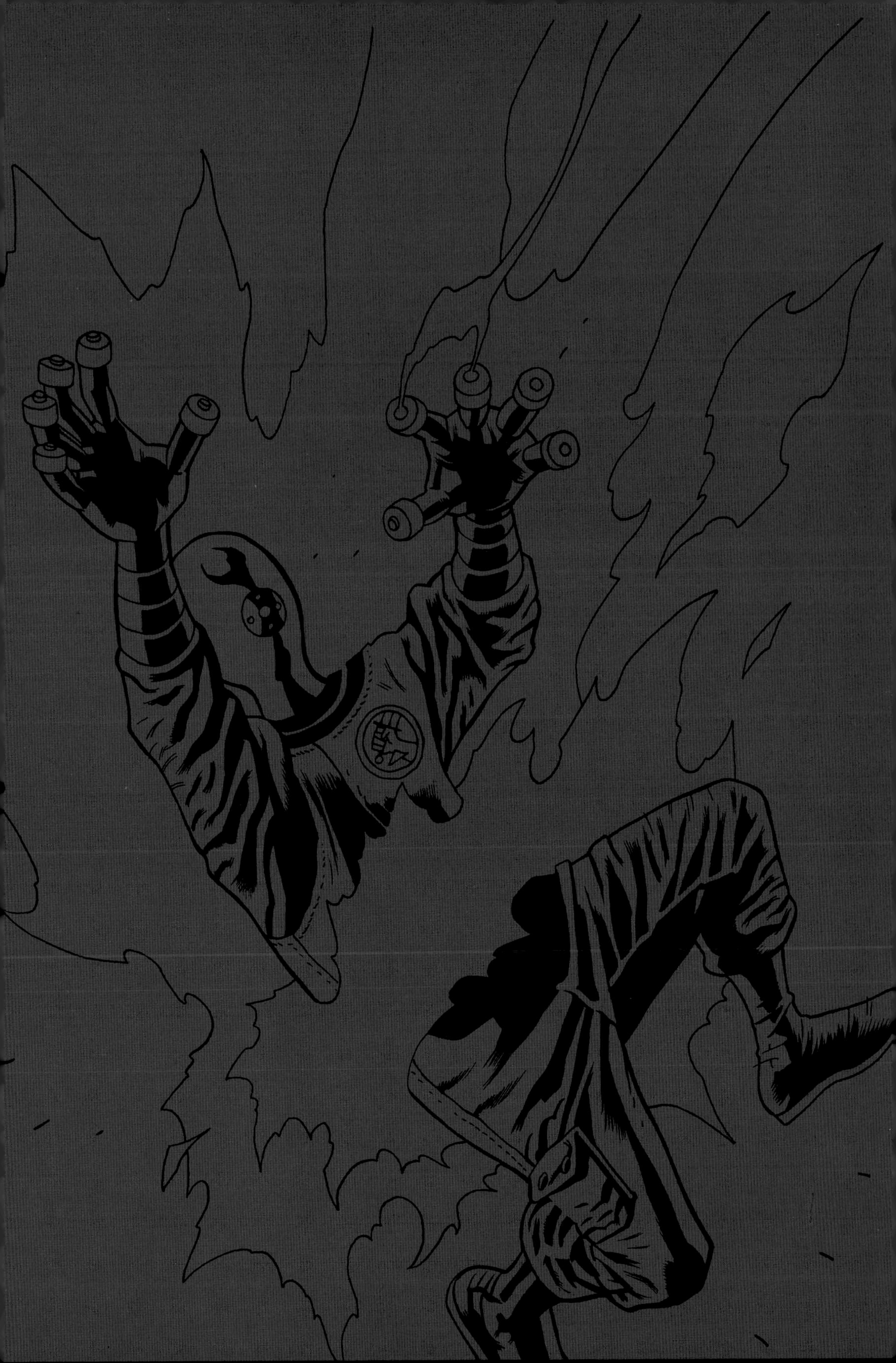

CHAPTER FIVE

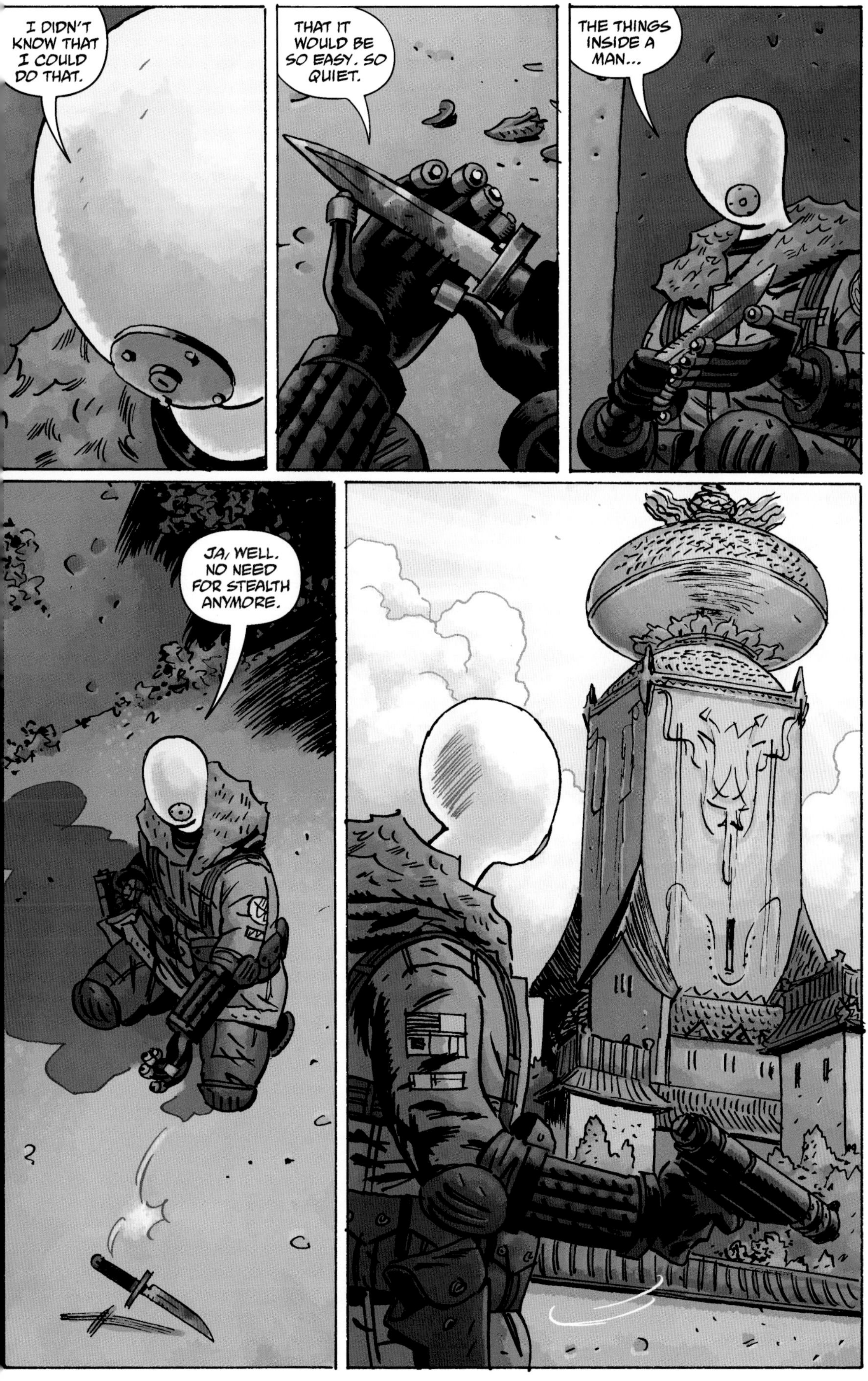
I DIDN'T KNOW THAT I COULD DO THAT.
THAT IT WOULD BE SO EASY. SO QUIET.
THE THINGS INSIDE A MAN...
JA, WELL. NO NEED FOR STEALTH ANYMORE.

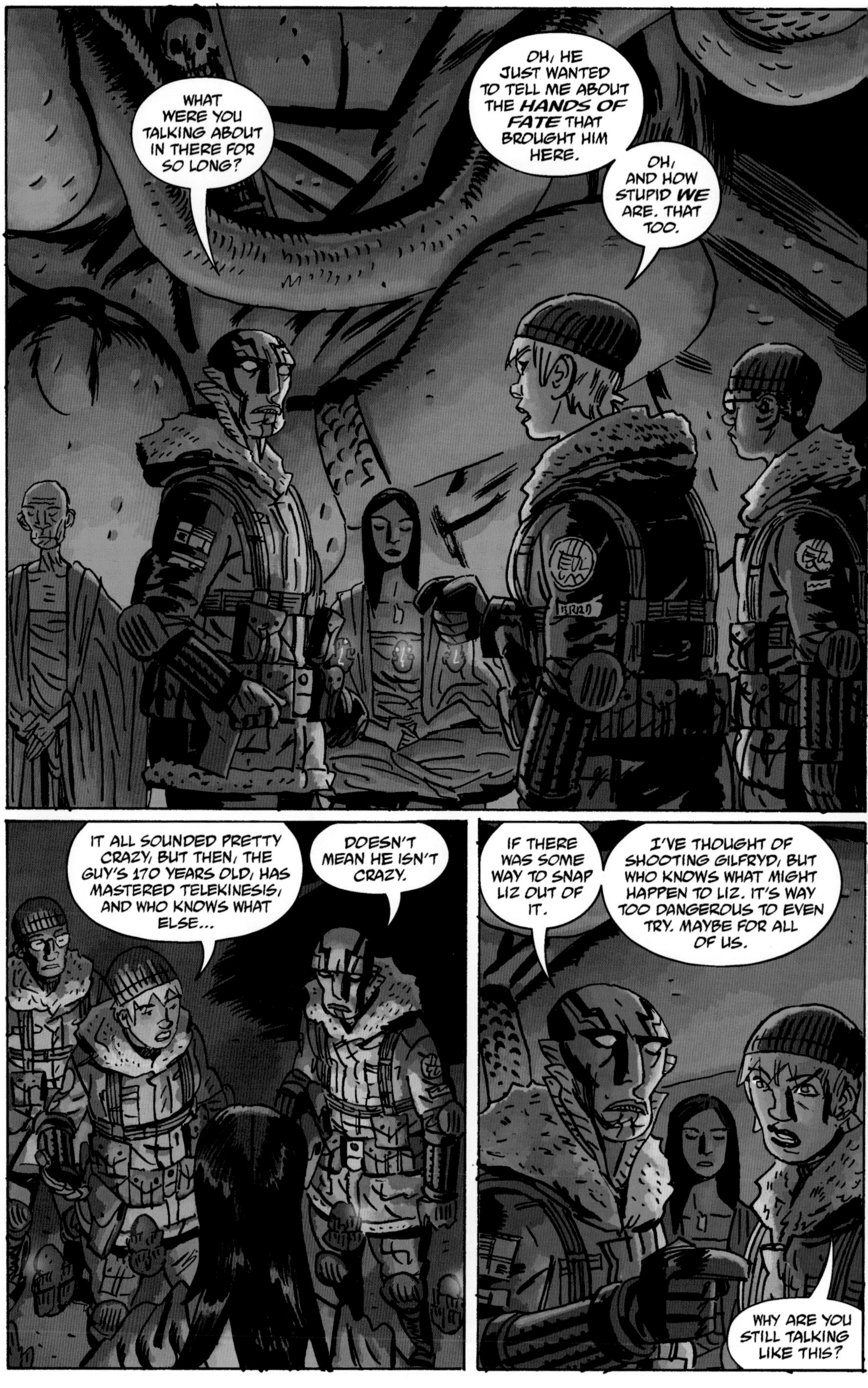
WHAT WERE YOU TALKING ABOUT IN THERE FOR SO LONG?
OH, HE JUST WANTED TO TELL ME ABOUT THE **HANDS OF FATE** THAT BROUGHT HIM HERE.
OH, AND HOW STUPID **WE** ARE. THAT TOO.
IT ALL SOUNDED PRETTY CRAZY, BUT THEN, THE GUY'S 170 YEARS OLD, HAS MASTERED TELEKINESIS, AND WHO KNOWS WHAT ELSE...
DOESN'T MEAN HE ISN'T CRAZY.
IF THERE WAS SOME WAY TO SNAP LIZ OUT OF IT.
I'VE THOUGHT OF SHOOTING GILFRYD, BUT WHO KNOWS WHAT MIGHT HAPPEN TO LIZ. IT'S WAY TOO DANGEROUS TO EVEN TRY. MAYBE FOR ALL OF US.
WHY ARE YOU STILL TALKING LIKE THIS?

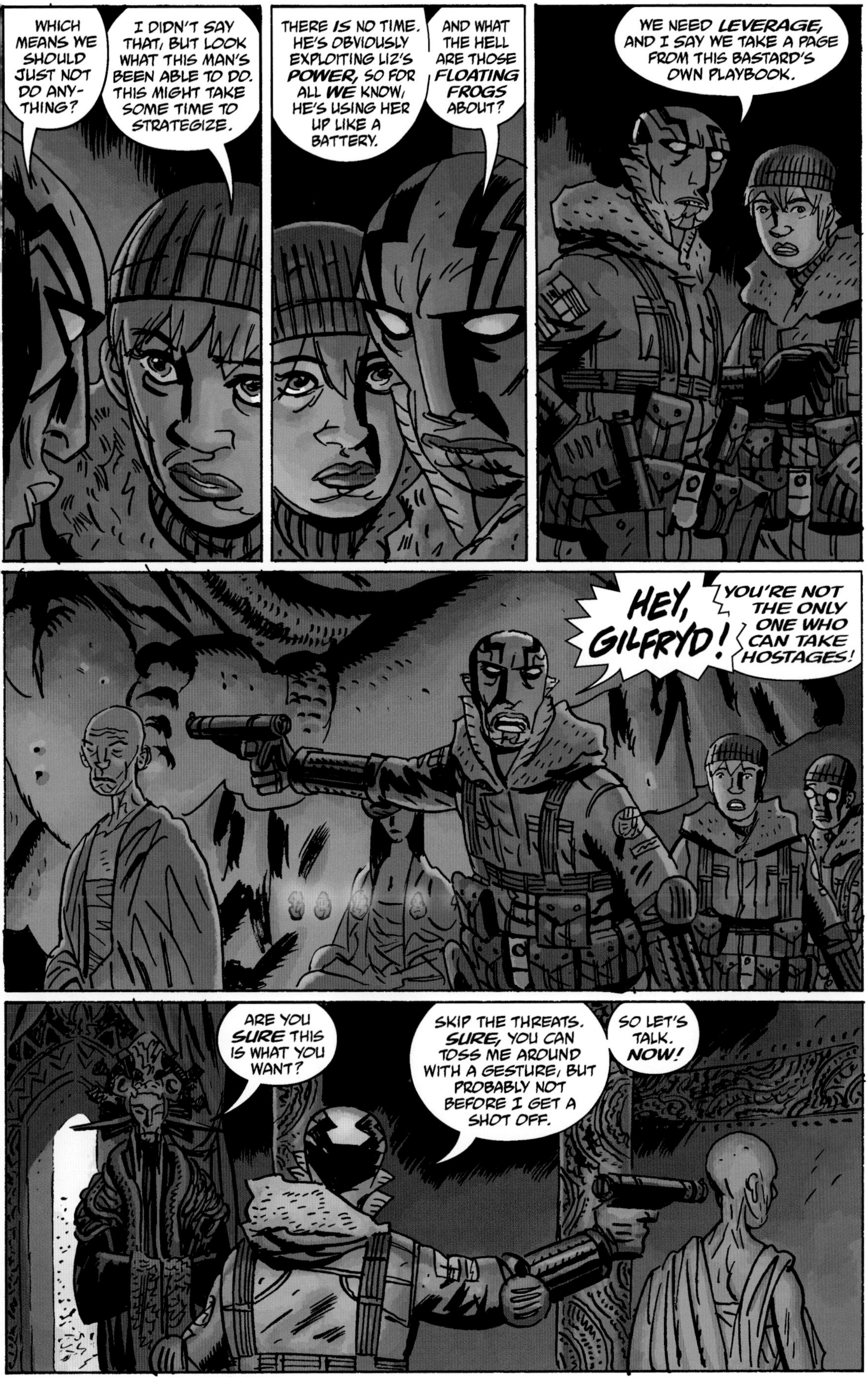

WHICH MEANS WE SHOULD JUST NOT DO ANY-THING?
I DIDN'T SAY THAT, BUT LOOK WHAT THIS MAN'S BEEN ABLE TO DO. THIS MIGHT TAKE SOME TIME TO STRATEGIZE.
THERE IS NO TIME. HE'S OBVIOUSLY EXPLOITING LIZ'S POWER, SO FOR ALL WE KNOW, HE'S USING HER UP LIKE A BATTERY.
AND WHAT THE HELL ARE THOSE FLOATING FROGS ABOUT?
WE NEED LEVERAGE, AND I SAY WE TAKE A PAGE FROM THIS BASTARD'S OWN PLAYBOOK.
HEY, GILFRYD!
YOU'RE NOT THE ONLY ONE WHO CAN TAKE HOSTAGES!
ARE YOU SURE THIS IS WHAT YOU WANT?
SKIP THE THREATS. SURE, YOU CAN TOSS ME AROUND WITH A GESTURE, BUT PROBABLY NOT BEFORE I GET A SHOT OFF.
SO LET'S TALK. NOW!

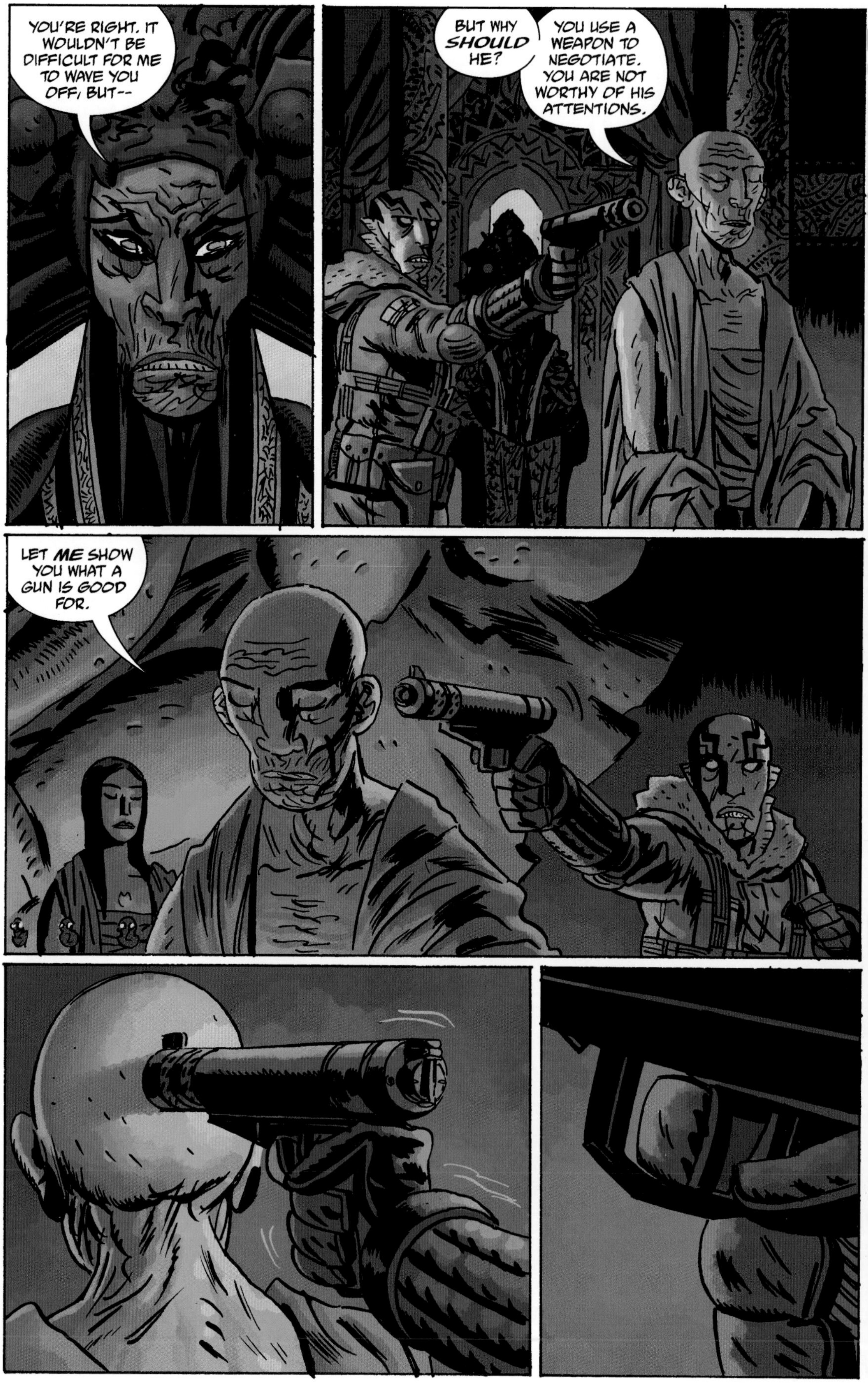
YOU'RE RIGHT. IT WOULDN'T BE DIFFICULT FOR ME TO WAVE YOU OFF, BUT--
BUT WHY *SHOULD* HE?
YOU USE A WEAPON TO NEGOTIATE. YOU ARE NOT WORTHY OF HIS ATTENTIONS.
LET *ME* SHOW YOU WHAT A GUN IS GOOD FOR.

WHAT THE HELL ARE YOU DOING TO HIM?

I HAVE NOTHING TO DO WITH IT, DOCTOR.

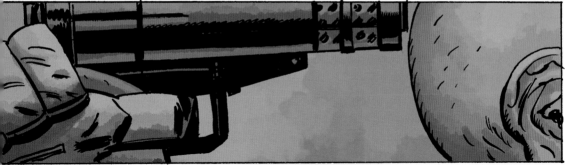

BLAM

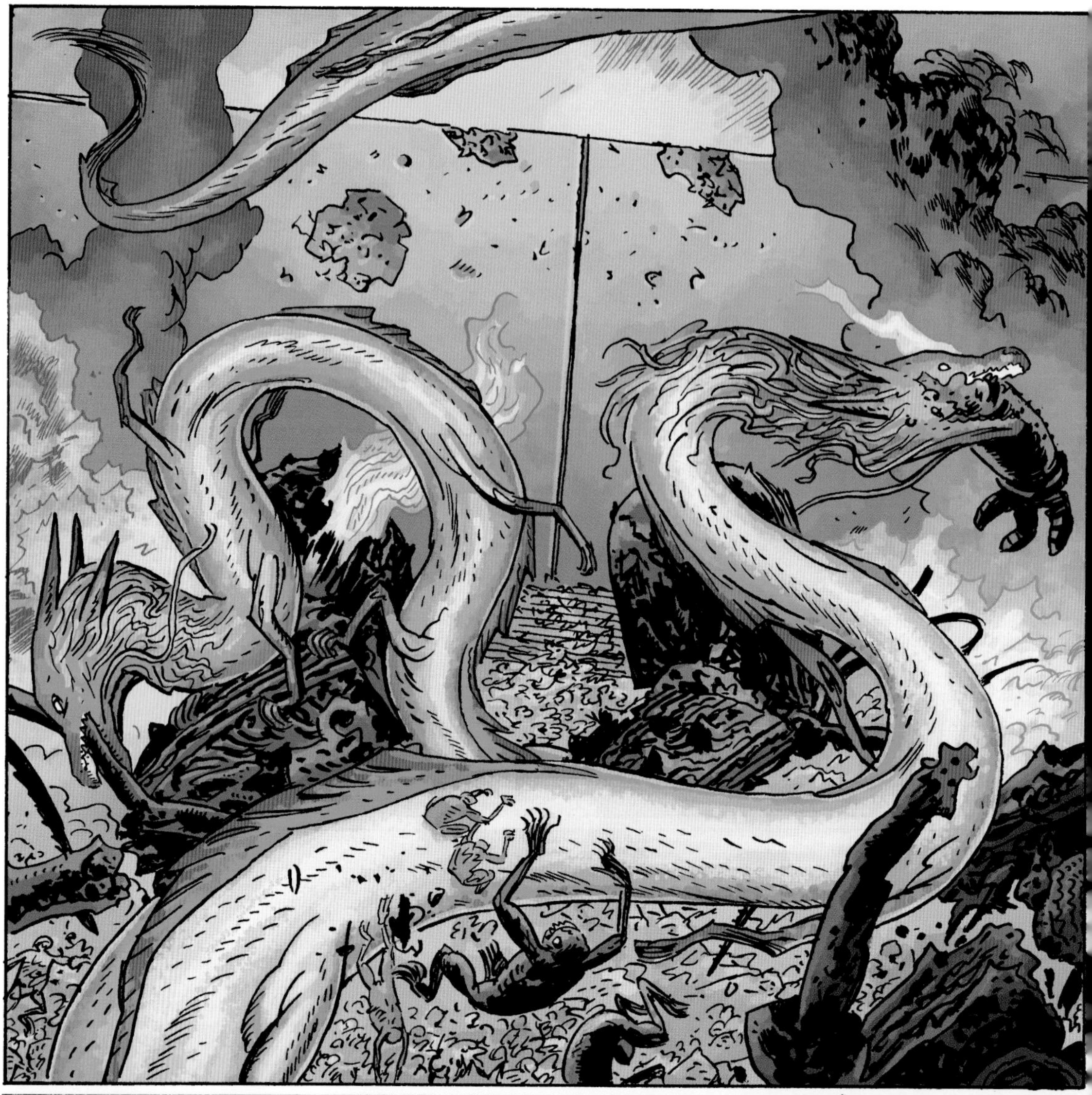

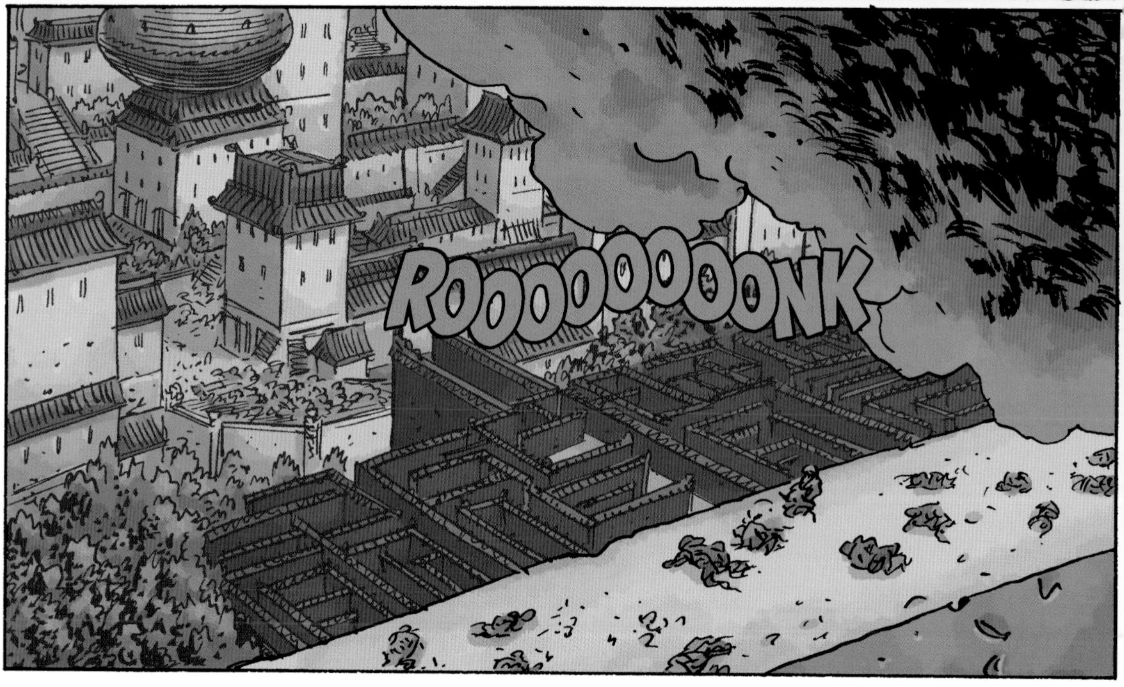
ROOOOOOOOONK

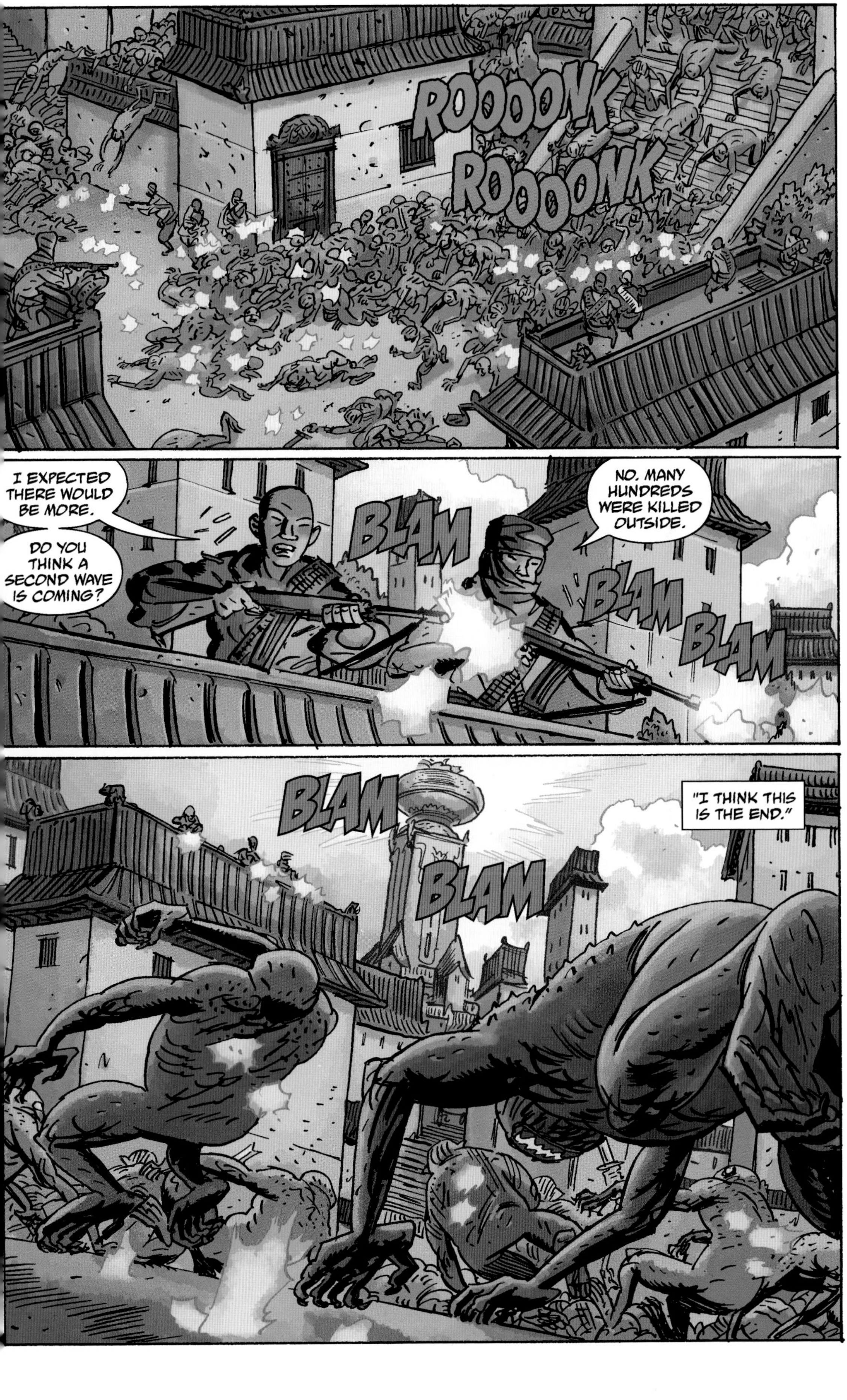
ROOOONK
ROOOONK
I EXPECTED THERE WOULD BE MORE.
DO YOU THINK A SECOND WAVE IS COMING?
BLAM
NO. MANY HUNDREDS WERE KILLED OUTSIDE.
BLAM
BLAM
BLAM
"I THINK THIS IS THE END."
BLAM

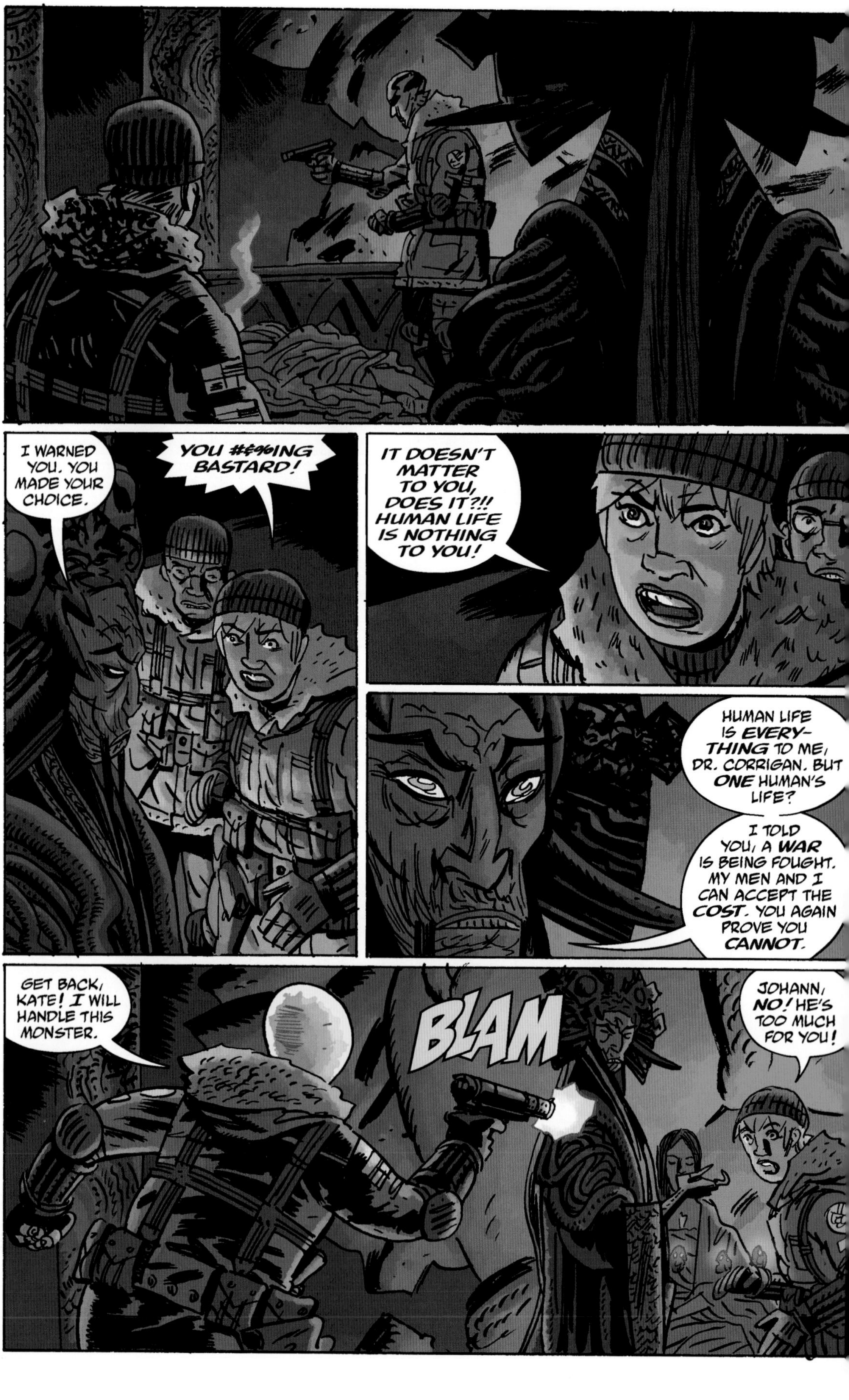
I WARNED YOU. YOU MADE YOUR CHOICE.
YOU #€%ING BASTARD!
IT DOESN'T MATTER TO YOU, DOES IT?!! HUMAN LIFE IS NOTHING TO YOU!
HUMAN LIFE IS EVERYTHING TO ME, DR. CORRIGAN. BUT ONE HUMAN'S LIFE?
I TOLD YOU, A WAR IS BEING FOUGHT. MY MEN AND I CAN ACCEPT THE COST. YOU AGAIN PROVE YOU CANNOT.
GET BACK, KATE! I WILL HANDLE THIS MONSTER.
BLAM
JOHANN, NO! HE'S TOO MUCH FOR YOU!

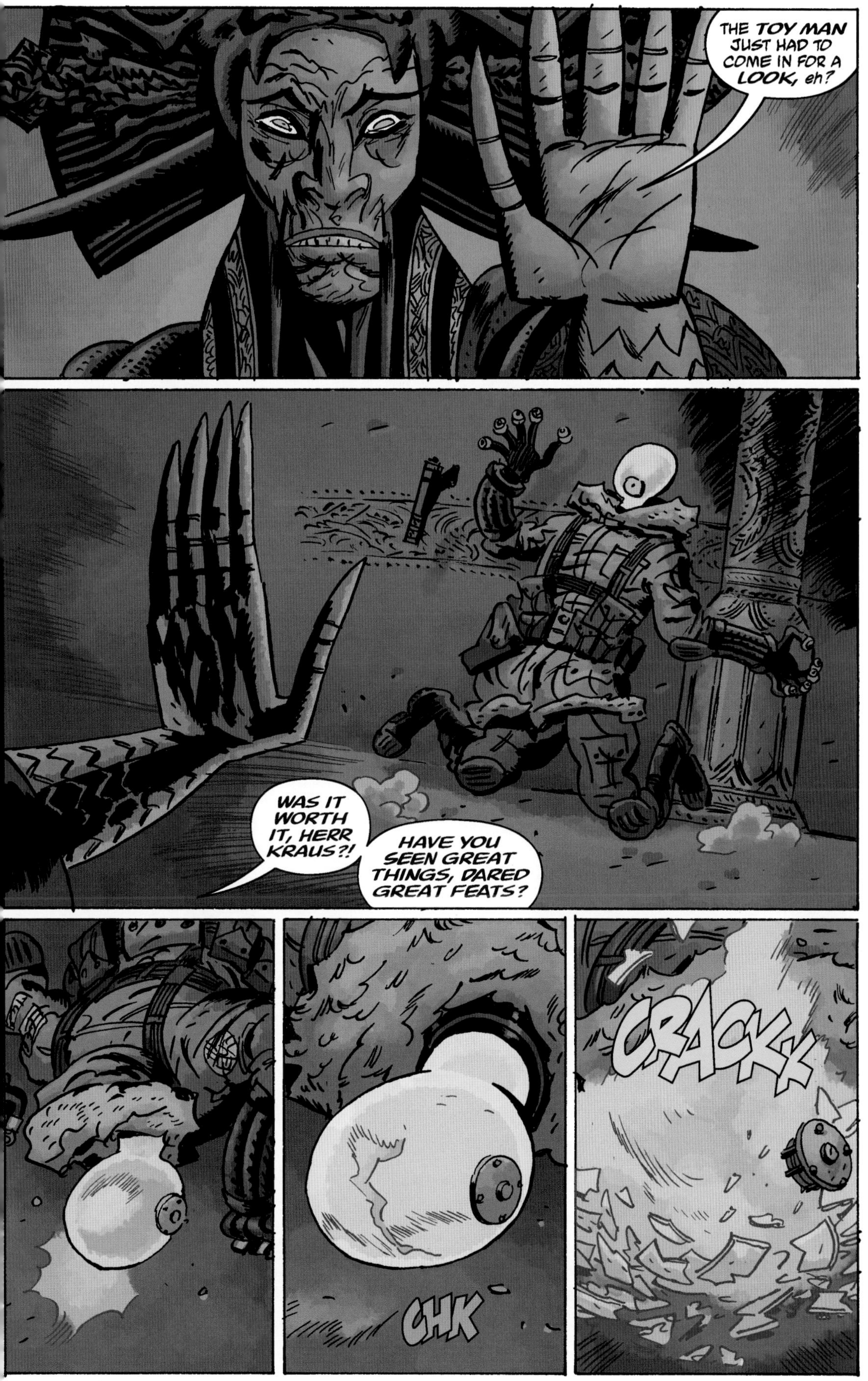
THE TOY MAN JUST HAD TO COME IN FOR A LOOK, eh?
WAS IT WORTH IT, HERR KRAUS?!
HAVE YOU SEEN GREAT THINGS, DARED GREAT FEATS?
CHK
CRACKK

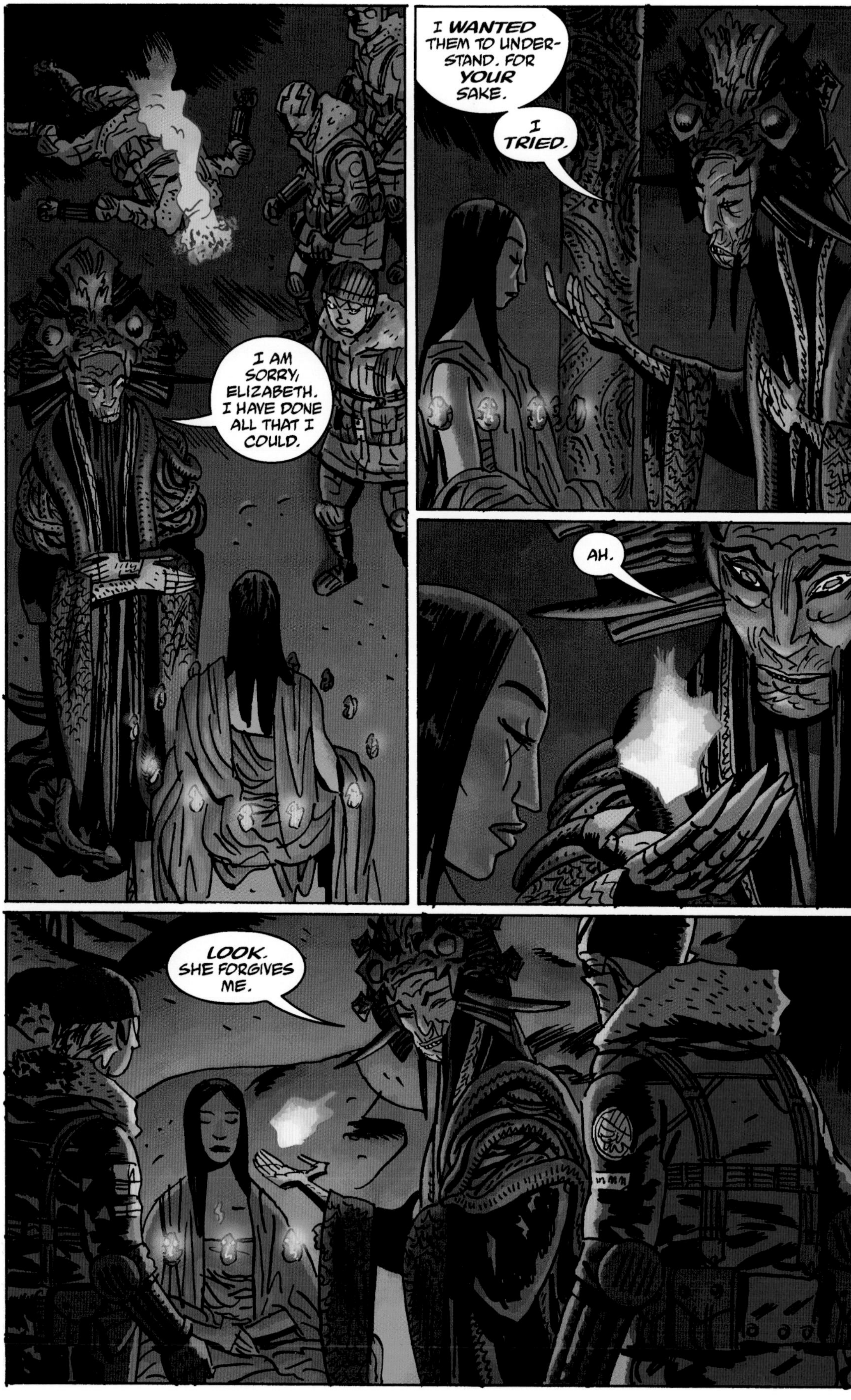
I AM SORRY, ELIZABETH. I HAVE DONE ALL THAT I COULD.
I WANTED THEM TO UNDER-STAND. FOR YOUR SAKE.
I TRIED.
AH.
LOOK. SHE FORGIVES ME.

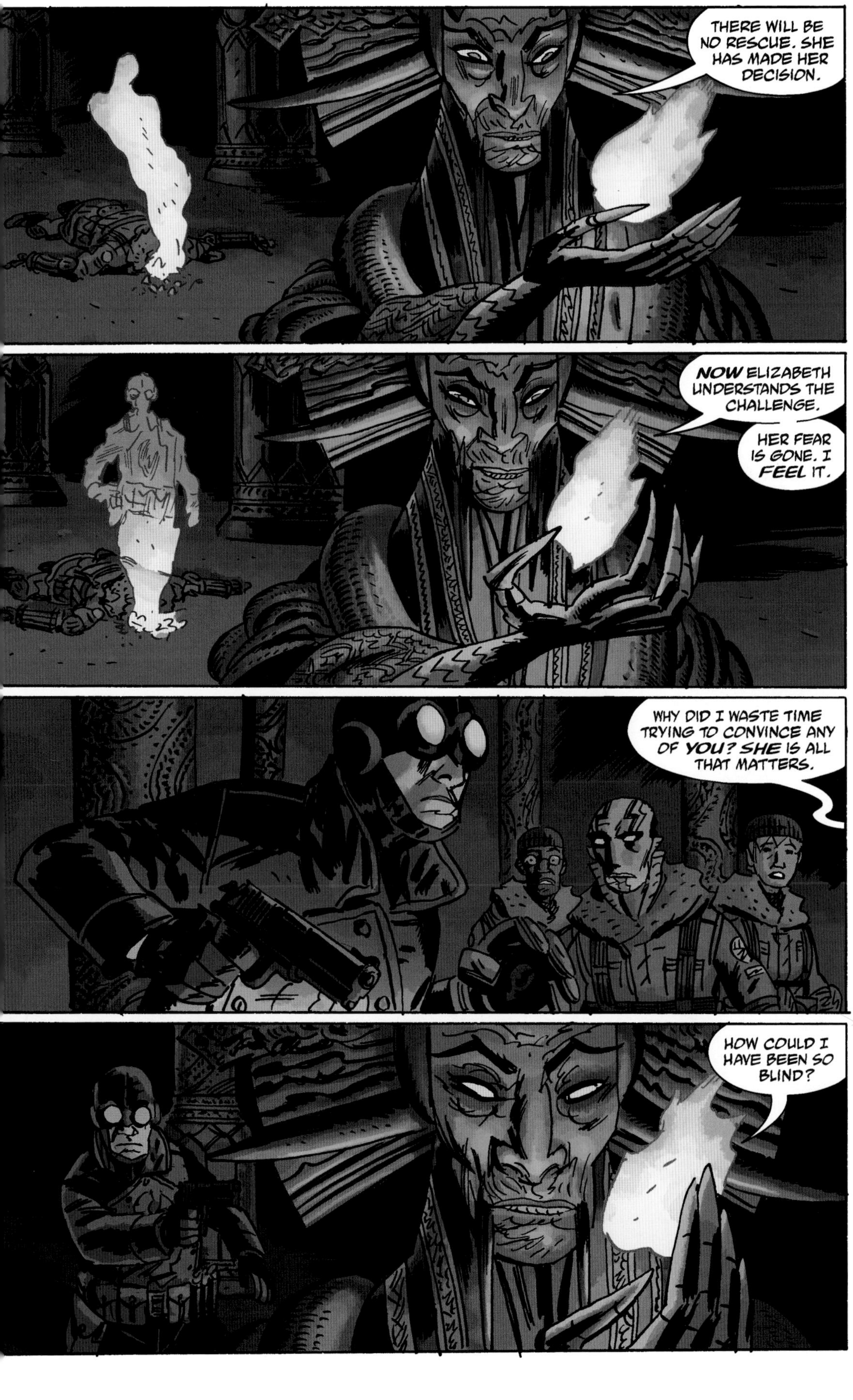

THERE WILL BE NO RESCUE. SHE HAS MADE HER DECISION.
NOW ELIZABETH UNDERSTANDS THE CHALLENGE.
HER FEAR IS GONE. I FEEL IT.
WHY DID I WASTE TIME TRYING TO CONVINCE ANY OF YOU? SHE IS ALL THAT MATTERS.
HOW COULD I HAVE BEEN SO BLIND?

FWOO

KSHHH

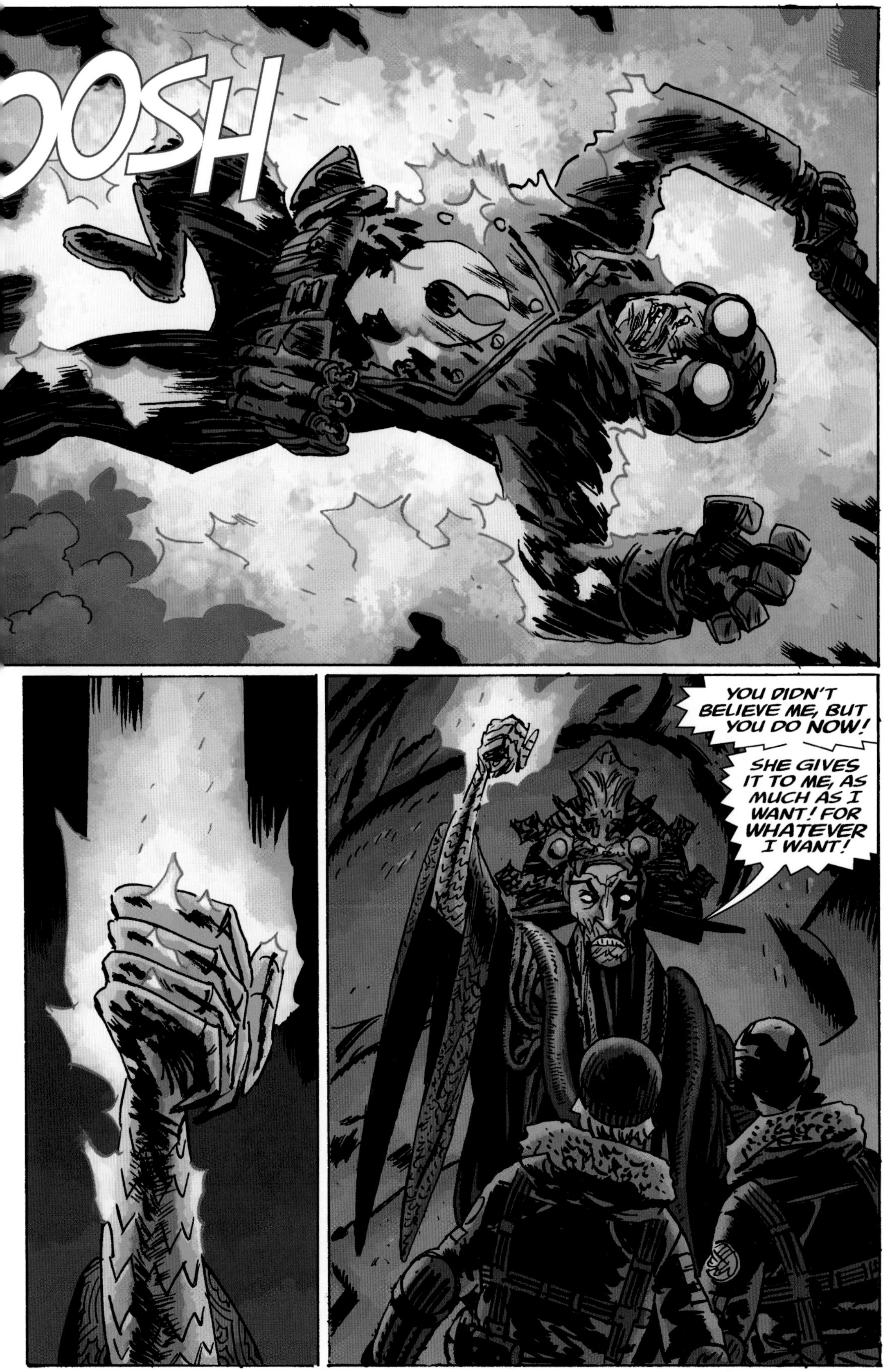
OOSH
YOU DIDN'T BELIEVE ME, BUT YOU DO NOW!
SHE GIVES IT TO ME, AS MUCH AS I WANT! FOR WHATEVER I WANT!

NOW YOU WILL *GO!*

YOU CAME FOR YOUR *FRIEND,* AND I HAVE LET YOU SEE HER.

BE *THANKFUL* FOR THAT, AND *GO!*

GO FIGHT YOUR *LITTLE BATTLES.* LEAVE THE *WAR* TO US.

#+*96¢ OFF!* WE'RE NOT FINISHED WITH YOU YET.

NO. OF *COURSE* NOT.

I COULD CHANGE *WATER* INTO *WINE.* IT WOULDN'T BE ENOUGH FOR *YOU.*

UNGGH!

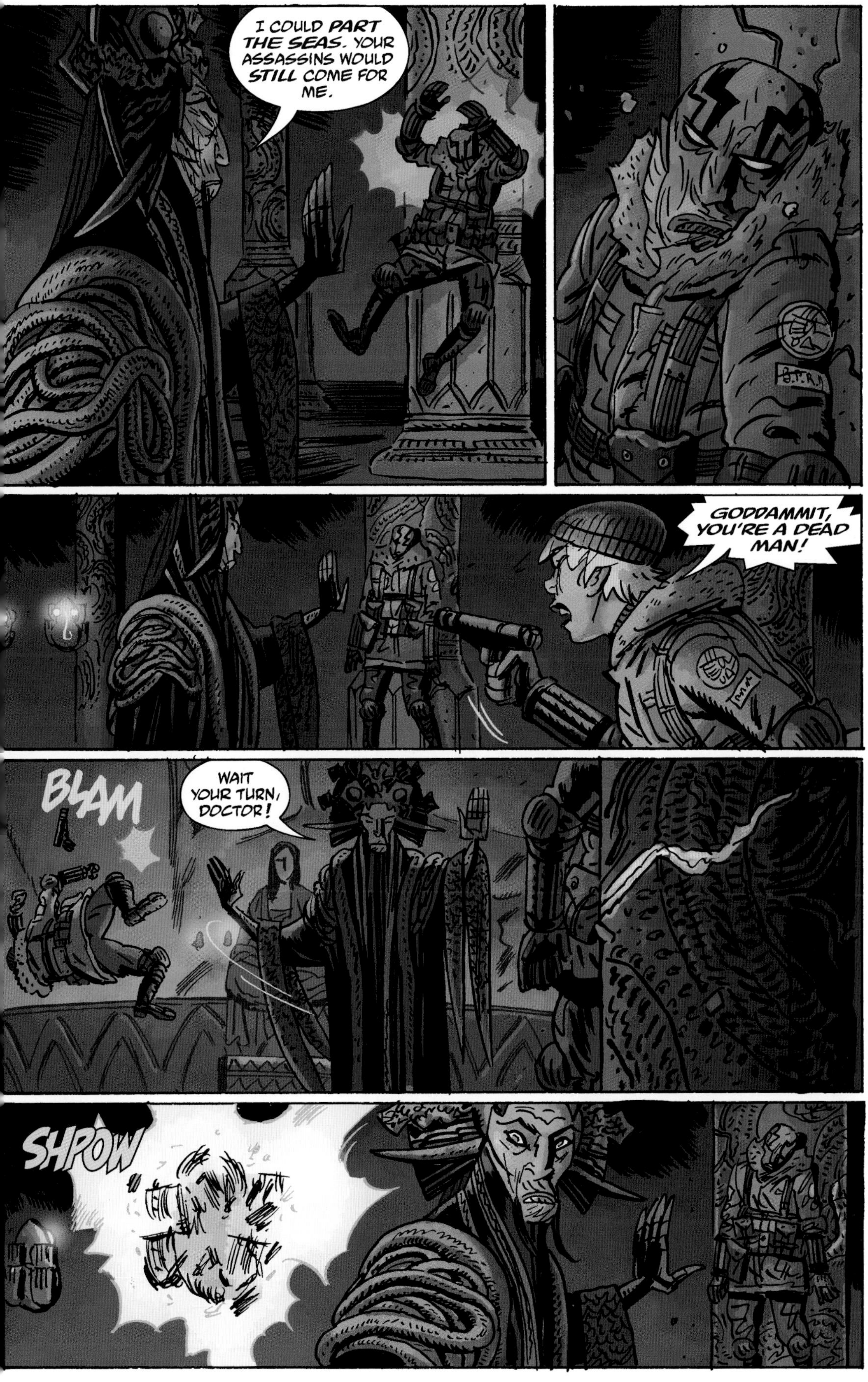
I COULD PART THE SEAS. YOUR ASSASSINS WOULD STILL COME FOR ME.
GODDAMMIT, YOU'RE A DEAD MAN!
BLAM
WAIT YOUR TURN, DOCTOR!
SHPOW

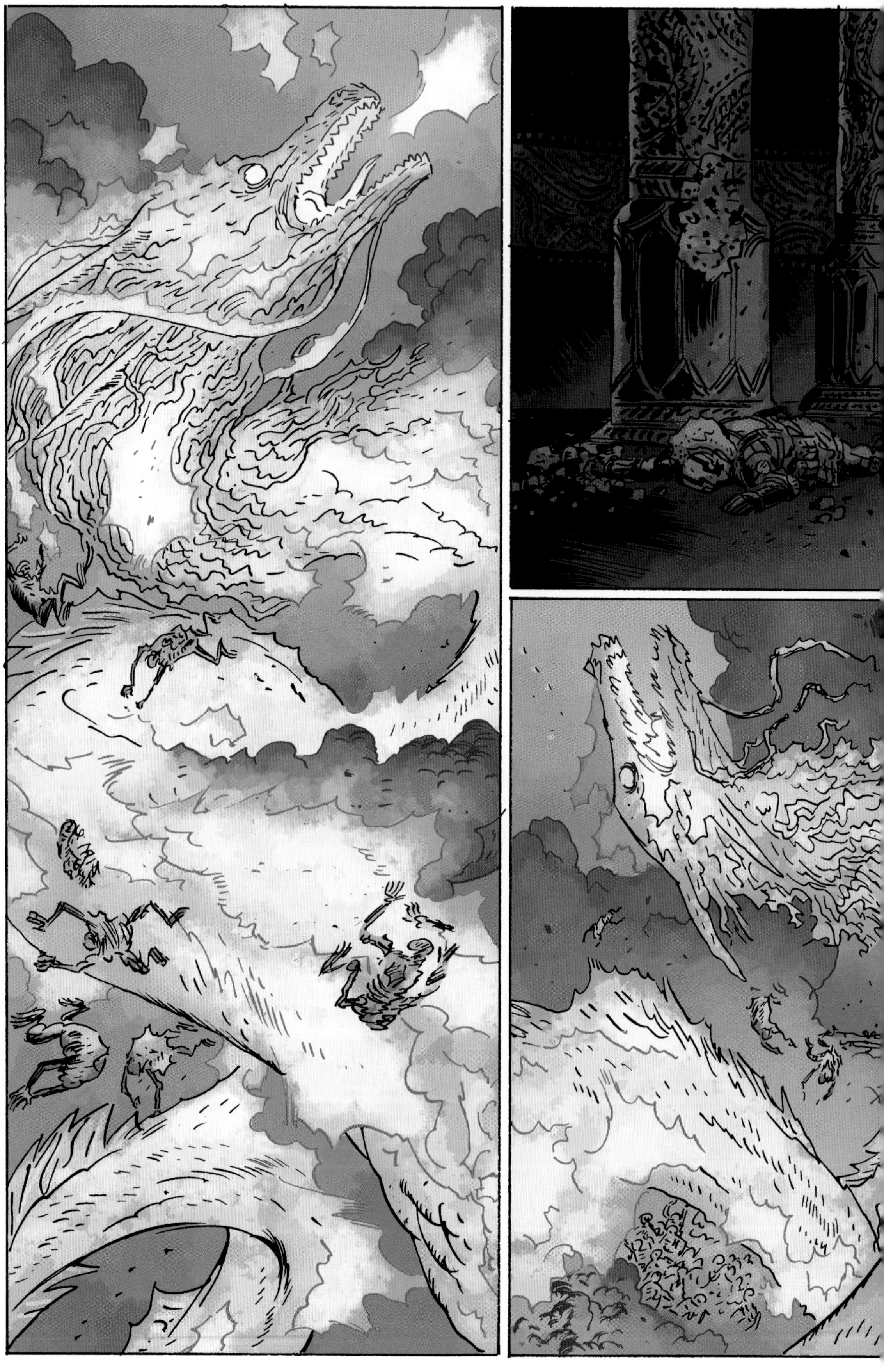

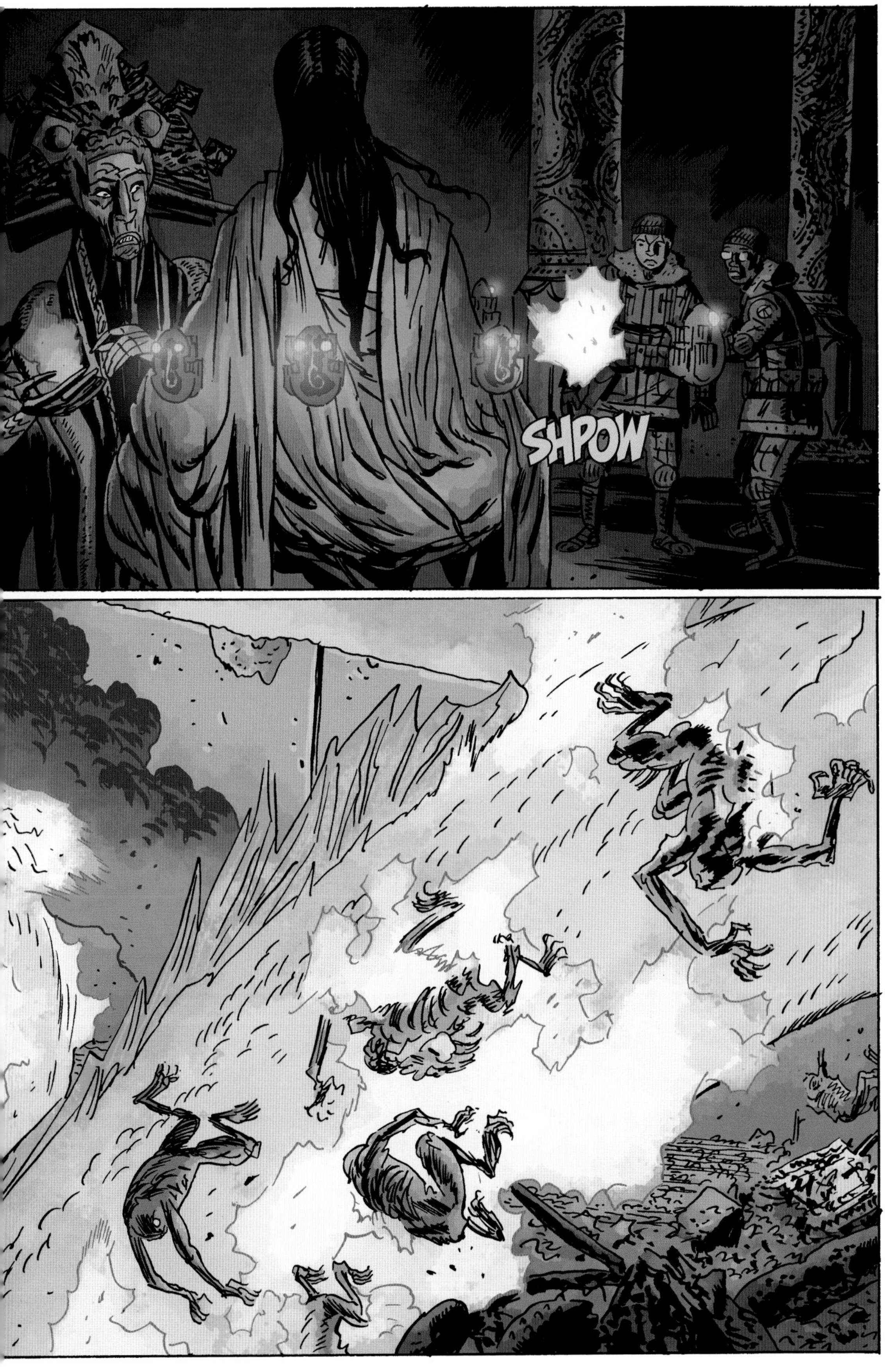
SHPOW

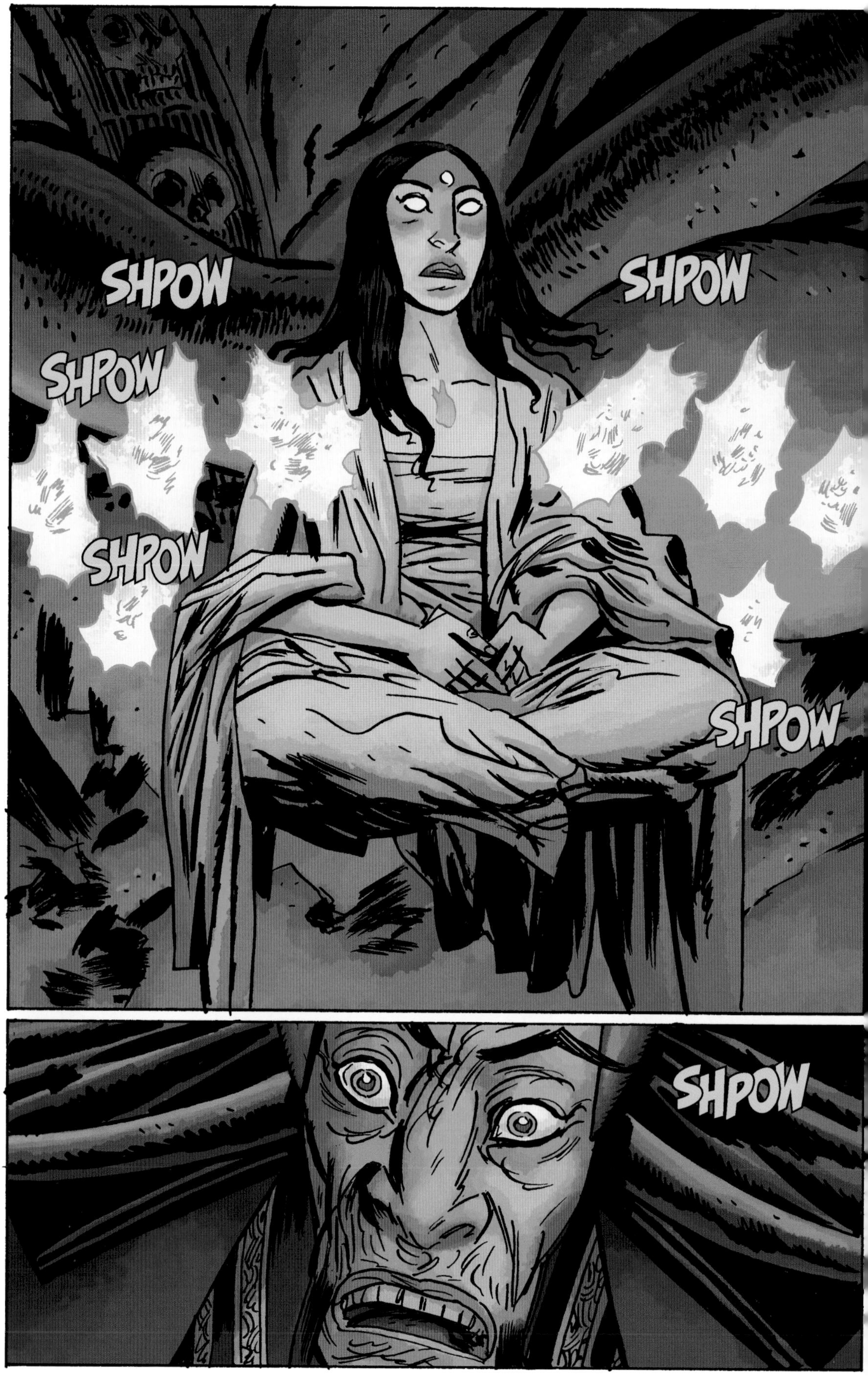
SHPOW
SHPOW
SHPOW
SHPOW
SHPOW
SHPOW

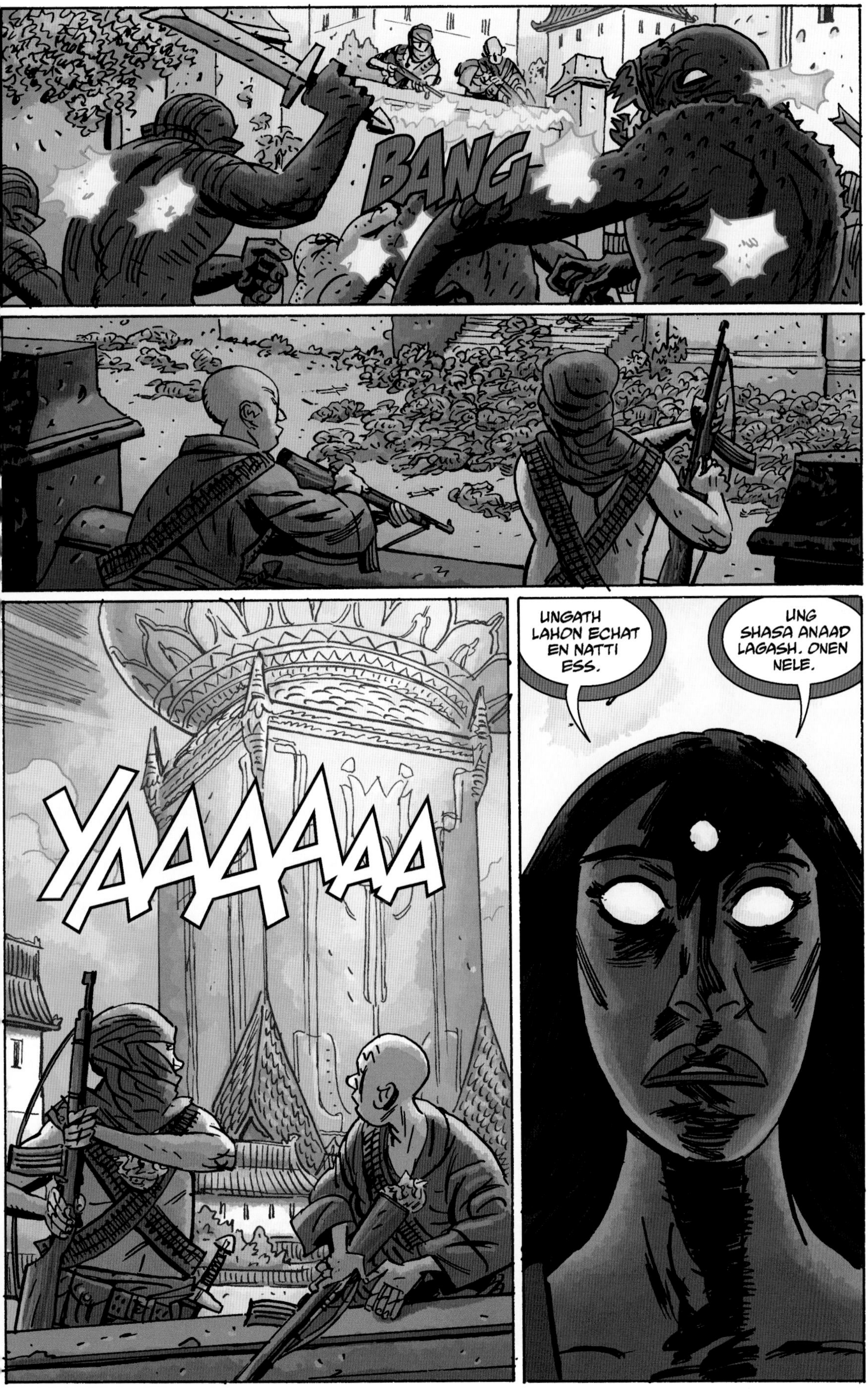
BANG
YAAAAAA
UNGATH LAHON ECHAT EN NATTI ESS.
UNG SHASA ANAAD LAGASH. ONEN NELE.

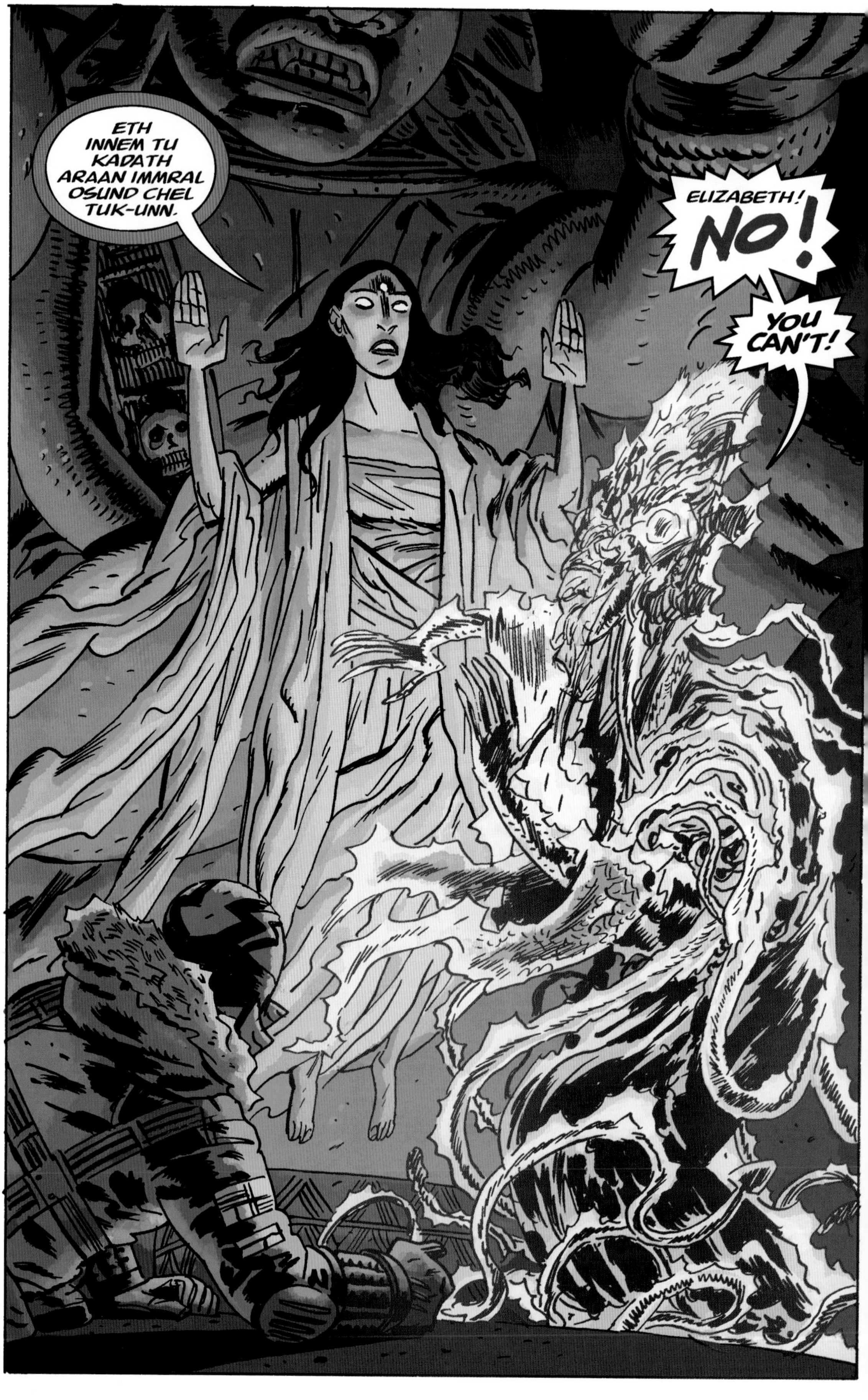
ETH INNEM TU KADATH ARAAN IMMRAL OSUND CHEL TUK-UNN.
ELIZABETH! NO!
YOU CAN'T!

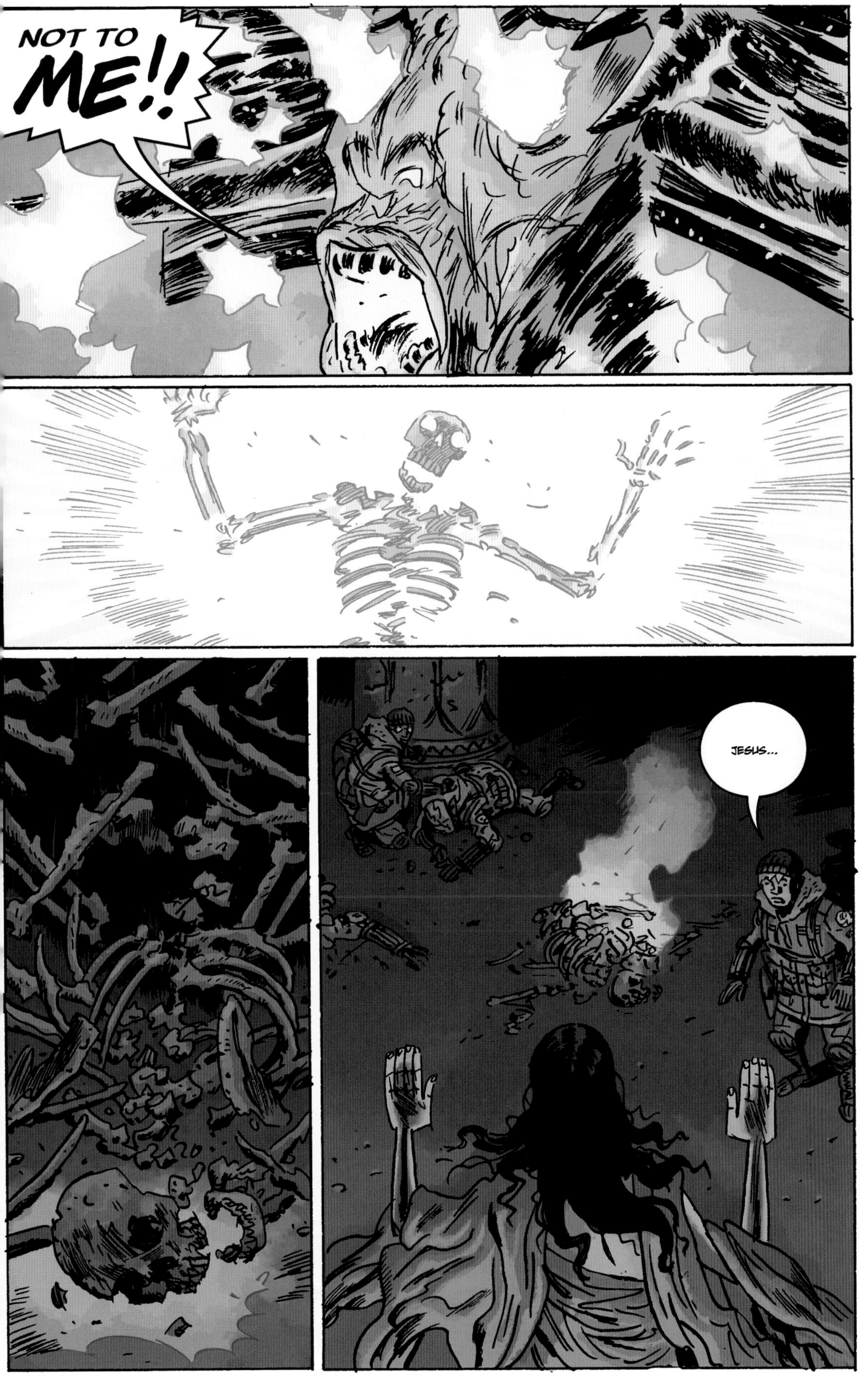
NOT TO ME!!
JESUS...

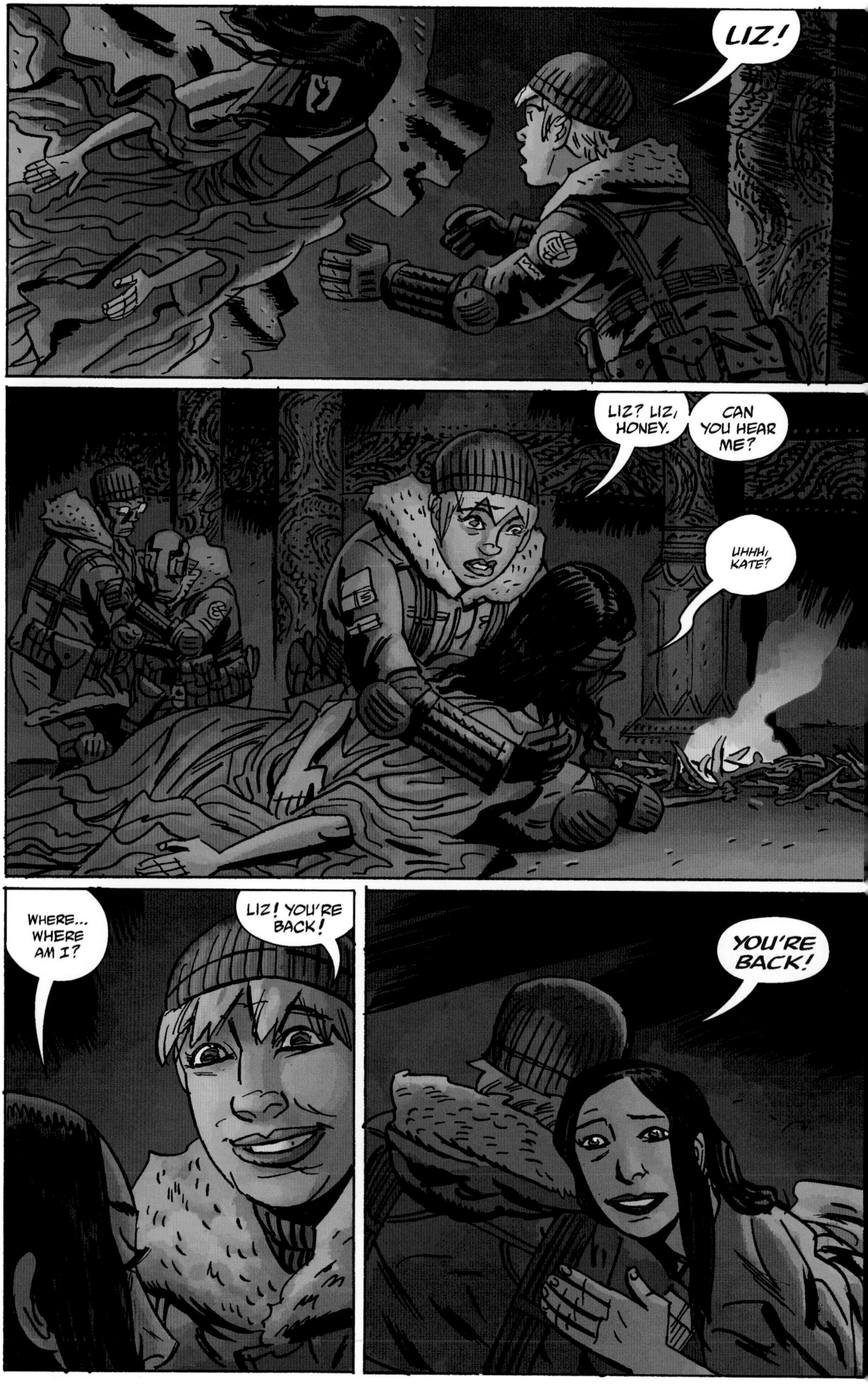
LIZ!
LIZ? LIZ, HONEY.
CAN YOU HEAR ME?
UHHH, KATE?
WHERE... WHERE AM I?
LIZ! YOU'RE BACK!
YOU'RE BACK!

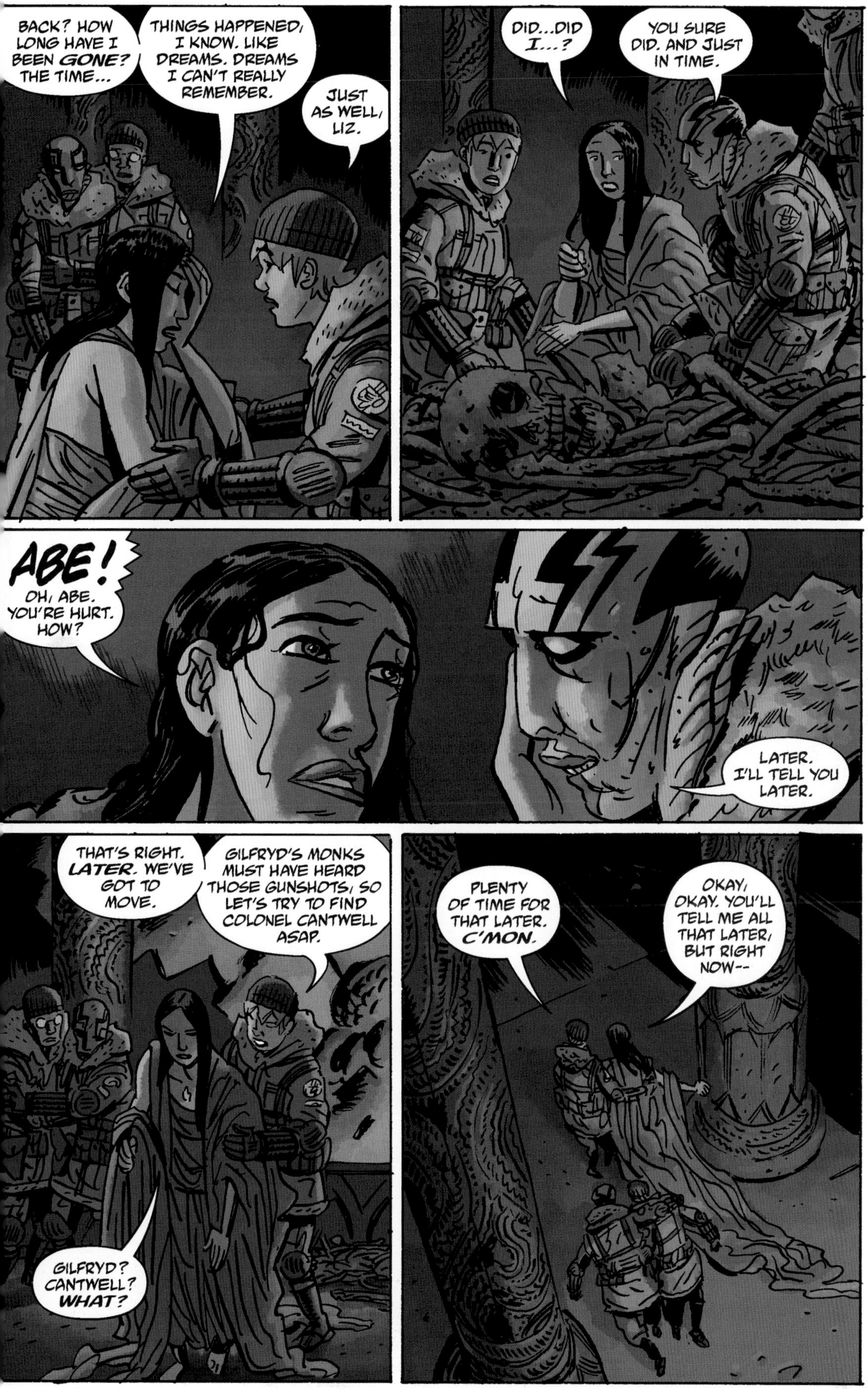
BACK? HOW LONG HAVE I BEEN GONE? THE TIME...
THINGS HAPPENED, I KNOW. LIKE DREAMS. DREAMS I CAN'T REALLY REMEMBER.
JUST AS WELL, LIZ.
DID...DID I...?
YOU SURE DID. AND JUST IN TIME.
ABE! OH, ABE. YOU'RE HURT. HOW?
LATER. I'LL TELL YOU LATER.
THAT'S RIGHT. LATER. WE'VE GOT TO MOVE.
GILFRYD'S MONKS MUST HAVE HEARD THOSE GUNSHOTS, SO LET'S TRY TO FIND COLONEL CANTWELL ASAP.
GILFRYD? CANTWELL? WHAT?
PLENTY OF TIME FOR THAT LATER. C'MON.
OKAY, OKAY. YOU'LL TELL ME ALL THAT LATER, BUT RIGHT NOW--

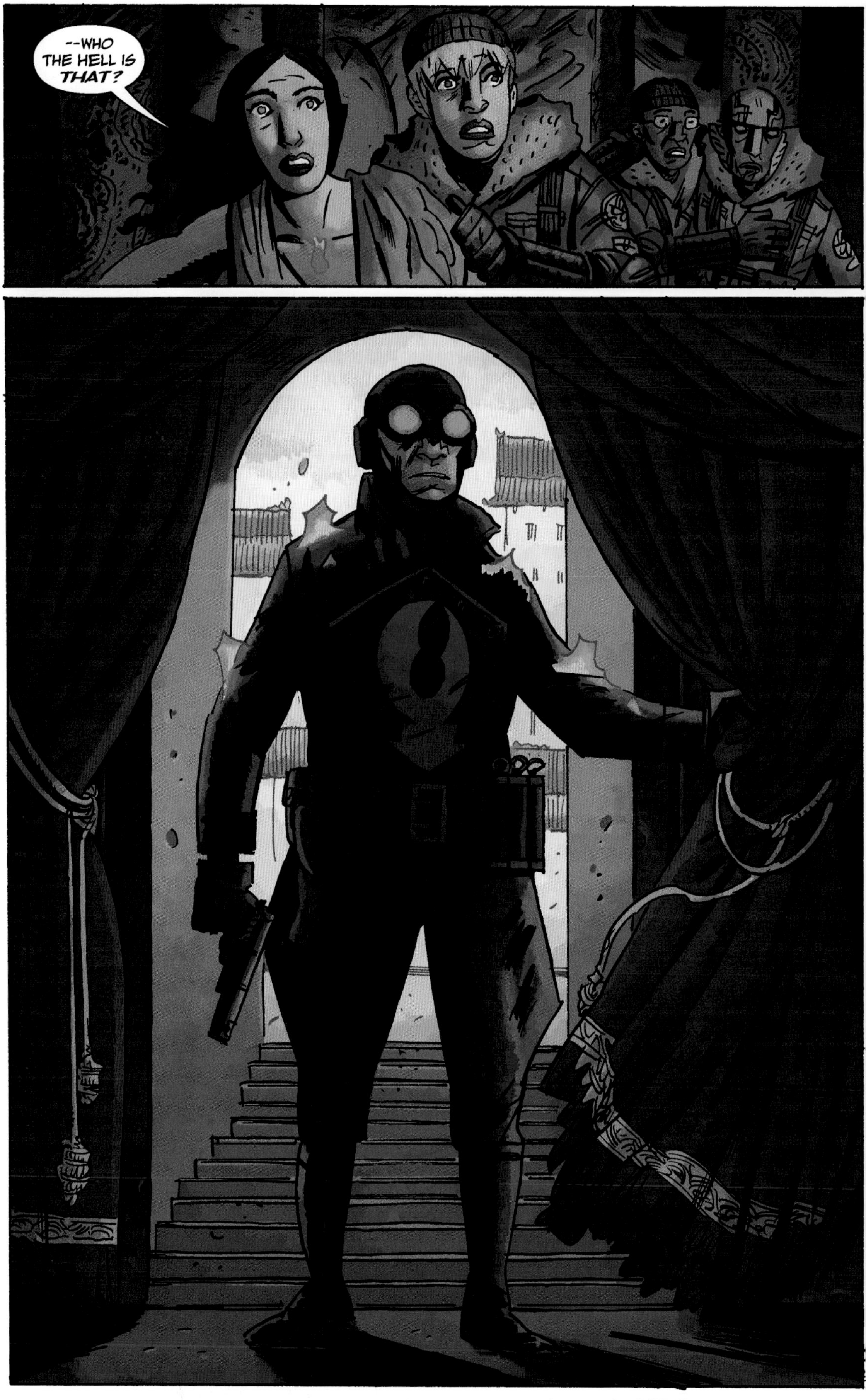
--WHO THE HELL IS THAT?

TO BE CONCLUDED IN B.P.R.D.: THE KING OF FEAR

B.P.R.D.™

SKETCHBOOK

Notes by Guy Davis

The army, the B.P.R.D., robot monsters, frog monsters, Hyperborean hordes and underworld beasts, monks that turn into yetis, all slugging it out while Abe and the gang find Liz and Memnan Saa at the temple of the Black Goddess—is it any wonder why I love getting to draw this book? Below: To me a rough character face is almost as much fun to draw as a monster; the colonel was loosely based on Ernest Borgnine, and you can't find a better rough character face than that—except maybe Richard Boone. Left: Mike's design for the statue.

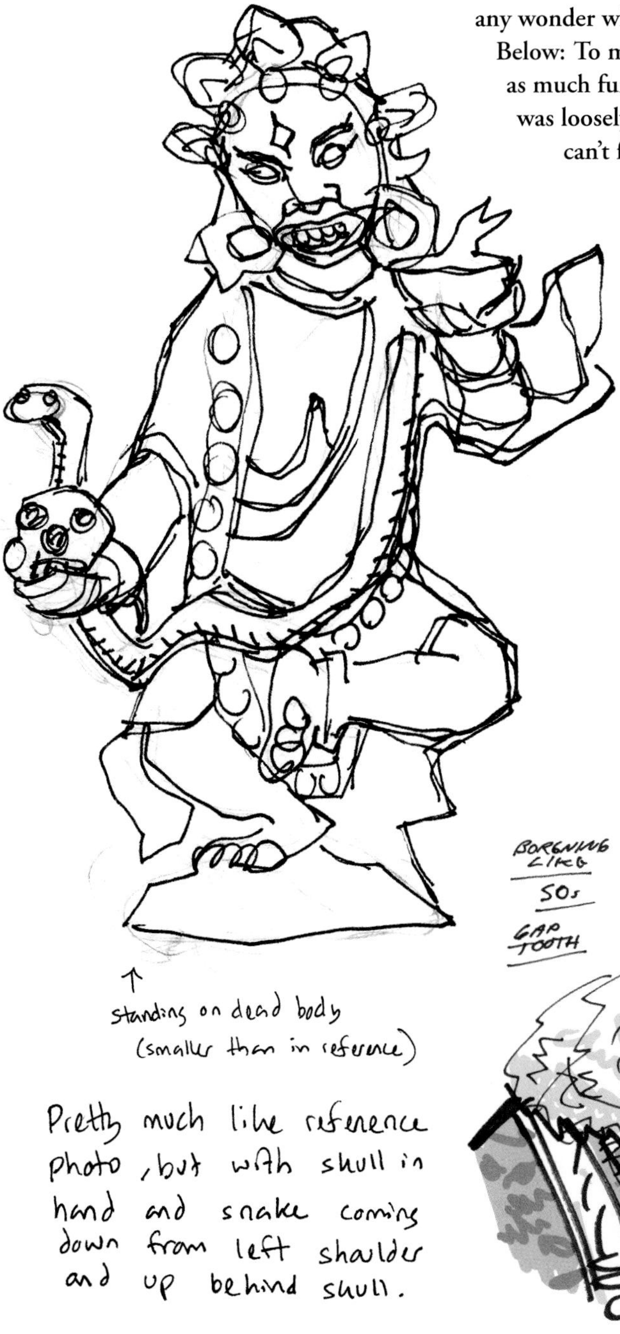
standing on dead body
(smaller than in reference)
Pretty much like reference photo, but with skull in hand and snake coming down from left shoulder and up behind skull.

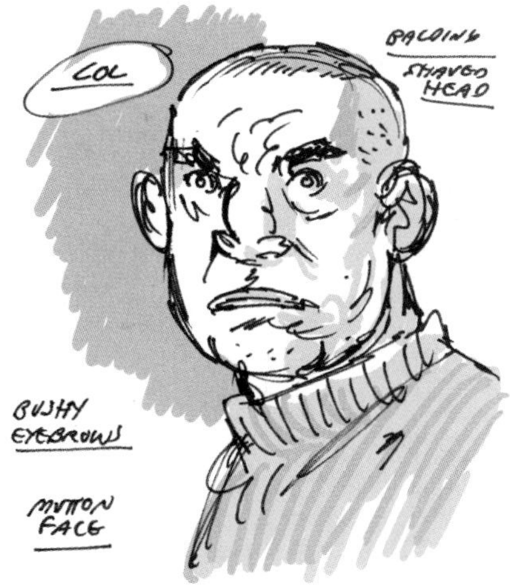
COL
BALDING
SHAVED HEAD
BUSHY EYEBROWS
MUTTON FACE

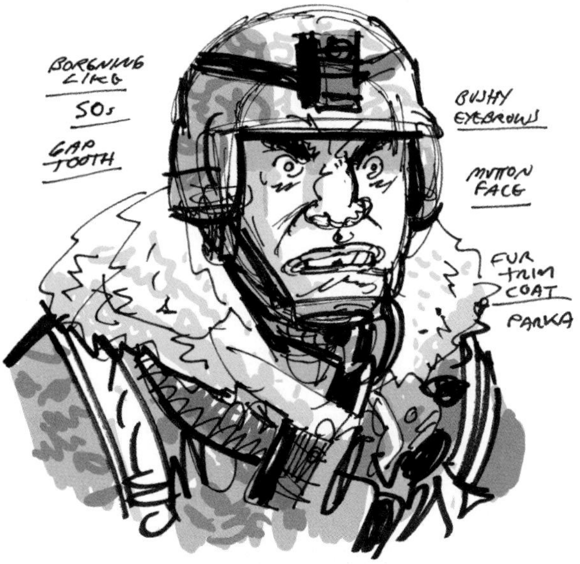
BORGNINE LIKE
50s
GAP TOOTH
BUSHY EYEBROWS
MUTTON FACE
FUR TRIM COAT
PARKA

Mike wanted the designs for the dragons to have the long, twisting bodies of mythological Chinese dragons. I based the faces on moray eels to make them seem like something more biologically than fantasy based, and the body poses in the story were inspired by a couple of pet ferrets.

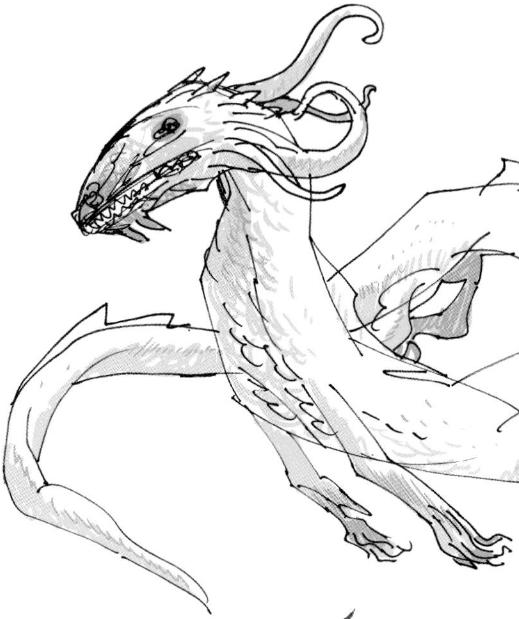

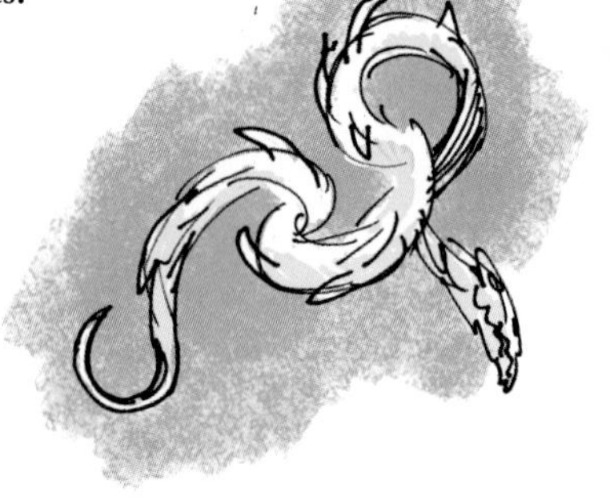

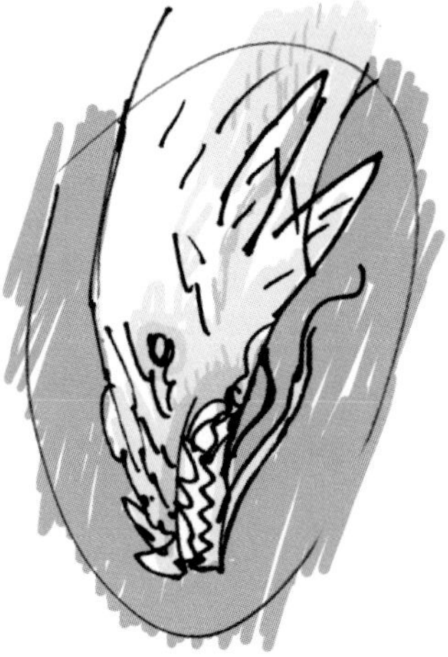

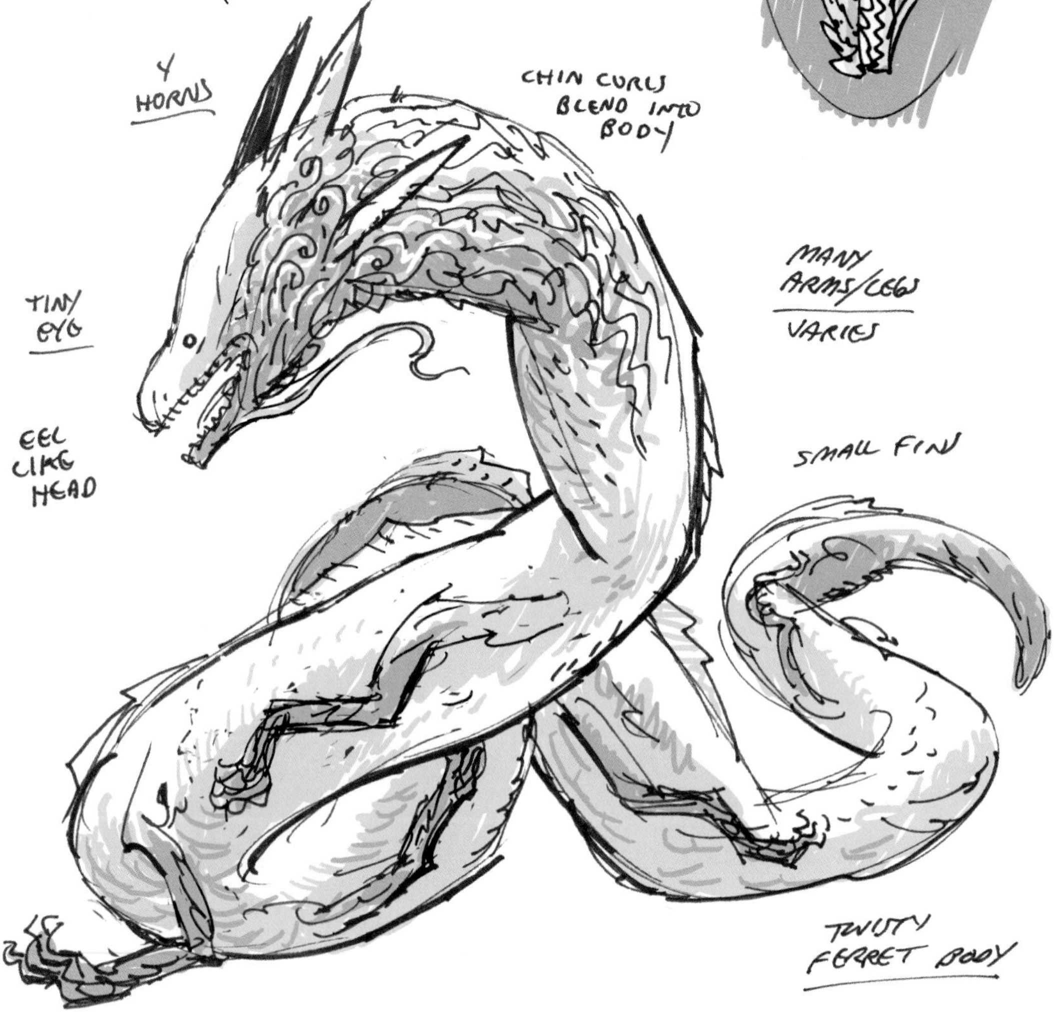
4 HORNS
CHIN CURLS BLEND INTO BODY
MANY ARMS/LEGS VARIES
TINY EYE
EEL LIKE HEAD
SMALL FIN
TWISTY FERRET BODY

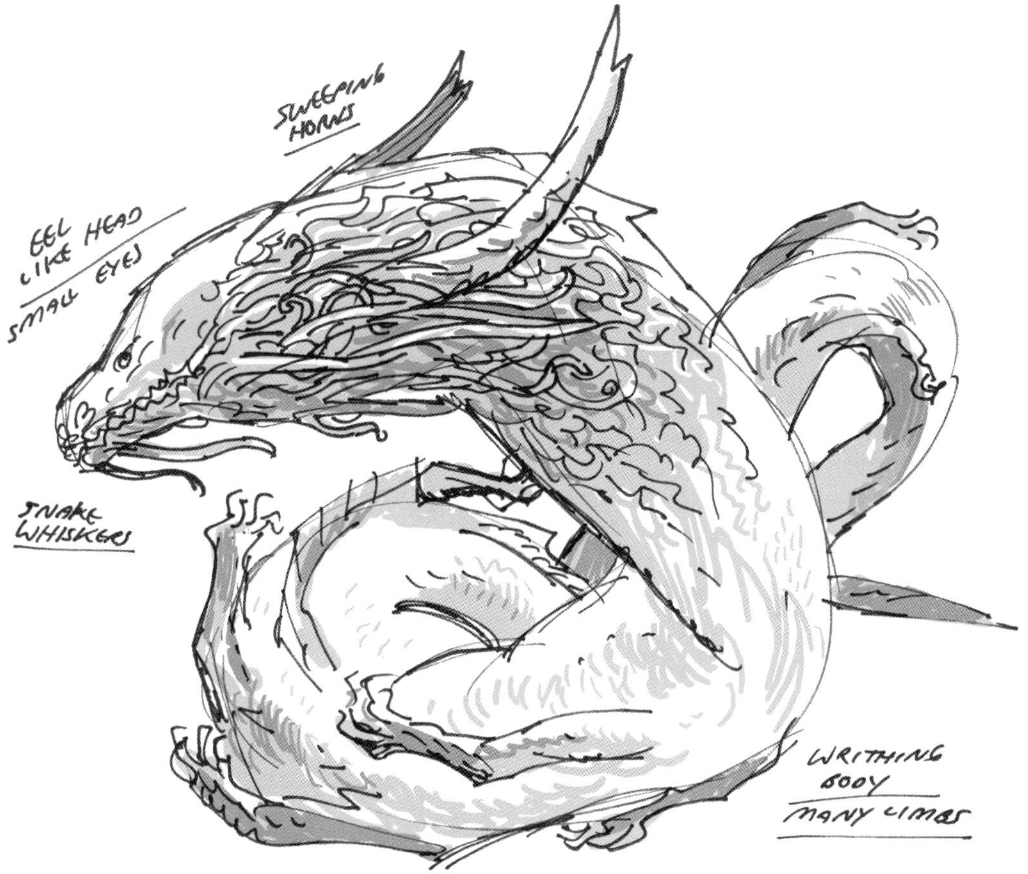
SWEEPING HORNS
EEL HEAD LIKE
SMALL EYES
SNAKE WHISKERS
WRITHING BODY
MANY LIMBS

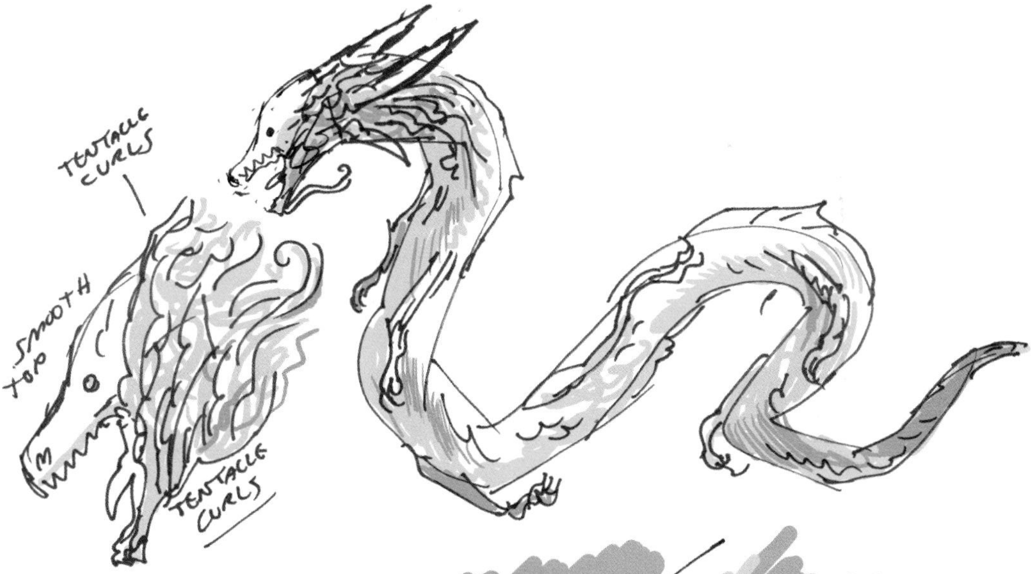
TENTACLE CURLS
SMOOTH TOP
TENTACLE CURLS

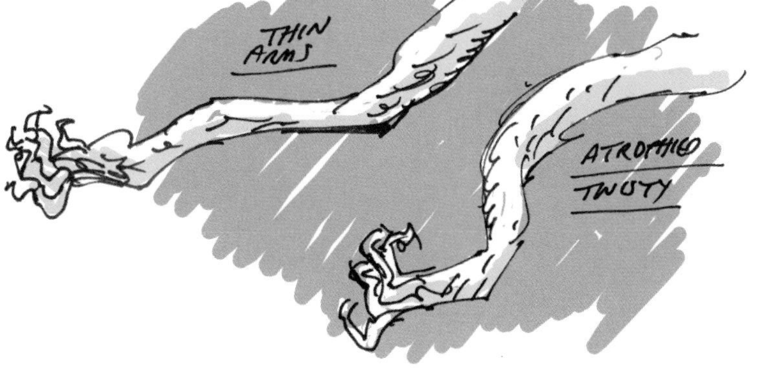
THIN ARMS
ATROPHIED
TWISTY

In the script, John had the dragons forming from smoke pouring out of the frogs' mouths, but I thought the frogs deserved to suffer a bit more and sketched out the idea of their tongues swelling and turning into a dragon's body—and because John and Mike spoil me, they let me do it!

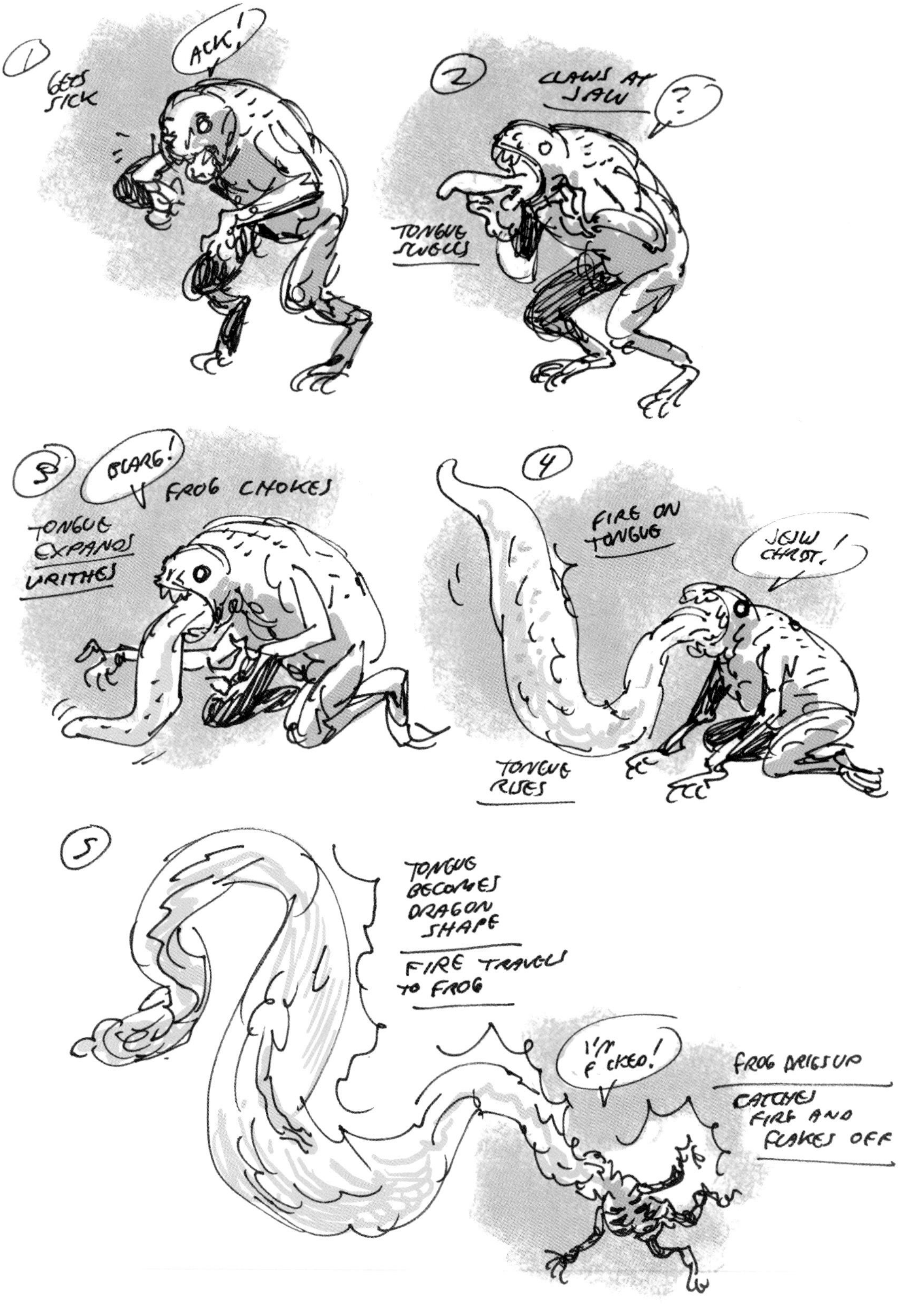

1
GETS SICK
ACK!
2
CLAWS AT JAW
?
TONGUE SWELLS
3
BLARG!
FROG CHOKES
TONGUE EXPANDS
WRITHES
4
FIRE ON TONGUE
JESUS CHRIST!
TONGUE RISES
5
TONGUE BECOMES DRAGON SHAPE
FIRE TRAVELS TO FROG
I'M F CKED!
FROG DRIES UP
CATCHES FIRE AND FLAKES OFF

Mike's great designs for the Hyperboreans were all established from *Hollow Earth.* For a bit I thought about giving some of them armor for their big attack, but the huge fight scenes were already cluttered enough without adding more details to them.

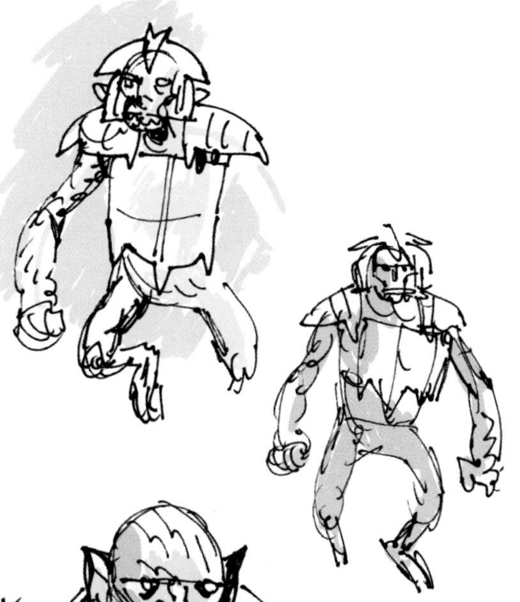

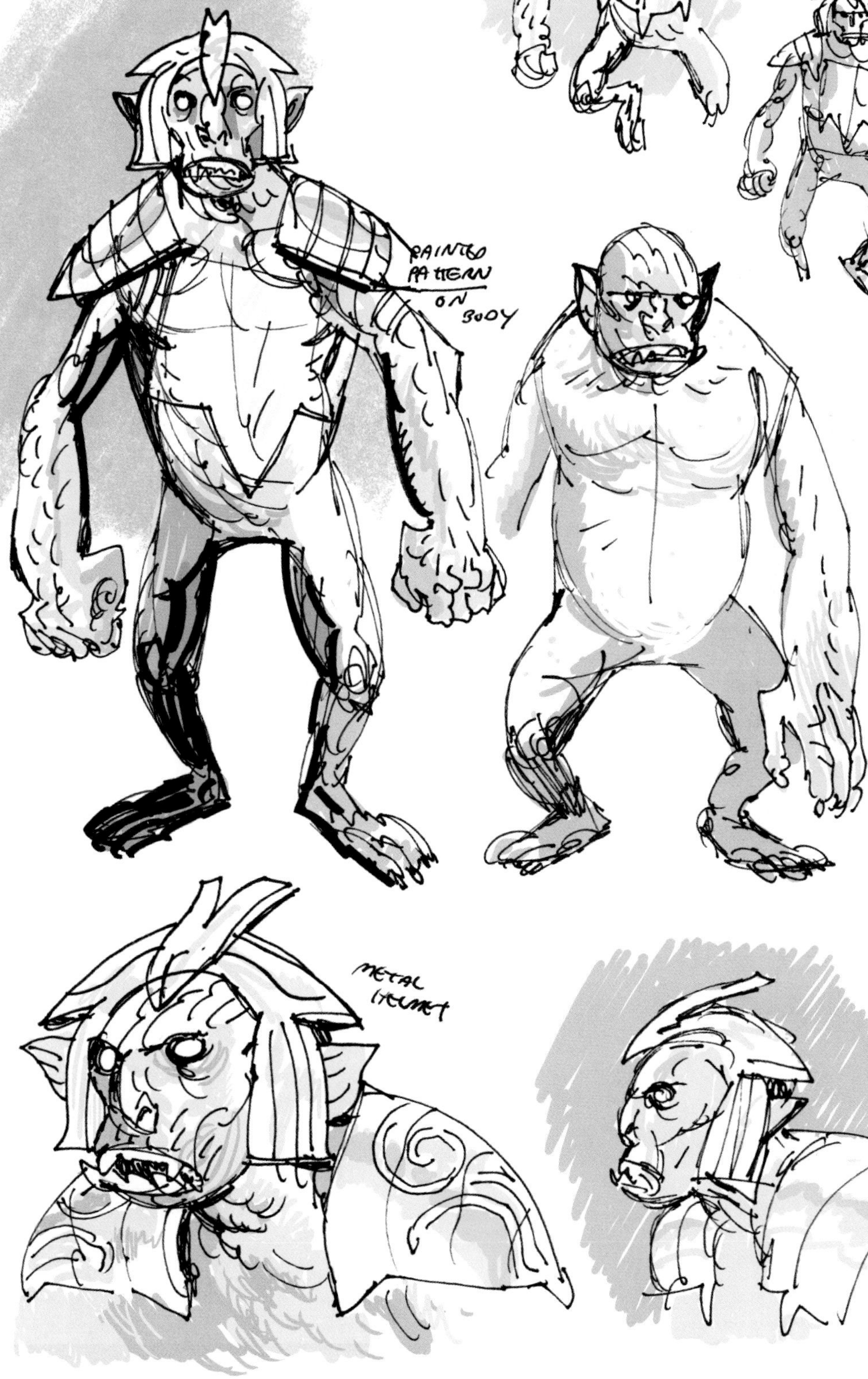
PAINTED PATTERN ON BODY
METAL HELMET

For Memnan Saa's temple robes I wanted something more grand and ominous than what he had before, keeping the living snakes as adornment, but adding a crazy headdress and making the lot black.

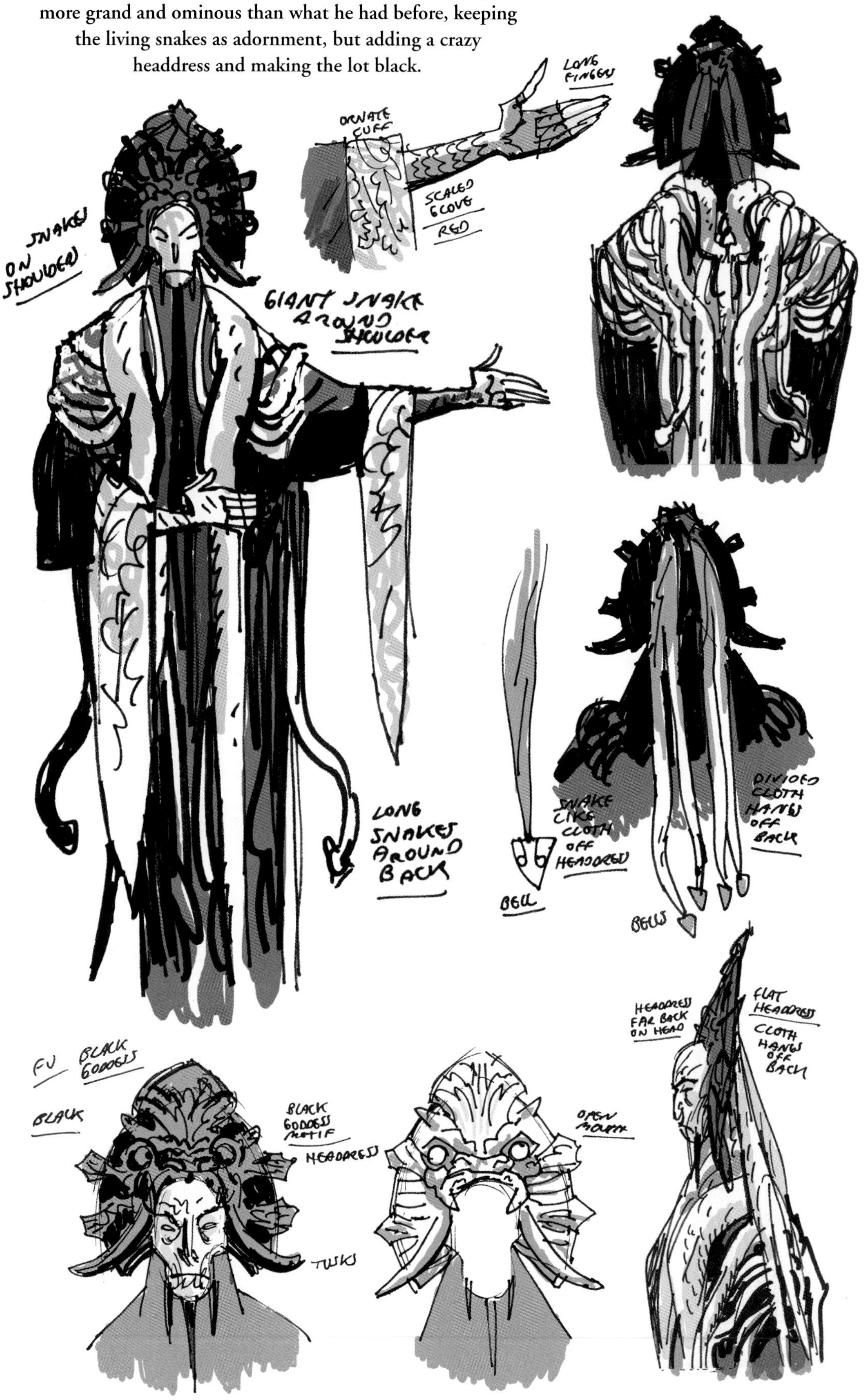
LONG FINGERS
ORNATE CUFF
SCALED GLOVE
RED
SNAKES ON SHOULDERS
GIANT SNAKE AROUND SHOULDER
LONG SNAKES AROUND BACK
SNAKE LIKE CLOTH OFF HEADDRESS
BELL
DIVIDED CLOTH HANGS OFF BACK
BELLS
HEADDRESS FAR BACK ON HEAD
FLAT HEADDRESS
CLOTH HANGS OFF BACK
FU BLACK GODDESS
BLACK
BLACK GODDESS MOTIF
HEADDRESS
TUSKS
OPEN MOUTH

Liz's robes for the temple of the Black Goddess were based on the monks and also the King of Fear from *Hollow Earth*.

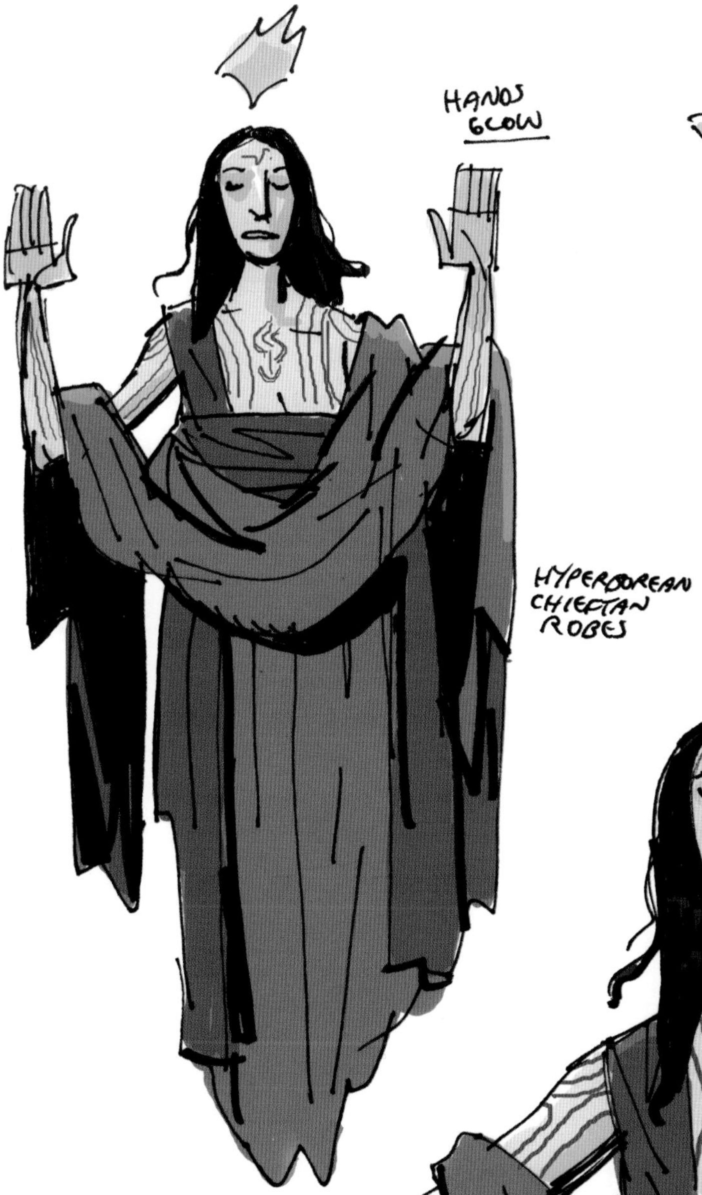
HANDS GLOW
HYPERBOREAN CHIEFTAN ROBES

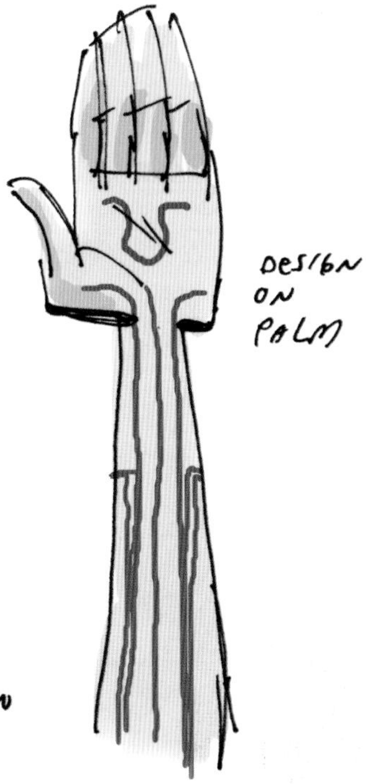
DESIGN ON PALM

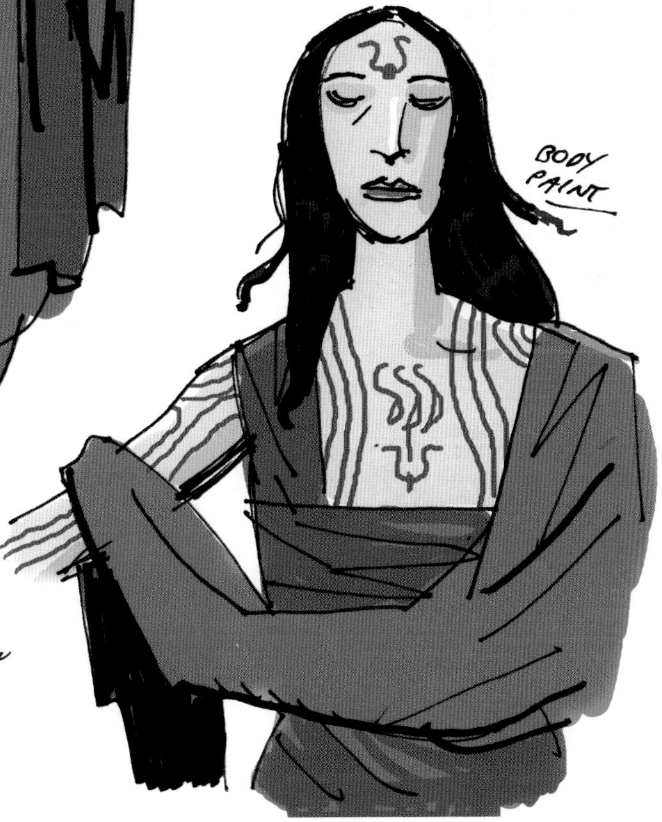
BODY PAINT

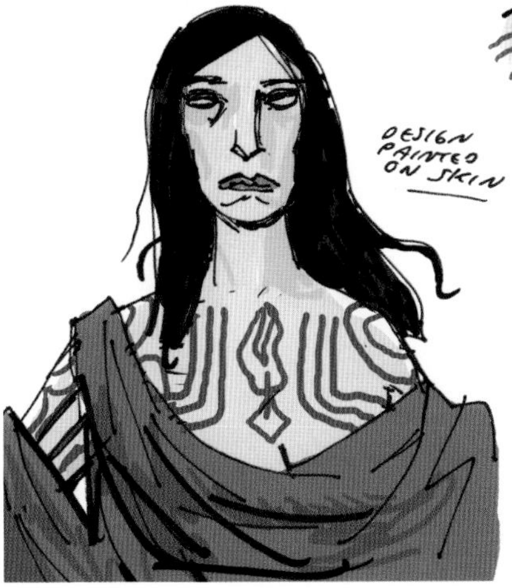
DESIGN PAINTED ON SKIN

At first I thought of having her painted with symbols and tribal markings, but it looked too cluttered and the idea really got out of hand with the sketch to the left! Yikes!

For the Lobster Johnson flashback, I sketched up a few bizarre villain-thugs, but then John liked the idea of showing off the Steel Hawk again.

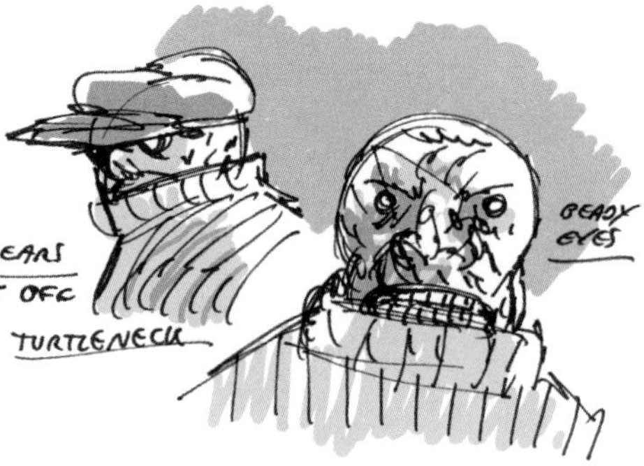
NO EARS
CUT OFF
TURTLENECK
BEADY EYES

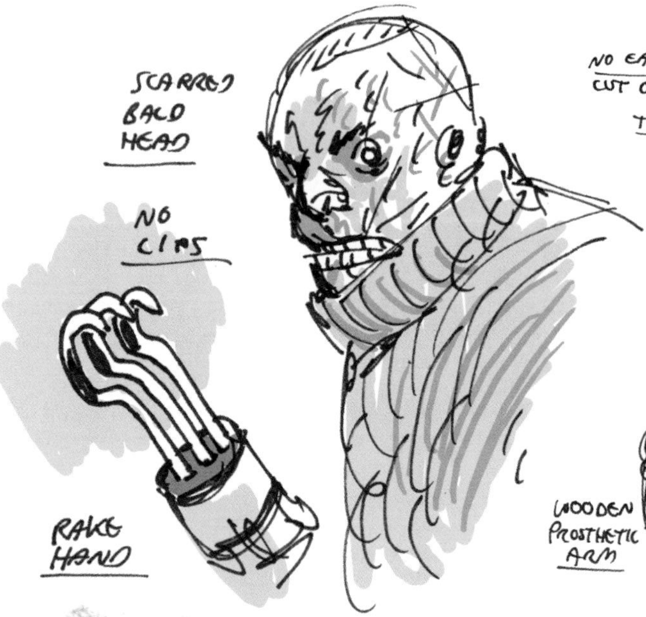
SCARRED BALD HEAD
NO LIPS
RAKE HAND

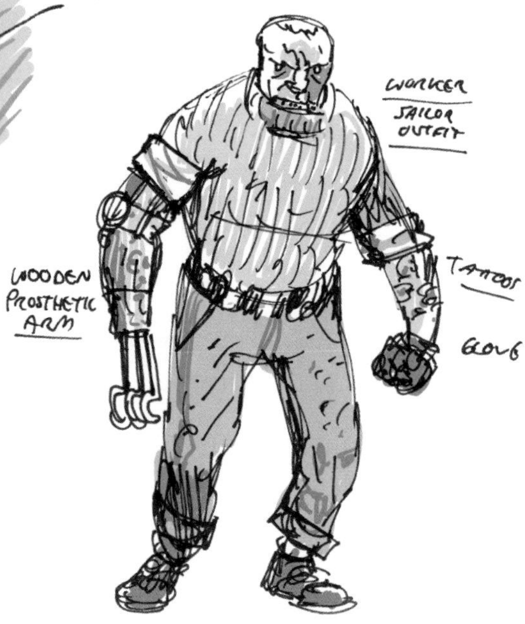
WORKER
SAILOR OUTFIT
WOODEN PROSTHETIC ARM
TATTOOS
GLOVE

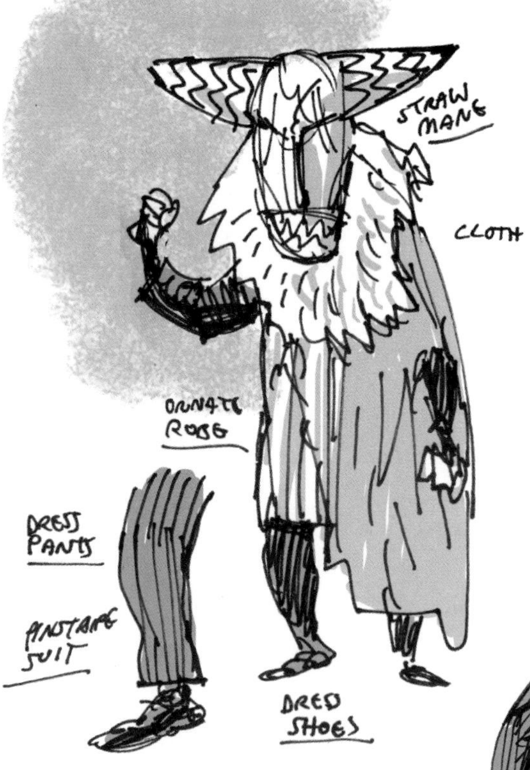
STRAW MANE
CLOTH
ORNATE ROBE
DRESS PANTS
PINSTRIPE SUIT
DRESS SHOES

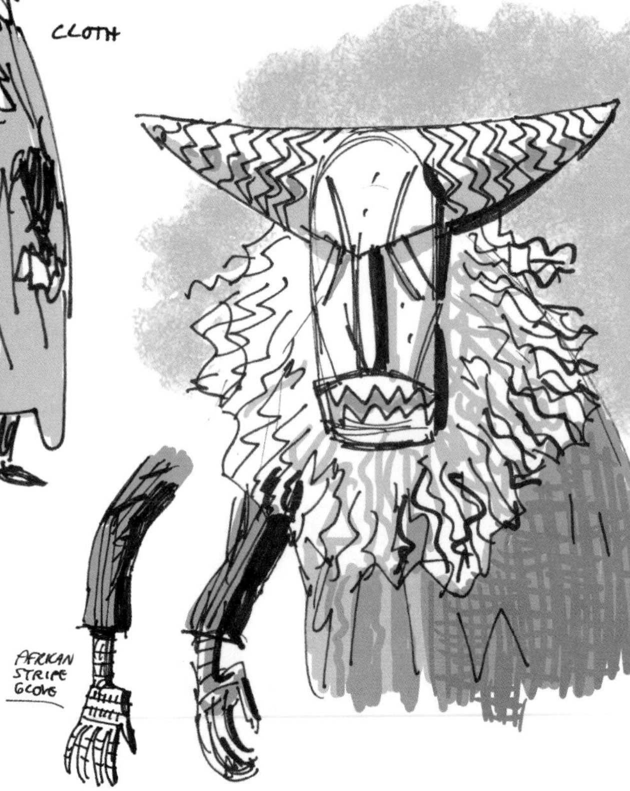
AFRICAN STRIPE GLOVE

I have no idea what the story is behind this guy—something from John's great imagination—but you don't need to ask me twice to draw something like that!

BLACK GODDESS
COVER SKETCHES

MIGNOLA

ISSUE 1

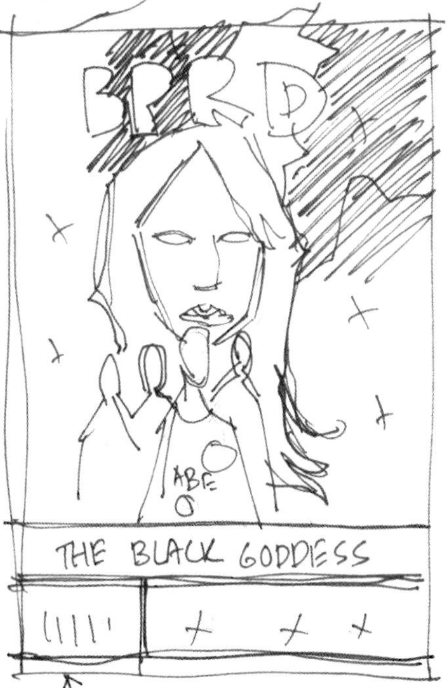
BPRD
ABE
THE BLACK GODDESS

↑ UPC symbol on its side

- TEAM SHOT OF ABE, JOHANN, KATE AND DEVON (YOUNG BLACK GUY FROM UNIVERSAL MACHINE).
- KATE IN STREET CLOTHES.
- EVERYBODY ELSE IN FIELD UNIFORM
- LIZ HEAD LARGE IN BACKGROUND with FLAME from head or rising behind head - LIZ HEAD IS COLORED DARK - APPEARING GHOST-LIKE OUT OF BLACK BACKGROUND WITH EYES OPEN FOR COLOR.

Issue 2

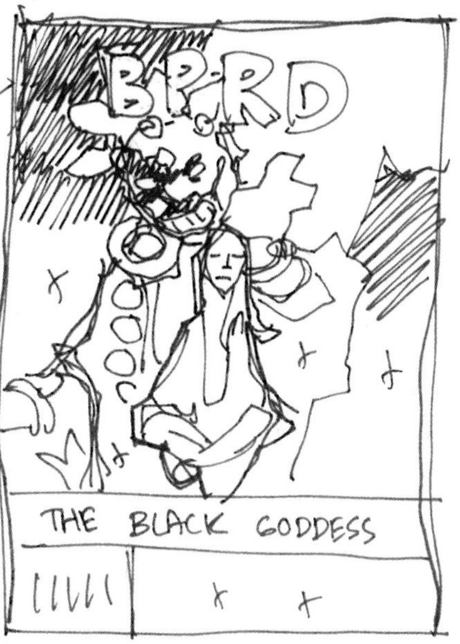
BPRD
THE BLACK GODDESS

- LIZ* FLOATS IN SOME KIND OF LOTUS POSITION IN FRONT OF GIANT IMAGE OF BLACK GODDESS STATUE - SEEN IN MY DARKNESS CALLS EPILOGUE AND TOWARDS END OF THE ISLAND.
- GODDESS STATUE HOLDS BOWL OF FIRE BEHIND LIZ'S HEAD TO CREATE Effect similar to cover of issue 1.
- GODDESS IS DARK, Blending into BLACK BACKGROUND AS LIZ HEAD DID ON ISSUE 1 cover. STATUE EYES (3 of them) open for color.

* GUY needs to design robe for Liz to be wearing -- or I can do that. Hyperborean Fashion!

ISSUE 3

ROARING YETI ↓

one of Memnan Saa's Minions

BPRD GUY ↓

FROGS   FROGS

THE BLACK GODDESS

* The Memnan Saa guy should be dressed similar to the henchmen in Lobster Johnson — with or without head covering. That's up to you.

• THE BIG IDEA HERE IS THE CONTRAST BETWEEN A BPRD SOLDIER ON ONE SIDE (in uniform with machine gun) and one of Memnan Saa's guys* in loincloth and old (1930s?) bolt-action rifle. The two guys are back to back with hoard of frog guys in background. They are surrounded by impossible odds.
 — It would be great if you could position the guys so we see BPRD symbol on soldier (on chest or uniform shoulder) and skull and snake symbol on chain around the neck of the other guy — same symbol on henchmen in LOBSTER JOHNSON miniseries.

• In background is large symbolic image of roaring yeti — same type of creature seen in first issue of LOBSTER JOHNSON.

Mike gave me a solid little layout to work with, but my first problem was that big yeti. I drew several sketches with his head at the angle Mike showed in his thumbnail sketch, but none of them worked. I finally tried drawing him straight on and made him larger. I made faces into a mirror until I got an expression that was suitably monstrous. The light from my drawing lamp created just the right shadows.

Scott and Mike seemed to like the sketch but asked me to make the B.P.R.D. guy bigger and suggested a sword instead of the bolt-action rifle. One more change was made digitally after I finished the inks: the medallion looked too much like a tattoo so the production people enlarged it.

This one went pretty smoothly since most of the changes were caught before I started the finished pencils. And I loved inking all that yeti fur.

—Kevin Nowlan, cover artist

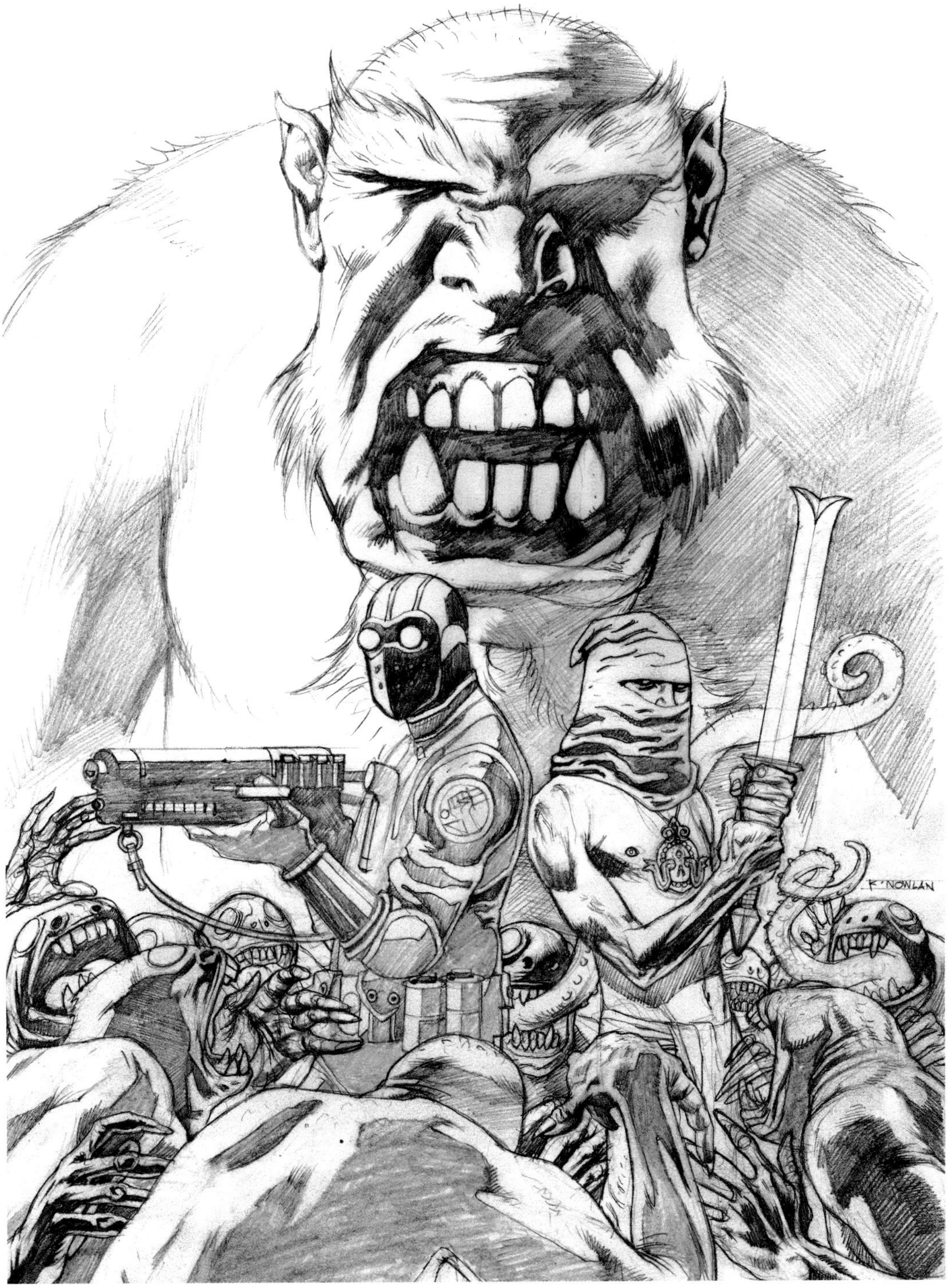
K'NOWLAN

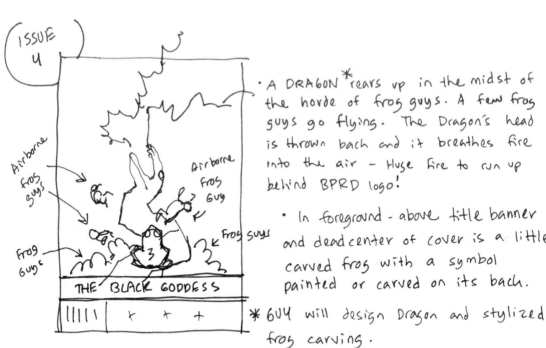

ISSUE 4

- A DRAGON* rears up in the midst of the horde of frog guys. A few frog guys go flying. The Dragon's head is thrown back and it breathes fire into the air — Huge fire to run up behind BPRD logo!

- In foreground - above title banner and dead center of cover is a little carved frog with a symbol painted or carved on its back.

* GUY will design Dragon and stylized frog carving.

Airborne frog guys

Airborne frog Guy

Frog guys

Frog guys

THE BLACK GODDESS

ISSUE 5

— Johann hangs in the air —
As though thrown back by some unseen force — And he is engulfed in flame. He is on fire but we see enough of him to clearly recognize him.
Fire fills a lot of the cover and background is BLACK.

THE BLACK GODDESS

Kevin — when you've seen these sketches give me a call and we'll talk about them. Thanks --

MIKE M.

I liked the idea of Lobster Johnson crawling out of the fallen body suit of Johann for his big reveal in the fifth chapter, but the layout and pacing of the page didn't work for it. Below: A closer shot of Lobster Johnson for the final page of *Black Goddess*; I pencilled this at the last minute wanting a more dramatic shot—but it wasn't clear enough where he was coming from and we went with the original panel.

—Guy Davis

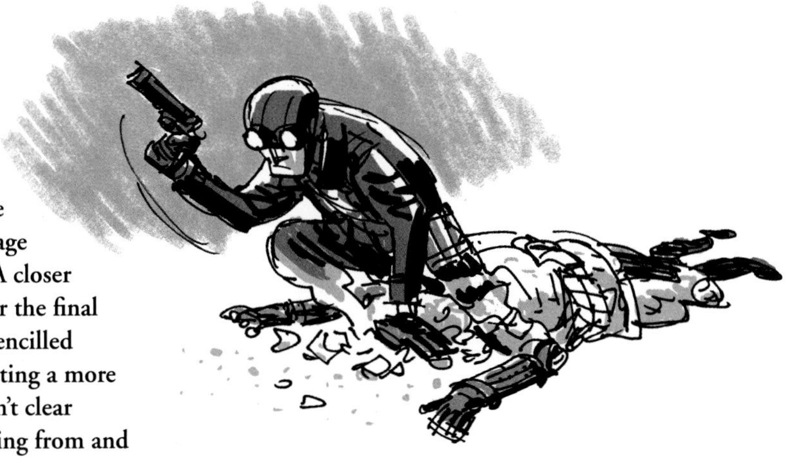

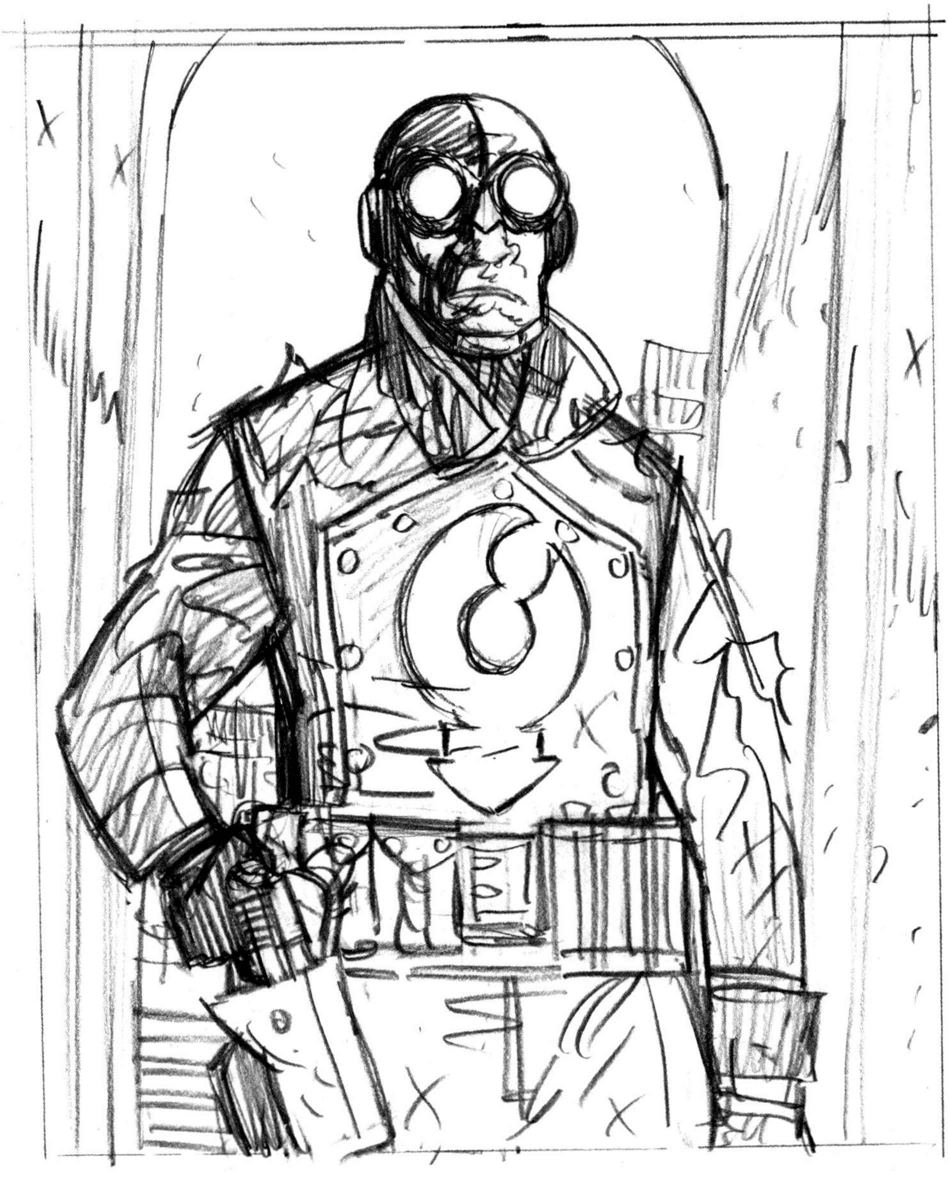

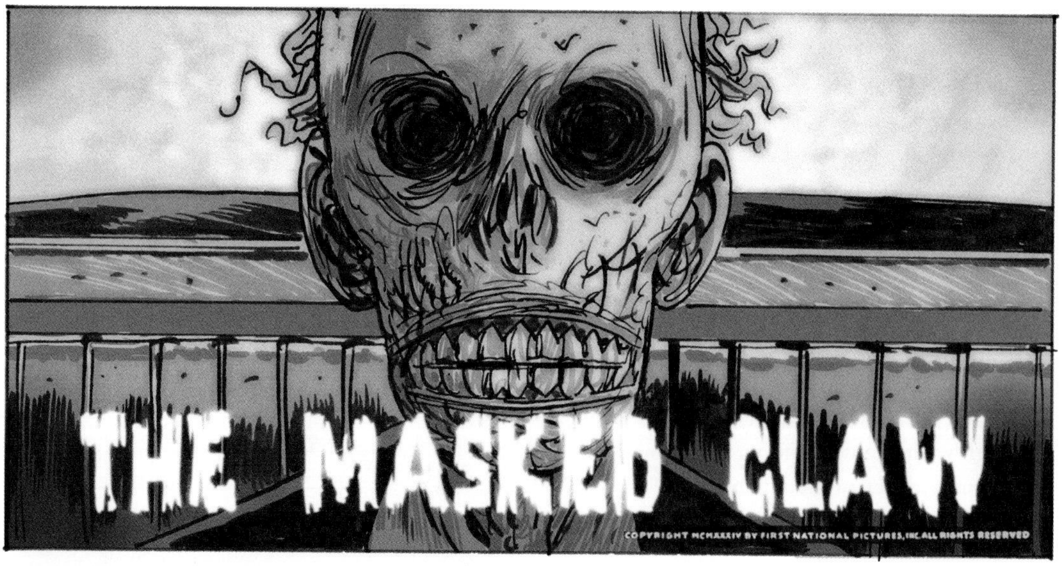
THE MASKED CLAW
COPYRIGHT MCMXXXIV BY FIRST NATIONAL PICTURES, INC. ALL RIGHTS RESERVED

LATCHKEY MEMORIES FROM CRAB POINT

When I was growing up in the seventies, before cable television and DVDs—hell, even VCRs—there was just good ol' television and none of that crap reality TV that's sucked the imagination out of entertainment. No, sir, back then we had shows like *Space: 1999*, *The Outer Limits*, *UFO*, and *Police Woman*—not to mention Monster Week, with a different Godzilla film every day at four! The afternoons were ruled by kids' shows. I remember running home from school to catch reruns of *Lost in Space*, *Ultraman*, *Captain Scarlet*, and the oddest of the bunch, *The Masked Claw*—which, I didn't realize till years later, was the cut-up and dubbed version of the Mexican Lobster Johnson films!

They still called him Lobster Johnson in the show and credits—but *The Masked Claw* must have been a catchier title. I haven't seen it in ages and still look for it on YouTube, but even all these years later I vividly remember the opening: there'd be a clap of thunder, and lightning would form the claw symbol as a huge black town car drove over a dusty hill. It was like the Green Hornet's Black Beauty, with a saucy woman all in black behind the wheel, and a corpse in the back seat! How cool was *that?* Then the camera would pan through the front windshield to the back seat and close in on the gnarled (and very fake) face of the corpse as the theme rang out in a chorus of baritones accompanied by a trio of guitars and Mexican trumpets:

Out of the night
When crime is alight
Comes the hero known as Lobster Johnson!

This defender of law
Uses his gun and a claw
So all would fear—Lobster Johnson!

Lobster! Lobster! Lobster!

The chant would fade out and we'd settle in with a mouth full of Smarties to see his latest adventure.

It was black and white, but we weren't spoiled by color TV too much—as long as the shows were entertaining and action packed, we didn't complain! And these were the most action-packed, violent, and surreal shows on the TV set. Not surreal in a druggy *H.R. Pufnstuf* or *Lidsville* way—but surreal like a darker *Eraserhead*, Dali-painting way, if Dali dressed up like a Mexican wrestler, which he might have done.

The best part was they never really explained who or what Lobster Johnson was, so we all had our own stories and histories made up in our heads about who he was. Anyhow, he would be driven into town by his saucy assistant/wife/daughter—I'm not sure what she was, and she didn't speak, sort of like Vulnavia from *The Abominable Dr. Phibes*—who was like a curvier Vampira, dressed all in black with a plunging neckline and crazy Emma Peel catsuit—monsters and Mexican wrestlers could only carry a show so far! She would just transport this corpse around to a troubled spot where wrongs needed to be righted. And then at night, through a slow fade of old fifties camera trickery, the corpse would become Lobster Johnson!

A beefy Mexican wrestler with the claw symbol on his bare and oily chest, ready for a fight!

And Lobster Johnson would fight every type of weird thing you could imagine: Space men, giant robots, monsters (even Frankenstein and Dracula would get beat up). Mummies seemed to pop up a lot, probably because it was an easy costume to throw on some extras, and Lobster Johnson would always step back in mock surprise and exclaim, "Mummies!" as if he never had seen them before—even though he had just pummeled them in the previous episode. That turned out to be a more memorable catch phrase than "Beware the Claw of Justice" when we'd play the Lobster at recess. We'd randomly jump back from anyone and yell, "Mummies!" in surprise, before throwing staged punches. He even fought Death and the Devil in the last couple of episodes! Now that's tough, and the Devil wasn't just a guy in a red suit—it was this really messed-up giant papier-mâché head with huge black eyes and a twisted, nightmarish grin. No wonder I ended up drawing the stuff I do!

I don't remember much of the specific plots—the original films had been cut up to make two or three episodes of the TV series, and TV stations at the time didn't really care what was on each day to entertain the little bastards, so most of the time the pieces would be shown out of order. Lobster Johnson would fight a bad guy dressed as a skeleton with a fedora at the end of one episode, and the next would start up with him in the clutches of some marsh monster or space man!

But it didn't matter. Most plots revolved around evil scientists and saucy villainess ladies robbing banks or trying to kill people, but they were all just excuses for Lobster Johnson to show up and start cracking monster heads—that's what we all were waiting to see! Once that eerie theremin sound started, and the camera panned to the back seat and those hollow corpse eyes, we knew the fun was about to start!

It was fight time, and not the old fisticuffs sort of Bam! Pow! *Batman* crap, but wrestling moves that no kid should imitate—but we all did, with no serious injuries. He'd usually just shoot the random thugs or smack them to death with a shovel or something handy, but for the main villains and monsters it was time for a physical beating of suplexes, kicks, and chops, with each fight ending with him lifting the monster over his head for a final toss. When they got up for another go, he'd give them the "Claw of Justice"—wow! That was the best! He'd grab their face in his meaty hand and, with an overblown *crunch* sound effect, he'd dispatch them by *crushing their face!* And that was that,

Saucy!

"Mummies!" They had Creature from the Black Lagoon hands—could they be mummified Creatures from the Black Lagoon? The mind reels at how cool that could be!

The transformation of Lobster Johnson!

Bolts versus Brawn! Those old movie-serial robots from *Undersea Kingdom* turned up everywhere!

The messed-up-looking Devil!

Mummies!

The Claw of Justice!

CRUNCH! Take that, space man!

no handing them over to the police—what would the police do with mummies anyhow?—just a *crunch*, and then, as he stood triumphant, he'd fade away, and we'd see him as the corpse again in the back seat of that huge black car being driven off into the distance, leaving only a cloud of dust! The moral was obvious to any kid watching it—be good, or you'll get shot or have your face crushed! Lesson learned!

I used to think these shows were a delusional product of growing up in the wilds of Crab Point, Michigan. But all these years later, I still have the two cheapo rack toys they put out, the kind of thing you'd only find in the dire and unloved toy-shelf spot at a supermarket—but I cherished that LoJo cap pistol, and one of those plastic "Parachute Lobster Johnsons" that you'd throw in the air and hope the parachute would open before it hit you on the head. And the cool thing was that he actually did parachute in a couple of episodes—these made sense, as opposed to the *Star Trek* ones they made with Spock in a parachute!

So all these years later I get to draw the classic Lobster Johnson in *B.P.R.D.*, and it's great fun, but part of me still misses his bizarre Mexican cousin! Hopefully they'll put these old shows out again, but they probably won't hold up—looking back, they weren't that great to begin with, but they were fun, and they had imagination, or at least guts to make something so messed up to begin with. Maybe if Guillermo del Toro finally does the remake, there'll be renewed interest in the old show—and I know I want to get the job redesigning those mummies!

Guy Davis
Crab Point, Michigan

MYSPACE DARK HORSE PRESENTS VOLUMES 1–4
Various

The online comics anthology *MySpace Dark Horse Presents* sees print in these four volumes—each collecting six issues of the ongoing series. Top talents from the industry like Mike Mignola, Joss Whedon, Eric Powell, Adam Warren, John Arcudi, and many others bring new visions and stories. They are joined by some of the freshest new talent out there today—found on MySpace! These are premier comics unlike anything else! *myspace.com/darkhorsepresents*

$19.95 EACH
VOLUME 1: ISBN 978-1-59307-998-7 | VOLUME 2: ISBN 978-1-59582-248-2
VOLUME 3: ISBN 978-1-59582-327-4 | VOLUME 4: ISBN 978-1-59582-405-9

SOLOMON KANE VOLUME 1: THE CASTLE OF THE DEVIL
Scott Allie, Mario Guevara, Dave Stewart, Mike Mignola

Robert E. Howard's vengeance-obsessed Puritan begins his supernatural adventures in the haunted Black Forest of Germany in this adaptation of Howard's "The Castle of the Devil." When Solomon Kane stumbles upon the body of a boy hanged from a rickety gallows, he goes after the man responsible—a baron feared by the peasants from miles around. Something far worse than the devilish baron or the terrible, intelligent wolf that prowls the woods lies hidden in the ruined monastery beneath the baron's castle, where a devil-worshiping priest died in chains centuries ago.

$15.95 | ISBN 978-1-59582-282-6

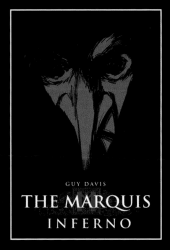

THE MARQUIS VOLUME 1: INFERNO
Guy Davis

In eighteenth-century Venisalle, faith governs life and death, and the guilty hide their shame behind masks, showing their faces only in the secret rites of the confessional. It is to this stronghold of the Inquisition that the souls of Hell have escaped to possess the living, spreading sin, murder, and chaos. Amid the carnage, one man is blessed with the clarity to recognize the demons that prey on his countrymen—and the means to return them to the fires of Hell. Features an introduction by *Hellboy* creator Mike Mignola and a 56-page sketchbook. Also includes a full-color cover gallery featuring the work of Matt Wagner, Mike Mignola, Charles Vess, Teddy Kristiansen, Kelley Jones, and Michael Gaydos!

$24.95 | ISBN 978-1-59582-368-7

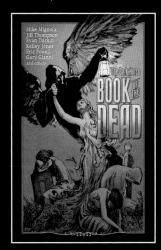

THE DARK HORSE BOOK OF THE DEAD
Mike Mignola, Guy Davis, Scott Allie

Mike Mignola presents a *Hellboy* yarn combining Shakespeare and grave robbing in this follow-up to Dark Horse's Eisner-nominated *Book of Hauntings* and *Book of Witchcraft*. Also returning this volume are Jill Thompson, who won a 2004 Eisner for her painted work in *Hauntings*, and her collaborator Evan Dorkin, with another occult canine adventure. New additions for this volume include *The Goon* creator Eric Powell, celebrated *B.P.R.D.* artist Guy Davis, and the artist who spent the last twenty years making superhero comics more scary—Kelley Jones. Cover artist Gary Gianni also returns, mixing prose with comics, with a rare tale by the man ultimately responsible for Dark Horse's biggest hit in years—*Conan* creator Robert E. Howard.

$14.95 | ISBN 978-1-59307-281-0

AVAILABLE AT YOUR LOCAL COMICS SHOP OR BOOKSTORE! • To find a comics shop in your area, call 1-888-266-4226.

For more information or to order direct visit darkhorse.com or call 1-800-862-0052 Mon.–Fri. 9 AM to 5 PM Pacific Time. Prices and availability subject to change without notice.

DARK HORSE COMICS ® *drawing on your nightmares*
darkhorse.com

HELLBOY

by MIKE MIGNOLA

HELLBOY LIBRARY EDITION VOLUME 1:
SEED OF DESTRUCTION AND WAKE THE DEVIL
ISBN 978-1-59307-910-9 | $49.99

HELLBOY LIBRARY EDITION VOLUME 2:
THE CHAINED COFFIN AND THE RIGHT HAND OF DOOM
ISBN 978-1-59307-989-5 | $49.99

HELLBOY LIBRARY EDITION VOLUME 3:
CONQUEROR WORM AND STRANGE PLACES
ISBN 978-1-59582-352-6 | $49.99

SEED OF DESTRUCTION
WITH JOHN BYRNE
ISBN 978-1-59307-094-6 | $17.99

WAKE THE DEVIL
ISBN 978-1-59307-095-3 | $17.99

THE CHAINED COFFIN AND OTHERS
ISBN 978-1-59307-091-5 | $17.99

THE RIGHT HAND OF DOOM
ISBN 978-1-59307-093-9 | $17.99

CONQUEROR WORM
ISBN 978-1-59307-092-2 | $17.99

STRANGE PLACES
ISBN 978-1-59307-475-3 | $17.99

THE TROLL WITCH AND OTHERS
ISBN 978-1-59307-860-7 | $17.99

DARKNESS CALLS
WITH DUNCAN FEGREDO
ISBN 978-1-59307-896-6 | $19.99

THE WILD HUNT
WITH DUNCAN FEGREDO
ISBN 978-1-59582-352-6 | $19.99

THE CROOKED MAN AND OTHERS
WITH RICHARD CORBEN
ISBN 978-1-59582-477-6 | $17.99

THE ART OF HELLBOY
ISBN 978-1-59307-089-2 | $29.99

HELLBOY II: THE ART OF THE MOVIE
ISBN 978-1-59307-964-2 | $24.99

HELLBOY: THE COMPANION
ISBN 978-1-59307-655-9 | $14.99

HELLBOY: WEIRD TALES
VOLUME 1
ISBN 978-1-56971-622-9 | $17.99
VOLUME 2
ISBN 978-1-56971-953-4 | $17.99

HELLBOY: MASKS AND MONSTERS
WITH JAMES ROBINSON AND SCOTT BENEFIEL
ISBN 978-1-59582-567-4 | $17.99

B.P.R.D.

WITH JOHN ARCUDI AND GUY DAVIS

PLAGUE OF FROGS HARDCOVER COLLECTION VOLUME 1
ISBN 978-59582-609-1 | $34.99

THE DEAD
ISBN 978-1-59307-380-0 | $17.99

THE BLACK FLAME
ISBN 978-1-59307-550-7 | $17.99

WAR ON FROGS
ISBN 978-1-59582-480-6 | $17.99

THE UNIVERSAL MACHINE
ISBN 978-1-59307-710-5 | $17.99

THE GARDEN OF SOULS
ISBN 978-1-59307-882-9 | $17.99

KILLING GROUND
ISBN 978-1-59307-956-7 | $17.99

THE WARNING
ISBN 978-1-59582-304-5 | $17.99

THE BLACK GODDESS
ISBN 978-1-59582-411-0 | $17.99

KING OF FEAR
ISBN 978-1-59582-564-3 | $17.99

1946
WITH JOSHUA DYSART AND PAUL AZACETA
ISBN 978-1-59582-191-1 | $17.99

1947
WITH JOSHUA DYSART, FÁBIO MOON, AND GABRIEL BÁ
ISBN 978-1-59582-478-3 | $17.99

ABE SAPIEN: THE DROWNING
WITH JASON SHAWN ALEXANDER
ISBN 978-1-59582-185-0 | $17.99

LOBSTER JOHNSON: THE IRON PROMETHEUS
WITH JASON ARMSTRONG
ISBN 978-1-59307-975-8 | $17.99

WITCHFINDER: IN THE SERVICE OF ANGELS
WITH BEN STENBECK
ISBN 978-1-59582-483-7 | $17.99

NOVELS

HELLBOY: EMERALD HELL
BY TOM PICCIRILLI
ISBN 978-1-59582-141-6 | $12.99

HELLBOY: THE ALL-SEEING EYE
BY MARK MORRIS
ISBN 978-1-59582-141-6 | $12.99

HELLBOY: THE FIRE WOLVES
BY TIM LEBBON
ISBN 978-1-59582-204-8 | $12.99

HELLBOY: THE ICE WOLVES
BY MARK CHADBOURN
ISBN 978-1-59582-205-5 | $12.99

LOBSTER JOHNSON: THE SATAN FACTORY
BY THOMAS E. SNIEGOSKI
ISBN 978-1-59582-203-1 | $12.99

SHORT STORIES

ILLUSTRATED BY MIKE MIGNOLA

HELLBOY: ODD JOBS
BY POPPY Z. BRITE, GREG RUCKA, AND OTHERS
ISBN 978-1-56971-440-9 | $14.99

HELLBOY: ODDER JOBS
BY FRANK DARABONT, GUILLERMO DEL TORO, AND OTHERS
ISBN 978-1-59307-226-1 | $14.99

HELLBOY: ODDEST JOBS
BY JOE R. LANSDALE, CHINA MIÉVILLE, AND OTHERS
ISBN 978-1-59307-944-4 | $14.99

ALSO

THE AMAZING SCREW-ON HEAD AND OTHER CURIOUS OBJECTS HARDCOVER COLLECTION
BY MIKE MIGNOLA
ISBN 978-1-59582-501-8 | $17.99

BALTIMORE: THE PLAGUE SHIPS
WITH CHRISTOPHER GOLDEN AND BEN STENBECK
ISBN 978-1-59582-673-2 | $24.99

DarkHorse.com

AVAILABLE AT YOUR LOCAL COMICS SHOP OR BOOKSTORE! • To find a comics shop in your area, call 1-888-266-4226.
For more information or to order direct visit DarkHorse.com or call 1-800-862-0052 Mon.–Fri. 9 A.M. to 5 P.M. Pacific Time.
Prices and availability subject to change without notice.